S0-ADS-664

Conversations with Denise Levertov

Literary Conversations Series

Peggy Whitman Prenshaw
General Editor

Photo credit: © Chris Felver; courtesy of New Directions

Conversations with Denise Levertov

Edited by
Jewel Spears Brooker

University Press of Mississippi
Jackson

Copyright © 1998 by University Press of Mississippi
All rights reserved
Manufactured in the United States of America

01   00   99   98   4   3   2   1

The paper in this book meets the guidelines for permanence and durability of the Committee on Production Guidelines for Book Longevity of the Council on Library Resources.

Library in Congress Cataloging-in-Publication Data

Levertov, Denise, 1923–1997
    Conversations with Denise Levertov / edited by Jewel Spears
Brooker.
        p.   cm.—(Literary conversations series)
    Includes bibliographical references and index.
    ISBN 1-57806-073-7 (alk. paper).—ISBN 1-57806-074-5 (pbk. :
alk. paper)
    1. Levertov, Denise, 1923–1997—Interviews.   2. Women poets,
American—20th century—Interviews.   I. Brooker, Jewel Spears,
1940– . II. Title. III. Series.
PS3562.E8876Z464   1998
811'.54—dc21   98-15893
                                                                    CIP

British Library Cataloging-in-Publication data available

Books by Denise Levertov (not including small limited editions)

The Double Image. London: Cresset Press, 1946.
Here and Now. San Francisco: City Lights Books, 1957.
Overland to the Islands. Highlands, NC: Jargon, 1958.
With Eyes at the Back of Our Heads. New York: New Directions, 1959.
The Jacob's Ladder. New York: New Directions, 1961; London: Cape, 1965.
O Taste and See. New York: New Directions, 1964.
The Sorrow Dance. New York: New Directions, 1967; London: Cape, 1968.
Relearning the Alphabet. New York: New Directions, 1970; London: Cape, 1970.
To Stay Alive. New York: New Directions, 1971.
Footprints. New York: New Directions, 1972.
The Poet in the World. New York: New Directions, 1973. (Essays)
The Freeing of the Dust. New York: New Directions, 1975.
Life in the Forest. New York: New Directions, 1978.
Collected Earlier Poems 1940–1960. New York: New Directions, 1979.
Light Up the Cave. New York: New Directions, 1981. (Essays)
Candles in Babylon. New York: New Directions, 1982.
Poems 1960–1967. New York: New Directions, 1983.
Oblique Prayers. New York: New Directions, 1984; Newcastle upon Tyne: Bloodaxe Books, 1986.
Selected Poems. Newcastle upon Tyne: Bloodaxe Books, 1986.
Poems 1968–1972. New York: New Directions, 1987.
Breathing the Water. New York: New Directions, 1987.
A Door in the Hive. New York: New Directions, 1989.
New and Selected Essays. New York: New Directions, 1992.
Evening Train. New York: New Directions, 1992.
Tesserae: Memories & Suppositions. New York: New Directions, 1995. (Prose)
Sands of the Well. New York: New Directions, 1996.
The Stream & The Sapphire. New York: New Directions, 1997.
The Life Around Us. New York: New Directions, 1997.

Translations by Denise Levertov

In Praise of Krishna (co-translator, Edward C. Dimock, Jr.). New York: Doubleday, 1967; London: Cape, 1968.
Selected Poems of Guillevic. New York: New Directions, 1969.
Jean Joubert, *Black Iris.* Port Townsend, Wash.: Copper Canyon Press, 1988.

For Denise Levertov
in memoriam 1923–1997

Contents

Introduction

Denise Levertov emerged as a public figure at the end of the 1950s and the beginning of the 1960s and very quickly became a presence in our collective imagination. She was frequently in the news throughout the 1960s and 1970s and, with each passing decade, continued to hold our attention, serving as a reference point for Americans in discussions of American art and politics. She caught the imagination not only of her own constituencies in poetry, politics, and religion, but also of more centrist intellectuals and students throughout the country. Many were still fascinated with her when, just before Christmas in 1997, we heard the announcement on National Public Radio that she had died. She had been suffering from lymphoma for a number of years, but she had never stopped speaking out on timely issues and giving readings of her powerful poems.

At first glance, it may seem ironic that this English-born daughter of a Welsh mother and an Anglo-Russian father came to stand for so much that seemed American. But even in her mixed heritage and European origins, Levertov seemed in special ways "one of us." There are several possible explanations for Levertov's hold on our imagination—the language in her American poems, her fierce independence, her liberal politics, her role as gadfly to politically neutral intellectuals in situations of national concern, such as the war in Vietnam. Stephen Daedalus, in Joyce's *Portrait of the Artist as a Young Man*, claims that the artist, "like the God of the creation, remains within or behind or beyond or above his handiwork, invisible, . . . indifferent, paring his fingernails" (chap. V). Levertov believed, on the contrary, that artists must immerse themselves in history. She respected no boundaries between art and life and, furthermore, made the transgression of boundaries a centerpiece of her poetry. She was as involved in politics as she was in poetry, and she brought the same energy and passion to both. Being passionate about poetry was for her being passionate about life.

Levertov's ability to balance so many difficult issues and roles reminds us that in her youth she wanted to be a dancer. In several interviews, she discusses her love of the dance, and although she abandoned ballet, she retained the energy, the fluidity, the sense of coherence and rhythm that gives ballet so much tension and grace. As Henry James thought of writing in terms of painting, Levertov thought of poetry in terms of dance. In the interview with Walter Sutton, she quotes Pound's definition of *logopoeia* as "the dance of the intellect among words" and relates balance in composition to balance in dance. In some interviews, she actually performs her answers. For example, in the interview with William Packard, she explains that in poetry thinking and feeling work together, as in a dance, and then, in answer to a question about line lengths in poetry, she leaps up and dances a response by walking, skipping, circling, taking quick steps, hesitating, changing directions. The truth is she was always dancing, always keeping time in time, and it is clear from her poems and these interviews that the real dance for her was the dance of life itself. In "Among School Children," Yeats uses the image of the dance to stand for the unity of life. And how, he asks, "can we know the dancer from the dance?" How, indeed. It is the holistic quality of Levertov's dance that has compelled our imagination, that has attracted us to the dancer within the dance.

The complexity and intensity of Levertov's dance is evident in these interviews. She often speaks of the difficulty of balancing her writing and her family, her teaching and her activism, her commitments to friends and to ideas. She is captured in a memorable moment in the 1983 interview with Janet Tassel. Standing at her ironing board, with one eye on her dress and one on the interviewer, Levertov reveals that her life is indeed a delicate balancing act—commuting between the east and west coasts for teaching, answering her correspondence, caring in a meaningful way for her friends, her family, the peasants in El Salvador, and taking care of her own immediate needs, like ironing a dress and getting a much-needed new perm. "Wild, isn't it?" she says with "hoots of laughter." The interviewer is spellbound by the London accent, the gap-toothed smile, and by the awareness that this slim woman dancing around the ironing board is a major American poet. In other interviews, Levertov explains that her morals force her to be involved in the life around her. She sometimes wears message buttons, one of her favorites being "Picket and pray."

This collection of some twenty interviews with Levertov spans more than three decades, from the early 1960s through the middle 1990s. She was forty years old and already recognized as an important poet at the time of the first interview; she was past seventy and an icon of American culture at the time of the most recent. Levertov first made her mark as a poet in the late 1950s. Her poetry was recognized as distinctive and indeed brilliant, and her earliest interviews are focused not on her politics, but on her youth, her education, and her poetry. Born in England in 1923 of a Welsh mother and an Anglo-Russian Jewish father who had become an Anglican priest, Levertov was educated at home, largely by her mother, and in the Victoria and Albert Museum and London libraries, largely by herself. She began writing poetry as a child and published her first poem at sixteen. Levertov discusses her family background and her education at home in a number of interviews, especially those by William Packard, Maureen Smith, Sybil Estess, and Fay Zwicky. When Levertov was in her late teens, war enveloped Europe. "To avoid the draft, which in England conscripted women as well as men," she explains to Estess, "[she] joined the 'land army,' working primarily in the Civil Nursing Reserve." Her first book of poems, *The Double Image*, was published in England in 1946, just after the war. In 1947, she married an American, Mitchell Goodman, and the following year moved with him to New York City. She immersed herself in American life and letters, and within a few years had become a friend and an occasional guest of William Carlos Williams, the poet who more than any other became her mentor and the inspiration for her poetry. In 1956, within a decade of her arrival on these shores, she became a citizen and published her second volume of poetry, *Here and Now*. In the next five years, she published several more volumes of poetry (*Overland to the Islands* in 1958, *With Eyes at the Back of Our Heads* in 1960, and *The Jacob's Ladder* in 1961), received several prizes for her work, and became Poetry Editor of *The Nation*. By the beginning of the 1960s, she was widely recognized as one of the most accomplished poets of her generation.

The interviews in this collection begin in the early 1960s, in the middle of her life and at a point of transition from a private to a public person. The first two interviews are centered primarily on her poetry, and secondarily, on her newfound identity as an American. She reflects on her English background and on the difference between English and American speech. As she will continue to do, she pays homage to Williams as the "one who gave me the use of the American language," the one among the older modernists—Stevens, H.D., Pound, and Eliot—to whom she feels the greatest debt. In these and later interviews, she expresses her gratitude for his friendship and recounts her pleasure in visiting him and reading poetry with him, even after his stroke. In these first two interviews, she reveals that she is a combination of Modernist and Neo-Romantic. Her Romanticism can be seen in her commitment to organic form, to the senses, and to nature; her modernism in her

acceptance of Hopkins's notion of "inscape," in her attempt to deal with the
"I" in her text, in her qualified agreement with Eliot on the importance of an
"objective correlative," in her belief in the importance of having "something
to say." Of special importance in these interviews are the long and meticulous discussions of the craft of poetry. Levertov is expansive on the subject,
particularly with Packard, Estess, and Terrell Crouch. She lingers lovingly
on aspects of organic form, diction, rhythm, lineation, and line speed. She
discusses the manner in which poems take their being within her and gradually "crystallize into some phrases, some words, a rhythm."

During the 1960s, Levertov began what was to be a series of academic
appointments, primarily in Massachusetts and California. In response to
Packard's question about the effect of teaching on her writing, she explains
that it has had a profound effect "in bringing me into contact with the student
generation and political activism on the various campuses. If I hadn't been
teaching I might easily have found myself very isolated politically." During
the 1960s and 1970s, she and her husband were deeply involved in the campus protests against the war in Vietnam. She became a symbol of leftist
protest, speaking frequently at campus rallies and public demonstrations and
spending time in jail for her anti-war activities. In the 1960s, she traveled to
Moscow, and in 1972, she and fellow poet Muriel Rukeyser went to Hanoi.
Major blocks of her poetry, such as the "Life at War" sequence in *The Sorrow Dance* (1967), vividly present the horror of war and passionately maintain the immorality of involvement. The interviews of this period, like the
poetry in such collections as *Relearning the Alphabet* (1970) and *To Stay
Alive* (1971), reflect her political concerns and her anguish over public policy.

In the first interview focused on her politics, Levertov explains to E. G.
Burrows how she and Goodman became involved in *RESIST,* a national anti-
war organization formed to encourage young people to resist the draft while
the United States was at war in Vietnam. She also explains, in response to
critics and friends who felt she was sacrificing her poetic gifts, that there can
be no "separation between so-called political poetry and so-called private
poetry in an artist, who is in both cases writing out of his inner life." The
social usefulness of poetry comes up in most interviews after the middle
1960s, including those with Estess, Zwicky, Packard, Michael Andre, Maureen Smith, and Lorrie Smith. Levertov's involvement in causes did not end
with the collapse of the war in Vietnam. She was a major participant in the
anti-nuclear movement, the green movement, the El Salvador resistance, and
most recently the opposition to the Gulf War. In the interviews with Fay

Zwicky and with Terrell Crouch, Levertov discusses the dilemma of being at heart a pacifist but realizing that violence is necessary in wars of liberation. She accepts violence in the interest of social justice, but at the same time, she admits that it is deforming to the people who resort to it and moreover, that it tends to perpetuate itself. In the most recent interviews, she backs away from judging those who fail to take up politics, telling Jan Ross in 1990 that she does not demand that all poets write anti-war poems. As she remarks in a later interview, "Walt Whitman wrote about the Civil War; Emily Dickinson did not."

The anti-war movement was, of course, part of a larger social upheaval that included the feminist movement and the Civil Rights movement. Levertov says little about the Civil Rights movement, and she did not actively participate in the feminist movement. Her poetry, however, includes many poems about the situation of women, poems that may or may not be feminist in intent, but are clearly feminist in thrust. Many feminists, consequently, have claimed her as a source of inspiration. These interviews contain scattered references to feminism, with extended discussions in the interviews by Fay Zwicky and by Nancy Gish. In response to Gish's feminist readings of some of her poems, Levertov discusses gender neutral language and explains what sort of feminist she is and what sort she is not.

Levertov's longtime commitment to issues of peace and social justice, especially in Latin America, led her to liberation theology and to the Catholic left. Some of the friends she admired most in the peace movement were Catholics, and among the martyrs of the movement were people such as Archbishop Oscar Romero, murdered at the altar as he was saying Mass. She wrote the libretto for an oratorio, *El Salvador*, based on Romero's murder, and discusses it in the interview with Janet Tassel. Her religious inclinations, however, existed long before she became an activist. As the granddaughter of a rabbi and the daughter of an Anglican priest, she grew up in an environment rich in religious symbolism. Her mixed religious heritage is explored with fine sensitivity in the interview with Joan F. Hallisey.

Levertov's religious commitment is also consistent with her work as a poet. From beginning to end, she arrives in her poetry at insights that seem profoundly religious. These insights stem in part from her absorption of the natural supernaturalism of Wordsworth and the more orthodox supernaturalism of Hopkins, but in part too from the nature of her involvement with language. Like Goethe, she feels that the poet has the power to see and reveal in language what is present but hidden, what she calls in the interview with

Ian Reid the "open secret." In 1985, in the interview with Lorrie Smith, Levertov says "I now define myself as a Christian, but not a very orthodox one." And in the 1990 interview with Gish, she defends herself as a Christian, saying that her criticisms of the Vatican and of certain doctrines must be understood as criticism from within the church. She affirms in this and other interviews her belief in the Incarnation.

Interviews, by their very nature, tend toward repetition, but need not, on that account, call for an apology. As Lévi-Strauss argues in "The Structural Study of Myth" (1955), it is through repetition that patterns are revealed, through repetition that the myth behind the fact discloses itself. In this collection, the same question is sometimes asked by several interviewers. Several ask, for example, about Levertov's family, her European upbringing, her early success, her craft, her feminism, and increasingly her politics and her religion. But interestingly and perhaps inevitably in a respondent as intelligent as Levertov, she responds in different shades in different seasons. In taking these questions seriously at different times, in different moods, different circumstances, different places, she moves like a performer doing variations upon basic themes, variations subtle and continuously changing. Her answers disclose an unfolding story, the story of an artist glimpsed in moments of time. In the larger picture, her development as a poet from British Neo-Romantic to American original, her movement in politics from pacifism to acceptance of revolutionary violence and then back to pacifism, and her pilgrimage in religion from agnosticism to belief all take their place in a meaningful pattern. They become part of the dance, and as Eliot says in *Four Quartets*, "there is only the dance."

As with other volumes in this series, these interviews are virtually unedited. Typographical errors have been corrected, and the biographical and bibliographical blurbs prefacing the interviews have been removed as a redundancy.

In conclusion, I wish to express my thanks for the generosity of the interviewers and publishers who allowed reprinting of their work and thus made the present volume possible. Specific acknowledgments are included in the headnotes for individual interviews. On a more personal level, I am enormously grateful to Joan F. Hallisey, a dear friend whose sensitive readings have greatly enriched my understanding of Levertov's poetry. I am also grateful to Allison Payne and Rebecca K. Root, my students at Eckerd College, for help in collecting and organizing these materials. I appreciate the support that the dean of Eckerd College, Dr. Lloyd Chapin, has given me for this and other work, and the continuous encouragement over many years of my husband, H. Ralph Brooker. Finally, I am grateful to Denise Levertov herself—for her poetry and for her openness in speaking to her readers and friends.

JSB
January 1998

Chronology

1923	24 October, Denise Levertov born in Ilford, Essex, England to Paul Philip Levertoff, a Russian Jew who had converted to Christianity and become an Anglican clergyman, and Beatrice Spooner-Jones of Wales, a descendant of Angel Jones of Mold, a tailor and a preacher Educated at home (except for ballet lessons)
1935	At the age of 12, sends her poems to T. S. Eliot who responds with a letter of advice
1939	At 16, meets the poet and critic Herbert Read and begins correspondence with him
1940	Publishes first poem, "Listening to Distant Guns," in *Poetry Quarterly*
1943–44	Works as a civilian nurse in London during World War II
1946	Works in an antique store and a bookstore in London; publishes *The Double Image*, first book of poetry
1947	Serves as civilian nurse at British hospital, Paris, France; marries American writer Mitchell Goodman
1948	Moves with Goodman to New York City
1949	Birth of son Nikolai; inclusion of poems in Kenneth Rexroth's anthology *New British Poets*; friendship with Robert Creeley; publishes poems in Cid Corman's magazine *Origin* and in the *Black Mountain Review*
1950–51	Lives in Europe with Goodman who, supported by G. I. Bill, studies and writes
1952	Returns to New York
1955	Becomes a naturalized U.S. citizen
1956	Publishes *Here and Now*, second book of poetry and first American book

1957–58   Lives in Mexico

1958   Publishes *Overland to the Islands* and *5 Poems*

1960   Publishes *With Eyes at the Back of Our Heads*; receives Bess Hokin Prize from *Poetry Magazine* for "With Eyes at the Back of Our Heads"

1961   Publishes *The Jacob's Ladder*; receives Longview Award

1961–62, 1963–65   Serves as Poetry Editor of *The Nation*

1962   Receives Guggenheim Fellowship

1964   Teaches poetry at Young Men and Women's Christian Association (YMCA-YWCA) Poetry Center in New York City; receives Harriet Monroe Memorial Prize and Inez Boulton Prize; publishes *O Taste and See*

1964–66   Honorary Scholar, Radcliffe Institute for Independent Study, Cambridge, MA

1965   Teaches at City College of New York and at Drew University, Madison, NJ; co-initiates the movement of Writers and Artists Protest against the War in Vietnam; receives Morton Dauwen Zabel Memorial Prize from *Poetry Magazine*

1966   Publishes *Psalm Concerning the Castle*; receives American Academy of Arts and Letters award

1966–67   Teaches at Vassar College, Poughkeepsie, NY

1967   Publishes *The Sorrow Dance*; included in *Penguin Modern Poets* (with Kenneth Rexroth and William Carlos Williams); with Edward C. Dimock, Jr., translates *In Praise of Krishna*; edits *Out of the War Shadow* for War Resisters League

1968   Publishes *A Tree Telling of Orpheus, In the Night* (prose), *Three Poems* and *The Cold Spring*; Goodman indicted along with Dr. Benjamin Spock for opposing military draft

1969   Teaches at the University of California, Berkeley; participates in People's Park movement protests in Berkeley; translates Eugene Guillevic's *Selected Poems*; publishes *Embroideries*

1969–70   Teaches at the Massachusetts Institute of Technology; participates in Peace Movement

1970   Receives honorary doctorate from Colby College, Waterville,

ME; publishes *Relearning the Alphabet, Summer Poems 1969*, and *A New Year's Garland for My Students, MIT 1969–1970*; travels to Moscow

1970–71   Artist-in-residence at Kirkland College, Clinton, NY

1971   Publishes *To Stay Alive*

1972   Publishes *Footprints*; travels to Hanoi, North Vietnam with Muriel Rukeyser and Jane Hart at invitation of Women's Union and Writer's Union. On return, speaks at many American colleges about her experiences in Vietnam, including her knowledge of U.S. bombing of hospitals

1973   Elliston Lecturer at the University of Cincinnati, Cincinnati, OH; receives honorary doctorate from University of Cincinnati; publishes *The Poet in the World* (essays)

1973–79   Teaches at Tufts University, Medford, MA

1974   Divorces Mitchell Goodman

1975   Publishes *The Freeing of Dust*

1976   Receives Lenore Marshall Poetry Prize

1976–78   Serves as poetry editor of *Mother Jones* (San Francisco)

1977   8 June, death of her mother in Mexico; publishes *Chekhov on the West Heath* and *Modulations for Solo Voice*

1978   Publishes *Life in the Forest*

1979   Publishes *Collected Earlier Poems 1940–1960*; visits Australia for first time

1980   Elected to the American Academy of Arts and Letters; serves as delegate to World Peace Parliament, Sofia, Bulgaria

1981–83   Fannie Hurst Professor at Brandeis University, Waltham, MA

1981   Publishes *Pig Dreams, Wanderer's Daysong, Mass for the Day of St. Thomas Didymus* and *Light Up the Cave* (essays)

1981–94   Teaches at Stanford University

1982   Publishes *Candles in Babylon*

1983   Receives Elmer Holmes Bobst Award in poetry; publishes *Poems 1960–1967* and *El Salvador: Requiem and Invocation*

1984   Receives honorary doctorates from Saint Lawrence University, Canton, NY, and Bates College, Lewiston, ME; receives Shelley Memorial Award from Poetry Society of America; publishes *Oblique Prayers*

1985   Contributes translations to *Poets of Bulgaria*, edited by William Meredith

1986   Publishes *Selected Poems* in England

1987   Publishes *Breathing the Water* and *Poems 1968–1972*; receives honorary doctorates from Allegheny College, Meadville, PA, and St. Michael's College, Burlington, VT

1988   Translates Jean Joubert's *Black Iris*

1989   Publishes *A Door in the Hive*; receives honorary doctorate from Massachusetts College of Art, Boston

1990   Translates Jean Joubert's *White Owl and Blue Mouse*; receives Robert Frost Medal

1991   Receives Senior Fellowship from the National Endowment for the Arts

1992   Publishes *New and Selected Essays*; receives Lannan Award

1993   Appointed Professor at Large, Cornell University; receives honorary doctorate from University of Santa Clara (California)

1994   Receives Lifetime Achievement Award from Conference for Christianity and Literature

1995   Publishes *Tesserae: Memories & Suppositions* (prose); receives honorary doctorates from State University of Southern Connecticut and from Seattle University; Fellowship of the Academy of American Poets

1996   Publishes *Sands of the Well*

1997   Publishes *The Stream & the Sapphire* and *The Life Around Us* December 20. Denise Levertov dies in Seattle, Washington, from complications of lymphoma.

Conversations with Denise Levertov

Denise Levertov
David Ossman / 1963

From *The Sullen Art: Interviews by David Ossman with Modern American Poets*, ed. David Ossman (New York: Corinth Books, 1963), 73–76. Reprinted by permission of David Ossman.

Ossman: Can you give me your statement of faith as a poet? Your aesthetic?

Levertov: First of all, I believe that the gift of being able to write poetry must always be considered *as* a gift. It's a responsibility, whether one considers it given by God or Nature. It's something which the poet must take seriously. His responsibility is not to himself, not to his career, but to poetry itself. Therefore I believe in craftsmanship and care. And, as a craftsman, I feel that every piece of punctuation, every comma and every colon, is a serious matter and must be duly considered. Punctuation is a tool, all the parts of punctuation and of grammar are tools, and one must use them efficiently.

Ossman: Then you don't believe in some of the current poetry, in which the first draft is left intact, automatically written, including spelling errors?

Levertov: No, I certainly don't. I do feel that it's indispensable to a poet to have the initial gift, which is given to him, and over which he has no control. He either has it or he doesn't. And I believe that every poem must arise from a very deep level of the poet, otherwise it's not alive. It's not going to have life. It's not viable. Incidentally, I think that a part of the poet's equipment is the instinct for knowing when to *begin* writing the poem. A poem which is begun to be put on paper, to be crystallized, too soon, is going to be a poem which, if the poet has a sense of responsibility, is going to need an awful lot of revision. This can be avoided by waiting until the moment is ripe. Once he has crystallized, initially, the poem, then comes in the responsibility of his intelligence and his judgment. Total accidents (not spelling errors, that's just beneath contempt), but sometimes accidents of syntax, for example, could be functioning parts of the poem.

The poet has to look at the poem after he's written the first draft and consider with his knowledge, with his experience and craftsmanship, what needs doing to this poem. It *may* be complete in itself. He has to have antennae that are going to tell him. He has to feel out what he has there.

Ossman: How do you know, having just written a first draft, that you have a poem which is right and which will work?

Levertov: Well, when one has just written a first draft one may be elated, and one may wrongly think that it's right as it stands. But, of course, one has to wait and read it over the next day or the next week. Some people work slowly and some people work fast. I work rather fast. Then, I think one's experience tells one. One spends one's whole life writing poems (I started writing poems when I was a child and I'm sure many other poets did start young), and has years of reading and years of thinking about poetry and years of writing poems to help one. One doesn't really come out of the blue. It's a question of judgment. How does a painter know when his painting is finished? It's a matter of a synthesis of instincts and intelligence. You can't leave the intelligence out. But you can't *start* with the intelligence; if you start with the intelligence, you have nothing whatsoever. You have a dead baby.

Ossman: You say "you" and "one" much more than you say "I." Is this also a characteristic of your poetry?

Levertov: It has been pointed out to me recently that I have tended, in the past, to say "one" or "you" or to leave out those words altogether. But I do believe in the use of the "objective correlative," as Eliot called it. I don't believe that poetry is the raw expression of personal emotion. On the other hand, I don't mean to say that it can't be; but I think that a poet has to be skilled and experienced before he begins using "I." He can come to it eventually; and I'm just really beginning to let myself say "I" because I feel that now I can do it without the kind of crudity with which some people who have just begun to write poetry write about their own feelings.

I always feel that what such people should be doing, if they really want to be poets, is writing objectively. Writing about a chair, a tree outside their window. So much more of themselves really would get into the poem, than when they just say "I." The "I-ness" doesn't come across, because it's too crude, very often. For instance, the objective earlier poems of William Carlos Williams (who, in the ripeness of his old age has been saying "I" in a quite different way) say so much more than what they superficially appear to be saying. They're quite objective little descriptions of this and that, and yet, especially when one adds them together, they say a great deal about the man. In a much deeper, more impressive way than if he'd spent the same years describing his emotions. If a writer only describes how he feels, crudely, it's not very interesting. If he writes about the blackness of the sky and the dirtiness of the sidewalk, the experience is transferred, and we feel oppressed by these things, just as he did.

Ossman: What do you write about?

Levertov: I believe in writing about what lies under the hand, in a sense. I think that one should never sort of look around for subjects. I don't believe in the contrived, and I don't like to read poetry which seems to me contrived. Keats said "poetry should come as naturally as the leaves to a tree, or not at all," and I don't think he meant that poetry was a question of "warbling native woodnotes wild." I feel that he meant that poetry arises out of *need*, out of really having something to say about something that we—that the poet—that I—have actually felt or experienced. Not necessarily in the visual world—the external world—it can be an inner experience—but it must be something true.

Ossman: Do you find that more of your poems are about inner experience?

Levertov: I think that the poems in *Here and Now*, for example, a few years ago, were very much more about things in the outside world. In the last couple of years I've drawn on experiences equally real to me, but perhaps more private—dreams and inner experiences. But I also believe very much in the concrete image. It's almost hypocritical of me to say that I *believe* in it, because it is natural for me to express myself in concrete images, not in abstractions.

Ossman: Do you think there has been, in effect, a poetry renaissance?

Levertov: I don't really know if there's a renaissance. There seem to be more readers, perhaps, for poetry. I think there have always been people writing poetry, and I don't think that the best ones are necessarily those that are most in the public eye. There are a lot of good poets in all the alleged "schools" of poetry. There is a good variety. Scattered all over the country there are interesting poets doing good work. I don't know whether this constitutes a renaissance.

A Conversation with Denise Levertov

Walter Sutton / 1965

From *minnesota review* 5 (December 1965), 322–38. Reprinted by permission of Walter Sutton.

Since coming to the United States from England in 1948, Denise Levertov has won recognition as a leading American poet. Her books of verse include *The Double Image* (1946), *Here and Now* (1957), *Overland to the Islands* (1958), *With Eyes at the Back of Our Heads* (1959), *The Jacob's Ladder* (1961), and *O Taste and See* (1964). She is poetry editor of *The Nation* and has read and lectured at many colleges and universities. Miss Levertov lives in New York City with her husband Mitchell Goodman and their son Nikolai.

Sutton: One of the unusual things about your situation is that you have come to this country and established yourself here as a poet. Do you think that this is a difficult thing to do?

Levertov: I think that for me it was in a certain way very easy because, although I had a book published in England, I hadn't a deep sense of being English. I didn't really fit in because England has a very set social system in which most people know exactly who and what they are. Now, I had very mixed parents. My father was essentially a European and then he was a Jew who had become a Christian and finally an Anglican priest. This was a very strange uncategorizeable sort of fact, you know. And my mother was Welsh, and I didn't go to school, so I didn't share in the general English type of education. I was very conscious of lots of differences.

Sutton: And these differences have affected your poetry?

Levertov: Yes, Alfred Alvarez started off a lecture at the Guggenheim Museum the other evening by saying that he thought one of the differences between American poetry and English poetry was the fact that English poets had this initial sense, practically from birth, of who they were, and that American poets didn't have it, so that American poetry was often very much concerned with self-definition. And although I disagreed with almost everything else that Alvarez said, I think that this is probably true.

Sutton: Do you think that you were concerned with the problem of finding yourself, as the American poet does, even before you knew America?

Levertov: Not consciously so, but I think that I was able to become American because I wasn't really anything. I was many things and no one thing. I had a background more like the background of many Americans than that of a typical English person.

Sutton: Do you think that this distinction is still true of the younger English poet in relation to the young American poet?

Levertov: Well, I think that a lot of English poetry of at least the last fifteen years certainly doesn't have the vitality of American poetry, and there hasn't been very much interesting work done in England in the last decade or so. I think that there are a few younger English poets who are very interesting; but they are the ones who have been influenced, more or less, by American poetry. I've felt for a long time that English poetry absolutely needs a shot in the arm from America. But a lot of English poets, of course, feel very incensed if anyone suggests it to them.

Sutton: There has been more of a direct influence of American literature upon English literature in recent years. Is this also true of poetry?

Levertov: Yes. There are a very few English poets who have been influenced by Williams. But there is a problem because of the difference in the languages. They are two different languages in certain respects, and when I first came here, even though I had such an urgent sense that Williams had something for me, I couldn't "get it" at first. I had to accustom my ears to American speech and my whole nervous system to the pace of American life before it really began to come through to me.

Sutton: Of course, Williams' whole idea of form is based on the use of idiomatic American speech. Do you think there is any problem for the English poet in taking this sort of poetic and applying it?

Levertov: Well, let us suppose some English poet influenced by Williams to the extent that he, an English poet, is trying to write in the American idiom. I've seen this happen, and it's absurd. But, of course, the real lesson is that they could take the English idiom and do something with it; however, they haven't done so—up to now.

Sutton: It's like the English rock-and-roll or jazz singer singing Americanly. But you do think that the English poet could apply the same standard to the idiom which is natural to him?

Levertov: Yes, and I think that is something English poetry desperately needs because a great deal of it is written in what seems to me a literary language that lacks vitality. I have had further thoughts about the American idiom in the years since I first became influenced by Williams. I think that the idiom of whatever country is yours, whatever language is yours, does have to be the norm of your poetry, if the poetry is going to be fully alive and flexible. But I think it's a terrible mistake if you leave it at that and begin to get inhibited about the whole range of language. I think this has happened to some people who have been influenced by Williams. It certainly didn't happen to Williams himself.

Sutton: Do you mean inhibited as far as vocabulary or diction is concerned?

Levertov: Yes, the actual vocabulary or diction. There are lots of people who suppose that the idea of using the idiom as your rhythmic mainstay means that you confine yourself to the language as commonly spoken and deprive yourself of all the words in the dictionary, all the words you might happen to know. But you don't have to. It's your norm, it's your mainstay, but if you want to use "thee" and "thine," if you want to use abstruse words, if they really are yours in the sense that you know them and feel them to be the most precise words for what you're saying, you have not only a right but an obligation to use them.

Sutton: You think that an unrestricted range of vocabulary is in order so long as the words are appropriate to the sensibility of the writer?

Levertov: Yes, I think so. In a sense it is not a question of American idiom; it's a question of the individual's idiom, of writing in your own language within your own or up to the limits of your own range of vocabulary, not in some preconceived literary language.

Sutton: With your adjustment to American life do you feel that the American idiom is also yours, even if not to the same extent as it is for a native-born poet?

Levertov: I think it is to quite a large extent. I've long since got to the point where I'm not quite sure whether some actual idiom that I find myself using is English or American.

Sutton: I think that your adaptation to a new language is somewhat unusual. Do you know of any other English poets who have succeeded in making this kind of transition? What do you think about Auden's poems after his coming to the United States?

Levertov: Well, speaking of Auden, I don't like his later work; and it interests me so little that I think I've not examined it carefully enough to determine whether it is really English poetry or American poetry or what. It isn't very much of a poetry to me, whereas I grew up with his earlier work and there is lots of it that I loved as an adolescent. But take Thom Gunn. I think he has remained an English poet, really, even though he lives in the States and has been so heavily influenced by Winters and uses a lot of American objects in his poems and landscapes and so forth. But I think it is an English poetry—he's one of the best English poets, I would say, of this time.

Sutton: To return to Williams for a moment. You said that he had a great deal to offer you but that it took you a while to "get him." Could you say anything more about this problem or about the qualities of his poetry that attracted you?

Levertov: I had never really heard of William Carlos Williams until not very long before I came to the States. In Paris, in a bookstore that used to carry a lot of New Directions books, I came across Williams. And my husband also didn't know anything about Williams; we bought *In the American Grain* and the *Selected Poems*, and I had an *immediate* feeling that here was something, something that was going to speak to me. I found myself unable to read *In the American Grain* because I had no background whatsoever in American history, and I went on feeling that there was something there but that I couldn't yet come to grips with it. My husband took *In the American Grain* and began to read it voraciously, and it immediately became for him a tremendously important book, as it became for me later. Now, what I felt about the poems in those first eight months or so, between my first finding them and my coming to America, and perhaps even after that for a while, was that I literally didn't know how they would sound. I couldn't read them aloud. I couldn't scan them, you know. I didn't understand the rhythmic structure, and often I didn't understand the references, because there are a lot of specifically American references, which one forgets, you know, after one becomes familiar with them. After I had lived here for a little while, I picked them up again, and I found to my joy that I could read them—and I think it was simply that my ear had gotten used to certain cadences. Besides which they do reflect something about the pace of life, which is a hard thing to put one's finger on, but it's different. The pace of life, the movement of one's day, is different in America from the movement of one's day in Europe. As for what they meant to me positively, I had an obscure sense that, because my life was changing, if I was to remain alive as a poet, I was going to have to find ways of meeting and expressing this change in my work.

Sutton: Yes, and as for the pace or movement of the day, I was reminded of James's commenting in "The Art of Fiction" on the necessity for the novelist, or any writer, I suppose, to catch what he called "the strange irregular rhythm" of the life of his place and time.

Levertov: That's exactly it. Yes. And so Williams showed me a way.

Sutton: And the movement is not only the rhythm for the individual but also the rhythm of a place which changes with the passing of time.

Levertov: Yes, and then there is the interplay of the personal rhythm and the rhythm of the place and the time, or the Zeitgeist, or whatever you call it.

Sutton: This idea would suggest that Williams may have had a point in saying that the rhythm of the long line in Whitman was all right for Whitman but not for us. Would you agree?

Levertov: Yes, and this is why certain forms do become obsolete. The sonnet is not something that is wrong in itself; it's just that it expressed in its heyday something which doesn't exist in our day.

Sutton: Just as a minuet, for example, could not sound of this place or this time?

Levertov: Yes.

Sutton: Of course, some contemporary poets have made use of the Whitman long line. Do you think that this may be an error or failure in their work just as the attempt to resuscitate the sonnet might be?

Levertov: Well, I don't think that the Whitman long line is anachronistic. I think it can be used. You'd have to mention a specific instance. Were you thinking of Allen Ginsberg?

Sutton: Yes, and I think I agree with Williams that Ginsberg's long line is somehow not in keeping with the natural rhythm of speech in our time.

Levertov: But I don't think that Ginsberg distorts the natural rhythms of speech. I think that he's often very good. He's written a lot of junk too, and he doesn't know what's his good and what's his bad work. At his best I think he is necessary and powerful.

Sutton: In the long line.

Levertov: Yes. Well, it almost all is long line—

Sutton: Of course it's not only that the line is long but that his verse employs a parallel structure, like that of the King James Bible—a structure that Whitman could use in a bardic vein; but it's not typical of our time. Even pulpit preachers do not speak in this way today.

Levertov: Well, this brings us to the subject of organic form. If one is looking for a direct expression of one's personal experience, then the units of one's experience may be long units, and a long line, a long cadence, may be the appropriate natural expression, I suppose. I think it's a terrible thing to try to concentrate on the Zeitgeist all the time. Your own experience may be much at variance with the experience of the people around you. I think that people are going to do good work only if they stick to what they themselves really experience. It may happen that they are in tune with the times, or it may not.

Sutton: Do you mean that, although the sonnet, for instance, may be largely passé, it is not really right to outlaw or proscribe forms which might still be used organically?

Levertov: By a given individual.

Sutton: Now, Whitman's long line was in keeping with a spirit of expansiveness that he shared with his time (Josephine Miles describes it as a poetry of praise) and that is not typical of our time because of changed conditions. Though I suppose the long line can be used to express other moods, other needs, as well.

Levertov: I was thinking of some of Robert Duncan's poems which I love so much. Some of them make use of an irregular long line. There are poems also in which some lines are much longer than others. A long line doesn't necessarily express expansiveness. It may express a sudden piling up of perceptions that all come tumbling out together and hold together in a sort of molecular . . . what is the word I want?

Sutton: Fusion?

Levertov: No, a sort of adherence.

Sutton: As in a magnetic field?

Levertov: Well, that, of course, brings me to Charles Olson. And Olson sometimes uses, doesn't he, quite a long line, and he does it successfully, but it's not a poetry of praise, necessarily.

Sutton: And Pound also uses a long line sometimes.

Levertov: Yes, and then Paul Goodman has poems that he titles "Long Lines."

Sutton: It may be in part that Williams objected to the long line as such because it was not in keeping with the tempo of Williams' speech.

Levertov: Yes, very likely. And much that Williams said about the American idiom is not really borne out in his poetry because much of it rises way above the American idiom as it is commonly used. It's a kind of high language.

Sutton: We've been skirting the general subject of organic form. Would you like to talk about it?

Levertov: Well, my notion of organic form is really based on the idea that there is form in all things—that the artist doesn't impose form upon chaos, but discovers hidden intrinsic form—and on the idea that poems can arrive at their form by means of the poet's attentive listening, not only his listening but also his feeling, his meditating upon his experience, and by means of his accurate transcription of that experience into words.

Sutton: This is in keeping with the quotation from Emerson—"Asking the Fact for the Form"—that you used as the title of your Wabash College lecture.

Levertov: Yes. By meditation upon the object the form of the apparently, let us say, fluid or vague or formless object is discovered and can be transmuted into words. It's a kind of alchemy.

Sutton: Aside from Emerson, whom you say you hadn't read much, how did you come to your idea of organic form?

Levertov: My thinking about organic form really began with my being asked why I wrote the way I wrote, why I broke my lines the way I did. Something that I had done intuitively I began consciously to think about. I asked myself if there were principles upon which I was working, and I discovered that there were. . . . I found that I believed in the existence of form in things, and this I would call by Hopkins' word "inscape." The inscape of things is not always immediately apparent. The inscape is a part of the object itself, when you're looking, let's say, at a flower. The flower's there. It's a real flower. You're looking at it. You are aware of it with your senses. But your experience may also include all sorts of sounds that occur at the same time you're looking at the flower and that condition what you see in one way or another.

Sutton: Are you referring to actual sounds?

Levertov: Yes, let us say that you are looking at a flower, which strikes you as a joyful sight, but at the same time you may hear an old barrel organ in the street that is making a melancholy sound. Your impression of the joyfulness of the flower is going to be conditioned in some way by what you're hearing at the same moment. Moreover, you're going to have any number of associations.

Sutton: Then the physical object, which is the focus of the poem, exists in a context in the world of reality that cannot be ignored.

Levertov: Yes, it cannot be ignored. But I would like to make the point that it *shouldn't* be ignored, and so—things exist in time—one's experience is sequential. At the first moment of looking at the flower there's a sound going on that's qualifying what you see. . . . It may be a sequence or it may be more than a simple sequence that goes from *a* to *b* to *c* to *d*. It may turn upon itself. One's feeling about it, one's thoughts, may be repeated (even in the most diagrammatic way). The sound that you've become aware of may cease, and then begin again. I'd refer to it as a constellation rather than a sequence—or I'd use the word *harmonic* to distinguish it from *melodic*. Now the form of the poem can reflect this sequence.

Sutton: Could you call it a sequence of events?

Levertov: All right, call it events. They are events which exist on a sensuous, psychological, intellectual level—all at once. All of those things are happening to you at once. They are happening in sequence but on all those levels at once. And I have found that if you are attentive enough to what is happening to you, a poem can arise out of those events which will be found to have *form*. I call it organic form because it is not a form imposed but a form discovered in the relation of the events.

Sutton: I think this is a very good way of describing the composition of an organic poem.

Levertov: But what I have just said leaves out one very important factor—something I would have added to that lecture. There is something else in the writer besides the careful attention to experience and the transcribing of experience, and that is the "form sense." It is a phrase that I have heard used by the composer Stefan Wolpe, and my idea of what it means is influenced by my experience as a painter. (I used to paint when I was a young girl; I wasn't a good painter.) Now, I know that when you are painting, and I'm speaking of painting from an object, you can go along so far in what you feel to be a transcription of what you see. You've got this bowl and these apples delineated on the canvas, but the form sense comes in to tell you that there are too many strong lines, heavy colors, let us say, in one area of this canvas. Your eye is therefore drawn that way, and perhaps, in fact, your eye goes right out of the painting at the corner, it's drawn so far down. And you have a physical sense, closely allied, I feel, with gesture and with dance, that you have to strengthen the top right-hand corner of your painting, which is very pale and very thin, or has very few lines in it. And you're going to be adding brush strokes up there which are not a faithful transcription of what you've been looking at. They're a faithful transcription of what you feel must be there, you know; and this composing element operates in the composition of an organic form. It's like, not a counterpoint, but another tension that enters and holds the whole thing together. . . . Up to a certain point the poet writing organic poetry believes in faithfulness to the events. But at a certain point he is made, if you will, to distort the events to a certain degree in order to cut them off. It's exactly like a cutting of the umbilical cord. It's a kind of violence. It is a breaking of the connections, but it enables the new child to live on its own.

Sutton: So that the work can exist as an entity.
Levertov: Yes, as an autonomous entity.

Sutton: This has something to do then with "distancing," or detaching it from a continuum of perception.
Levertov: Yes, although I do think that in the experience from which a poem arises there is a kind of intensity which happens to itself and gives it a beginning and an end.

Sutton: That sets it off as an experience?
Levertov: Yes, it's to a certain extent detached from the continuum any-way. One's faculties are more aware during that time than they are at other times. But the other thing that's left out of the lecture is the presence of the Muse, the Unexpected. The lecture made it sound as though, given an ear and some skill, one could more or less sit down and write a successful poem if only one gave that kind of attention. But something else comes into the writ-ing of a poem that really comes off. This thing, the X factor, is constantly, or

maybe inconstantly, operating in the writing of poetry, and perhaps it is what Lorca called "holding a fire in your hand." What happens is a withdrawal, by the imagination, from that first act of attention to the events. The head of the imagination is drawn back like the head of a snake about to strike. There is a silent explosion, and a blue light fills the room. It's like what happens when the alchemists call up the spirits—But this isn't true, either; it's just a vague way of saying it. But the withdrawal of attention is not something that you can do on purpose. It's something that happens to you. If you follow along, then the *duende*, or Muse, may or may not appear. Your attention is drawn back, and *Wham!* You've got an image that enters and transforms the poem and brings it alive, sets it afire, and that you never by faithful attention could have discovered. It arises out of that faithful attention.

Sutton: By a spontaneous combustion.

Levertov: Yes. Now poems in which this doesn't happen, but which are written in this organic way with great care and precision, will have organic rhythm, will give something, will reveal something; and a lot of them, I think, are pretty good poems. But, in the first-rate poems, somehow the *method* breaks and something utterly unpredictable happens.

Sutton: Do you think that these first-rate poems have a fusion or unity that the others lack?

Levertov: Yes, and there will be a sudden illumination, as well— depending on the degree. A poem in which the intellect and conscious mind have predominated can be a very good poem, but not at deep levels. I think that what happens if one gets oneself into this state of meditation that I tried to describe to you is that you are reaching down deeper into your consciousness, or unconscious, and of course it's going to have a deeper effect on the reader because it's going to speak to him at that same level.

Sutton: I don't particularly want to inject the word *archetype*, but to what extent would you say that you are speaking in Jungian terms? The idea of the archetype has led to considerable simplification.

Levertov: Yes, you can get too dogmatic about it. You can read and learn what *the* archetypes are, you know, the wise old man and so forth, and put them in your work in a perfectly conscious way, but that's not what I mean. That's why I prefer not to use the term *archetype*, because of its connotations, but I am thinking of images that arise from very deep associations and that in some marvelous way seem to reach people. . . .

Sutton: Would you like to make any other comments on organic form?

Levertov: I would like to say that one of the most important things for me about this "asking the fact for the form" is that the form arises from the fact through the sound of the words. In other words, it's not a matter of merely connotative precision. I mean that every time there is a *choice* (and there is a constant choice, as a matter of fact) of words meaning the same thing, one must be able to choose the one that corresponds in sound the most closely to the thing being spoken of. It's what Pound, quoting Dante, says about words being buttery or shaggy. If one is speaking of something fine, thin, and sharp, one has to choose the words that have the finest, thinnest, lightest, sharpest sound, and not words that have round, dark, warm, thick sounds.

Sutton: Do you mean that there is an interaction between meaning or connotation and sound, that it isn't a matter of using the words for sound as sound, but rather for sound as an element integrally related to meaning and perhaps visual images as well?

Levertov: Yes, I'm increasingly uninterested in what Pound has called *phanopoeia*, as such—the poetry of the visual image. I think the visual image is terribly important, but it must be accompanied by the *melopoeia*, and *melopoeia* of a distinctly expressive kind, not just the musical over-and-aboveness that Pound speaks of in *How to Read*. Something closer to onomatopoeia, actually.

Sutton: But visual imagery is still important to you, isn't it, as a necessary element of poetry?

Levertov: Oh, yes, it's of great interest to me. I love to look at paintings, and I think I've lived through my eyes a great deal. But visual imagery can be overemphasized, and I think that its what dissatisfies me about so much of the poetry that Robert Bly and the *Sixties* group write. I like some of it very much, but Bly's whole point of view is too much based on *phanopoeia*. That's why he's so much interested in translation, because he really seems to believe in the possibility of turning a poetry into another language. Well, I've done some translation myself, and I know just how hard it is to do. What you can do is to create another poem which will have equivalent sounds. Not that I don't believe in the possibility of translation. But obviously the simplest thing that you can do in translation is to reproduce images—and the results are frequently very unsatisfactory because the sounds are not interesting and are not expressive. . . . And even apart from Bly and that group, the average critic tends to talk about what has been said and not about the sounds in which it is said . . . and the way the sounds can carry the emotion of the poem.

Sutton: The sound carries the burden, then?

Levertov: Yes.

Sutton: And you object to the neglect of what seems to you an important dimension of form.

Levertov: Yes, a tremendously important dimension.

Sutton: Contemporary criticism has strenuously concerned itself with the analysis of meaning and imagery. I suppose that meaning and visual imagery are elements of form that are easier to get at and deal with.

Levertov: Yes, I'm in the midst of writing about ways of listening because I've noticed something about many audiences, who, even though they are *enjoying* poetry readings—and, after all, there is a public for listening to poetry now—have been conditioned by analytical experiences with poems, in school, I suppose. The lines that will most often cause a murmur of approval are lines that confirm in an almost epigrammatic way something which the audience already knows or feels. And there are whole areas of poetry, modern poetry especially, that people with those particular listening habits are really cut off from. I'm thinking of a poem by Barbara Moraff, a young poet; it is not exactly a surrealist poem, but it is a poem that is simply not apprehensible by the intellect, and yet it really has a great deal to give one. One has to listen to it in a much less alert way. Negative capability is necessary in the reader as well as in the writer. And the effects of such a poem are subliminal; there are marginal effects, if you will, conveyed in the sound of the words. It's really a very beautiful poem, but the average intelligent poetry audience wouldn't get it, I think, because they have such alert intellects.

Sutton: Yes, and for the most part poetry has been more silently read in the modern age than in earlier times.

Levertov: That's one of the historical reasons. And then there's the obvious one that, beginning around 1910 or so, people like Pound and Hulme, and later Richards and the New Critics, were trying to educate people, so that they could use their intelligence in poetry. And that was very useful, but I think it's gone too far. There's been an overemphasis on those things, and people don't bring all of themselves to the listening.

Sutton: Of course, one of the problems in talking about sound is that traditional metrics and scansion aren't much help, especially with "free," or organic, verse. You need something more.

Levertov: Yes, one person, a poet whose work doesn't on the whole mean very much to me, has done some very useful things along those lines. That's Edith Sitwell, in, among other places, *A Poet's Notebook*, the notes of her anthology, *The Atlantic Book of British and American Poetry*, and her contribution to Peter Russell's collection of essays for Pound's sixty-fifty birthday. She's really talked about the function of vowels and consonants in conveying what the poet is talking about, and she's one of the few people who have ever done it.

Sutton: Vowels and consonants in relation to meaning and feeling.

Levertov: Yes, you can't leave feeling out of meaning—total meaning, that is. . . .

Sutton: Would you like to talk about one of your poems?

Levertov: I think I would. I'm choosing this poem because it's a short poem and I've talked about it before. It isn't an especial favorite of mine, but it seems to lend itself to exposition. It's called "The Tulips," and first I'll read the poem through, and then I'll go through it step by step, trying to explain why it's written the way it is.

> Red tulips
> living into their death
> flushed with a wild blue
>
> tulips
> becoming wings
> ears of the wind
> jackrabbits rolling their eyes
>
> west wind
> shaking the loose pane
>
> some petals fall
> with that sound one
> listens for

First, there was the given fact of having received a bunch of red tulips, which I put in a vase on the windowsill. In general I tend to throw out flowers when they begin to wither, because their beauty is partly in their *short* life, and I don't like to cling to them. But these particular flowers, tulips, go on being very beautiful as the changes take place in them. I thought of that sentence of Rilke's about the unlived life of which one can die; and, looking at these tulips, I thought of how they were continuing to be fully alive, right on into their last moments. They hadn't given up before the end. As red tulips die, some chemical change takes place which makes them turn blue, and this blue seems like the flush on the cheeks of someone with fever. I said "wild blue" because, as I looked at it, it seemed to be a shade of blue that suggested to me perhaps far-off parts of sky at sunset that seem untamed, wild. There seem to be blues that are tame and blues that are daring. Well, these three lines constitute the first stanza. . . . Then came a pause. A silence within myself when I didn't see or feel more, but was simply resting on this sequence that had already taken place. Then, as I looked, this process continued. You can think of it as going on throughout a day; but when cut flowers are in that state, things happen quite fast; you can almost see them move. The petals begin to turn back. As they turn back, they seem to me to be winglike. The flowers are almost going to take off on their winglike petals. Then "ears of the wind." They seem also like long ears, like jackrabbits' ears turned back and flowing in the wind, but also as if they were the wind's own ears listening to itself. The idea of their being jackrabbits' ears led me to the next line, which is the last line of this stanza, "jackrabbits rolling their eyes," because as they turn still further back they suggest, perhaps, ecstasy. Well, this was the second unit. Then another pause. The next stanza, "west wind / shaking the loose pane," is a sequence which is pure observation without all that complex of associations that entered into the others. The flowers were on the windowsill, and the pane of glass was loose, and the wind blew and rattled the pane. This is background.

Sutton: Is it part of the sound that comes in, as you mentioned earlier?

Levertov: Yes, although it doesn't really get into the poem quite as sound. Then again a short pause, and then, "some petals fall / with that sound one / listens for." Now, the petals fall, not only because the flowers are dying and the petals have loosened themselves, in death, but also because perhaps that death was hastened by the blowing of the west wind, by external circumstances. And there is a little sound when a petal falls. Now, why does the line end on "one"? Why isn't the next line "one listens for"? That is because into the sequence of events entered a pause in which was an unspoken question, "with that sound one," and suddenly I was stopped. "One what?" Oh, "one listens to." It's the sound like the breath of a human being who is dying; it stops, and one has been sitting by the bedside, and one didn't even know it, but one was in fact waiting for just that sound, and the sound is the equivalent of that silence. And one doesn't discover that one was waiting for it, was listening for it until one comes to it. I think that's all.

Sutton: I think the line also turns back with that "one." There is a kind of reflexive movement for me, as you read it, emphasizing the solitary nature of the sound. Now in your comments on this poem you have talked mostly about the meanings, the associations of the experience, and their relation to images.
Levertov: Also, though, about their relation to rhythm, about where the lines are broken and where the silence is, about the rests.

Sutton: Where the silences fall. Now, "variable foot" is a difficult term. Williams said that it involves not just the words or the phrases but also the spaces between them. Is that your meaning also? That a pause complementing a verbal unit is a part of the sequence of events?
Levertov: Yes, and the line-end pause is a very important one; I regard it as equal to half a comma, but the pauses between stanzas come into it too, and they are much harder to evaluate, to measure. I think that what the idea of the variable foot, which is so difficult to understand, really depends on is a sense of a pulse, a pulse in behind the words, a pulse that is actually sort of tapped out by a drum in the poem. Yes, there's an implied beat, and as in music, there is such a beat, and you can have in one bar just two notes, and in another bar you have, you know, ten notes, and yet the bar length is the same. I suppose that is what Williams was talking about, that you don't measure a foot in the old way by its syllables but by its beat.

Sutton: Though not by what Pound called the rhythm of the metronome?
Levertov: Well, there is a metronome in back, too.

Sutton: Is it like the mechanical beat of the metronome or the necessarily variable beat of a pulse? Is it a constant beat? Or is it a beat that accelerates and slows?
Levertov: Oh, it accelerates and slows, but it has a regularity, I would say. I'm thinking of *The Clock* symphony of Haydn. Well, there's where the pulse behind the bars is actually heard—*pum*-pum, *pum*-pum, and so on. But then, winding around that pum-pum, it's going *dee*-dee-*dee*-dum, and so forth. Well, I think perhaps in a poem you've got that melody, and not the metronomic pum-pum; but the pum-pum, pum-pum is implied.

Sutton: When you think of the variable foot, then, you think of beats rather than of the spacing of phrases or of breath-spaced units of expression?

Levertov: I've never fully gone along with Charles Olson's idea of the use of the breath. It seems to me that it doesn't work out in practice.

Sutton: Of course he thinks of this as one of the achievements of the modernist revolution—that Pound and Williams inaugurated the use of breath-spaced lines.

Levertov: But I don't think they really are breath-spaced. There are a lot of poems where you actually have to draw a big breath to read the phrase as it's written. But so what? Why shouldn't one, if one is capable of drawing a deep breath? It's too easy to take this breath idea to mean literally that a poet's poems *ought* by some moral law to sound very much like what he sounds like when he's talking. But I think this is unfair and untrue, because in fact they may reflect his *inner* voice, and he may just not be a person able to express his inner voice in actual speech.

Sutton: You think then that the rhythm of the inner voice controls the rhythm of the poem?

Levertov: Absolutely, the rhythm of the inner voice. And I think that the breath idea is taken by a lot of young poets to mean the rhythm of the outer voice. They take that in conjunction with Williams' insistence upon the American idiom, and they produce poems which are purely documentary.

Sutton: What do you mean by the inner voice?

Levertov: What it means to me is that a poet, a verbal kind of person, is constantly talking to himself, inside of himself, constantly approximating and evaluating and trying to grasp his experience in words. And I do it even in dreams. I have many verbal dreams in which I am, as it were, writing the scene as I dream it, and sometimes I don't get it right, and I find myself going back and dreaming the scene over until I've got the words right. That's one example of the inner voice.

Sutton: It sounds something like a frustration dream in which one can't get the words right.

Levertov: I find that it isn't so much a matter of frustration, though, because in such dreams I may have to go over a scene, but I do get the words right. I had a dream which was about frustration, but I don't think of it as my frustration because I don't feel frustrated. But this was the dream. There was a sort of young middle-aged man who was a college teacher, and he was a frustrated writer. He wasn't a poet. He was a novelist. He'd written a novel and he couldn't find a publisher for the novel, and he didn't really think he liked teaching all that much, but he was stuck in it for life. You know, I've met a lot of such people. And I was not identified in my dream with this person. I was dreaming it as though I was reading a story about him. And he wrote a poem. And this is what the poem said. I woke up directly from the dream and wrote it down, still half asleep, exactly as it had been in the dream, and I gave it this title, "Poem a Frustrated Writer Wrote." I think it's the one poem that I know by heart. It goes like this:

> Life, like a neglected tethered goat,
> it's eaten the hay,
> the Bible,
> an apple,
> my novel;
> now it stands there hungry
> waiting for dessert.

Sutton: Is it still uncollected?

Levertov: I certainly wasn't going to print it, but Jay Laughlin saw it and liked it and asked if he could put it in the New Directions annual, so it will be printed, but not in my book. . . . Would you mind giving me your definition of the inner voice?

Sutton: Well, I think that the inner voice (which reminds me also of Keats's "true voice of feeling") has to do with one's inner responses or thoughts. They are affected by the conventionalization of outward speech, but they are not controlled by it to the same extent.

Levertov: I agree, and that gives me an idea, and that is the inner voice does not necessarily make use of the syntax of intellectually logical speech. It makes all kinds of leaps and bounds because many things are understood. There are many "givens" and "understoods" in its speech and that is why poetry often departs from normal expository syntactical practice.

Sutton: It seems to me that we would still say that poetry has its "syntax." The relationships are still very important, but they are not to be explained or understood in the same way.

Levertov: Yes.

Sutton: The idea of going below the syntactical level suggests the idea of the Surrealists, the breaking through the level of rational definition and experience to that of the dream or the unconscious. Do you think of it in these terms also?

Levertov: Yes, but not in such a dogmatic and limiting way. Surrealism was present in poetry before there were Surrealists; and Surrealism, in removing rational limits, tended to impose others. I think that the most interesting poetry can move back and forth with perfect ease between the rational and the irrational.

Sutton: I'm suddenly reminded of Hawthorne's description of a state between sleep and waking where the conscious mind is in partial control and yet images rise spontaneously.

Levertov: Yes, I think that is very much the state in which poems get written. It's a heightened consciousness, but it's not a heightening of the intellect. It's a heightening of the total consciousness, which includes a heightening of the emotions and of sensuous perception. . . .

Sutton: We've mentioned music and painting and dancing. Would you say that the dance as an art has been important to you as a poet?

Levertov: I think the experience of dancing has come into the practice of poetry in one way, and perhaps in much the same way as my experience of painting. It's the feeling that one gets when one is dancing, when one is improvising, that (I'm going to make a dreadful pun) one good turn deserves another. I mean, if you've moved, whirling around, let us say, in one direction, you may feel that, in the context of what you've done before, you need to get over to the other part of the stage and make some parallel kind of movement there. . . . Also, in the dance there's a parallel with writing, sometimes. It's not really dance so much as gesture. Sometimes when I'm talking I feel that the person I'm talking to has to look at me (that's why I don't like to talk on the telephone) because sometimes in conversation I feel that only a gesture will do. Well, it is a strange thing for a poet, you know, really to be saying "words fail me" and to have to use his hands. While that is true about ordinary conversation, for me anyway, in a poem there are, through tone and rhythm and imagery—through all the devices of poetry—equivalents of gesture which don't exist in ordinary speech. They exist only in the heightened speech of poetry, and perhaps that is why a person who, believe it or not, can sometimes be extremely inarticulate, like myself, can be a poet, and in fact has to be a poet because the only way one can speak is through poetry since one cannot always be gesturing.

Sutton: Would you venture the generalization that writers, or people who do have facility in the written word, may sometimes tend to be less articulate in speech?

Levertov: I wouldn't want to make a generalization like that. I've known an awful lot of writers, and some of them are very articulate.

Sutton: You related your idea of achieving balance in the dance to your earlier comments on the need of balancing composition through the form sense.

Levertov: Yes, in organic poetry one of the things that happens is that a line will be repeated, say, like a refrain. Now a person might think, "What is organic about that? That is an imposed form." But it can be organic in one of two ways. First, the experience itself may include this element of repetition or recurrence, and the recurrence in the poem is a reflection of this fact. Or it may arise out of the form sense, of the need of having to balance. But in either case it happens at the same time. It's not that you write the poem organically according to your experience and then pick it up a week later and revise it without reference to your feelings, from a coldly objective point of view, looking to see whether it's properly balanced or not. I think this is bad practice and tends to pinch the life out of a poem. This sense of the need for balance should work during the actual process of writing, which may be a question of a half hour, or a day or week or month, but it is a continuing process. As long as you are hot in it, if this sense occurs, it is *part* of the whole constellation. It enters into it naturally as a part of the organic whole.

Sutton: When you are writing, do you think about the need for balance self-consciously, or do you just do it? Or don't you know?

Levertov: I think I don't know. Sometimes I'm aware and sometimes less aware. I think the form sense has a great deal to do with one's biology, one's nervous system, and therefore it probably is one of those things that one is born with; but of course there is a great deal that one is born with that one may or may not develop.

Sutton: Or about which one may or may not intellectualize. As you spoke about the dance I was reminded that the idea of poetry as a dance of words is a fairly common one.

Levertov: Yes, and of course Pound's definition of *logopoeia* is "the dance of the intellect among words." Incidentally, it's not strictly relevant, but all that Sir John Davies wrote about the dance in his poem "Orchestra," which is about the correspondences between things, is something that has spoken very deeply to me; and it is very closely connected in my mind with those things that I've gotten from Emerson and, I may say, also from Robert Duncan.

Sutton: You have mentioned a debt to some of the earlier modernist poets, Williams particularly, but also Wallace Stevens and H. D. Would you like to comment on what you responded to in any one or more of them?

Levertov: Well, just briefly and at random: I think we've gone into what Williams meant to me and how he opened doors for me. . . . He gave me the use of the American language. He showed me how it and the American idiom could be used; and, more than that, he gave me instance after instance of how one's most ordinary experience could be shown in the poem as it was, invested with wonder. From Stevens, whose longer philosophical poems I don't care for so much as I do for his shorter poems, I think I've gotten, over and over again, a sense of magic, the same almost surrealist magic that García Lorca has—a reminder of how, at a certain pitch of awareness of language, one can make marvelous leaps. Stevens distorts my senses, like Rimbaud, you know. There's some quality that I can't quite put my finger on that I have always responded to in Stevens, whom I also discovered in Paris, shortly before coming to America.

Sutton: Are these leaps to be understood in the sense of the shifting of illusory images?

Levertov: They aren't illusory, because they reveal reality.

Sutton: I said "illusory" because he often seems concerned with the idea of the poet as an illusionist or harlequin dealing in almost kaleidoscopic effects.

Levertov: Yes, I think that's so. You see, I've often thought that if I could roll Wallace Stevens and William Carlos Williams into one, the ideal poet would then exist.

Sutton: What would this act bring together? The idea implies a contrast. There's something of each that you like; there's also a difference?

Levertov: That's a hard one. If I isolate a quality like realism in Williams, it seems to denigrate him by leaving out all his music, which is very important. So is Stevens' music. But the qualities that distinguish them in a way are realism, of a certain kind, in Williams and, as you say, the most marvelous illusionism in Stevens. But I don't think that's quite it.

Sutton: Of course, no one who is not Williams or Stevens could bring together the music of both—as neither one of them could, for that matter.

Levertov: In a way, since I admire them both very much, and love their work, and knew Williams personally and loved him very dearly, it sounds as if I'm saying that they are incomplete, but I'm not complaining of incompleteness. When I say that this would be the ideal poet, I mean an impossibly *ideal* poet, you know.

Sutton: Yes, the "complete" poet. As for Williams' realism, although he makes use of the commonplace, he enhances it.

Levertov: Oh, but he doesn't enhance it. He reveals it in its uncommonplaceness. Perhaps you could use the terms "classic" and "romantic," with Williams as the classic and Stevens as the romantic. Or with Williams as sunlight and Stevens as moonlight. That's why I'm saying that the ideal combination is impossible because one doesn't want to mix these things. But just let me put it like this: When I read Williams I don't feel that there's anything missing, but when I read Stevens I feel that there is some quality he has which maybe Williams doesn't have. It isn't felt as a lack in Williams.

Sutton: And of course there are qualities in Williams that Stevens doesn't have.

Levertov: Of course. There is to my mind a good deal more lacking in Stevens than there is in Williams.

Sutton: Why?

Levertov: Well, too much of Stevens is philosophical poetry; and it gets to be tiresome, I think.

Sutton: Because aesthetics is often the subject of his poems?

Levertov: Well, I don't mind that either. If that is what a poet is genuinely preoccupied with, then he ought to write poems about it. Unless it just remains a subject, you know, as it sometimes does in Stevens. In his long poems, there isn't to me the illuminating synthesis of form and content. The content remains content, or separable subject matter. There's too much of those poems that one could paraphrase, but the short poems are unparaphrasable. . . .

Sutton: You have said that H. D. has meant a good deal to you.

Levertov: But I'm not really speaking of her best known poetry, the early Imagist poetry, but the later poems, the poems in the war trilogy called *The Flowering of the Rod*, *Tribute to the Angels*, and *The Walls Do not Fall*. . . . There are certain things about the music of poetry and its relation to meaning which I think one can learn from those later poems. They're very simple— you might almost think them prosy on the surface, and yet if you read them out loud there's the most marvelous music that arises out of them, like incense. And they're terribly neglected. In the *Selected Poems* that Grove Press put out there are bits of them, but I don't think they're in print as complete books at the moment. My copies were given to me by Norman Holmes Pearson. They were printed in England, and so far as I know they have never appeared as complete books in the United States.

Sutton: Do you like Pound's work?

Levertov: I feel that I have learned more from Pound's criticism than from his poetry. Although I read it, I don't trace in myself any direct influence from his poetry. Yet I constantly reread *The ABCs of Reading* and have found it very useful, very practical.

Sutton: This is in keeping with Eliot's judgment of . . .

Levertov: Oh, it's not a judgment of his poetry. I was just thinking of it quite egotistically.

Sutton: Well, Eliot did comment that Pound's importance for him was primarily as a critic, by which he did not mean simply his prose writings. I believe he also suggested that the poetry had a critical interest for him.

Levertov: But he did also call him *il miglior fabbro*, "the better craftsman."

Sutton: Yes, he did. But do you feel that you have not responded in the same way to his poetry as you have to that of Stevens or Williams?

Levertov: I wouldn't quite say that. I have responded to it as a reader, but as a poet I feel that I have not learned from his poetry. This is not to suggest that there isn't something there to learn.

Sutton: Do you have any particular preference among his poems or between his earlier and later poems?

Levertov: No, the poetry of Pound that I most admire is all over the *Cantos*—early, middle, and late. There is a great deal of the *Cantos* that I don't understand and that doesn't really come through to me, but there are parts throughout that I think are marvelous poetry.

Sutton: Do you think the *Cantos* are radically incoherent?

Levertov: I don't think so. I don't see why I should assume that they are. But I think I don't understand them.

Sutton: You do think that they are poetry, however?

Levertov: Oh, yes, although I'm sure it isn't all on the same level. It has lots of ups and downs.

Sutton: I was thinking of an unsympathetic critic who referred to the later cantos as simply static thrown out by Pound's madness.

Levertov: It seems to me that there is a fashionable trend at the moment to denigrate the *Cantos*. But what seems to me to be poetry in them continues to seem to be that, and therefore I'm willing to give the benefit of the doubt to the parts that I don't understand. That's all I can say, really.

Sutton: One poet of the same generation that we haven't discussed is T. S. Eliot.

Levertov: Oh, Eliot.

Sutton: Yes.

Levertov: Well, I read Eliot pretty intensively when I was still living in England, and I'm sure that when I was very young I must have, just by osmosis, you know, not in any conscious way, been influenced, like everyone else to some extent, by Eliot; but he hasn't gone on being one of the important sources for me. A lot of Eliot that meant something to me twenty years ago, or fifteen years ago, doesn't wear very well. You know, in a way, the simple fact of his having dried up puts him at a remove. Those who went on writing throughout their lives, like Williams and Stevens and H. D., thereby somehow establish a claim upon and a rapport with the reader. But Eliot, by drying up when he did and yet still being around, you know, like a ghost at the party, sort of lost touch. It's an unfair thing to say. What if he had died at that age? Would his poetry still be relevant to us? I really don't know, but . . .

Sutton: But he doesn't have a contact with the coming generation, you think, and his work doesn't run into theirs?

Levertov: Yes, and there's his conservatism, his critical ideas, and so forth. His idea of the objective correlative is an important one, but a lot of his critical ideas are not very congenial to me.

Sutton: And in that respect you are probably typical of other poets of your generation, don't you think?

Levertov: I think so, but of course there are, I suppose one can say, at least two main groups of poets of my generation. And the other one I am thinking of (I am sure there are more than that) includes the poets grouped around or influenced by Robert Lowell. They write a confessional poetry—a poetry that isn't interested in sounds or philosophical ideas or images as such, but in psychology from a confessional point of view.

Sutton: This is a link with Eliot.

Levertov: And those poets continue to have a very respectful attitude to Eliot. Of course, Robert Duncan, who is a poet very close to me and from whom I feel I have learned a great deal, has paid homage to Eliot quite explicitly in a poem like "The Venice Poem." Eliot was very important to him at that time, and hasn't been discarded, but I think Eliot is not so important to any of the people I'm associated with as the other ones that we have mentioned—and Cummings isn't either.

Sutton: Would you say that Eliot is more important to the poets of the Academy than to the poets outside?

Levertov: Yes, and I think it's not so much because of his poetry as such, but because of the intellectual position that he took up and that they use as a sort of backing.

Sutton: His conservatism.

Levertov: Yes.

Sutton: As you have been talking about your and other poets' greater interest in figures like Williams and Stevens and Pound and H. D., I was thinking that it is ironic that Williams should have regarded *The Waste Land* as such a permanent blight on the poetic landscape and that he should have felt himself at such a disadvantage in relation to Eliot as an influence on contemporary poetry.

Levertov: He certainly did feel at a disadvantage. He said so explicitly in a number of places, mistakenly I am sure.

Politics and the Poet: An Interview with Denise Levertov

E. G. Burrows / 1968

From *Michigan Quarterly Review*, 7:4 (1968), 239–42. Reprinted by permission of *Michigan Quarterly Review*.

EGB: Denise Levertov is the author of some seven volumes of poetry and I think, without question, one of America's leading poets today. She has also been very much involved in recent years in an organization called RESIST, and on behalf of the defense of her husband (her husband being Mitchell Goodman) and others indicted for assisting in resistance to the draft. Perhaps, Denise, you could fill us in on what RESIST is, and I will ask you how this has affected your life in recent years.

DL: Mitch and I have been involved in anti-war activities for three or four years, but RESIST has only come into being during the last year. How it started is more or less like this: its origins occurred spontaneously and unconnectedly in several places at the same time. For example, in New York, Grace Paley and Carl Bissinger and some other people associated with the Greenwich Village Peace Center started an organization called SUPPORT IN ACTION, which is now the New York local of RESIST. They started that about a year ago to support local New York draft resisters. This time last year, my husband was in Stanford for ten weeks teaching in a special program called the VOICE project, and while he was there he met some of the young men who for reasons of conscience are resisting induction and opposing the whole selective service system, not merely seeking conscientious-objector status but refusing to cooperate with the selective service system at all.

He was very impressed with them. There were some active people on the staff of the faculty and in the Bay area who were also forming adult support organizations in connection with these young men, people who felt it shouldn't be the young that take the whole brunt of the struggle but that if these young men were going to be put in jail they were going to be the people standing up with them and saying "we aid, abet, and counsel these young men and what befalls them must befall us. We're not going to let them disappear alone into jail, we're going to put our bodies on the line to the fullest

28

extent of our ability." And he became during that period of two months or so very active with this group.

When he came back East, he was expecting that a similar movement would spring up in the big eastern colleges as it had at Stanford and Berkeley, but nothing seemed to be happening. So in the middle of the summer he and I and a summer neighbor in Maine, Henry Braun, who is a writer and poet and teaches at Temple University, Philadelphia—we got together, in our kitchen as a matter of fact, and sat around and wrote (Mitch did most of the writing, Henry and I made suggestions, offered our support and collusion) a kind of Call to professional people above draft-eligible age to form a support-group of this kind. We got this reproduced at a local printing shop, and we sent it out to a mailing list of about 300 people we sort of summoned out of memory and our own address books. In the meantime (we were rather isolated there in the country), a group of Eastern intellectuals—people including Dwight MacDonald, Noam Chomsky, and Seymour Melman—got out the Call to Resist Illegitimate Authority, which was printed in *The New York Review of Books* and in *The New Republic* and one or two other places. The content of this Call was almost identical with ours. The content *was* identical, the wording was slightly different. So we got together with them instead of duplicating our efforts. My husband felt that we should have some specific action which would be coördinated with the planned turn-in of draft cards across the country on October 16, [1967]. The first action we planned was to be on October 16. Then he went down and talked with Coffin at Yale and with one or two other people. Instead, they came up with the idea of doing it a few days later so that we would have time to collect all those draft cards that had been turned in across the country on the 16th, and that a group of very eminent and respectable people from various professions should take these draft cards to the Justice Department. And that's what we did. We added our little mailing list to the large mailing list that RESIST had already accumulated, and we asked people to come to Washington on that day. Six hundred people from all over the country, including many heads of departments—for example Donald Kalish from UCLA, head of the Philosophy Department—several Nobel prize winners in the sciences—I think Albert Szent-György is one of those—and many clergy, doctors, teachers, mostly college teachers but also quite a number of high-school and possibly even some elementary teachers—a number of very well-known writers including (as you know by now) Norman Mailer and of course Robert Lowell, who was very supportive throughout—quite an imposing array of people, including Dr. Spock—went to the Justice Department where we had secured an appointment with an assistant attorney general, man name of McDonough, I think, and a delegation of these people, plus some young representative resisters from different places in the country, took the thousand draft cards, which at that time had been gathered, in to this man and had their interview with him. Meanwhile the rest of us had a meeting on the steps outside. The organization, RESIST, which is the adult support-group to distinguish it from "The Resistance," which is the organization of young men of draft age, at that time was extremely loosely knit and had a sort of temporary office in New York, and subsequently developed a steering committee and a regular office with a full-time secretary in Cambridge, Mass.

EGB: Did the actual indictment of the individuals follow very quickly after this?

DL: No, it didn't. That occurred—the March on the Pentagon was on the 21st of October, so our thing was the day before—and the indictments didn't come until the fifth of January [1968]. In fact, in Mitch's case at least, the actual envelope with the official letter of indictment didn't arrive until considerably after that time. The first we heard of it was when some TV and news-service people called up and asked for interviews. They all arrived one after another the evening of the fifth, but we had received no official notice at all. Then, as you probably know the arraignment took place in Boston on the 29th of January, and then a period was allotted for the filing of motions, thirty days to the defense and thirty days to the prosecution. . . .

My husband welcomed the indictment, even though it's a plaguey thing to be mixed up with. But when he undertook the actions which led to his indictment, he knew what the odds were. He knew what he was doing could cause him to be indicted, and he knew what the penalties were. He welcomed it because the trial has seemed a valuable opportunity to publicly air certain issues.

EGB: Denise, you've been traveling around the country speaking on behalf of this organization as well as doing poetry readings. Has there been a decided effect on your artistic life from being involved in this sort of activity?

DL: In some ways it's the other way around. I have found myself as a poet, long before this particular involvement, saying things in poems which I think have moral implications. I think that if one is an articulate person, who makes certain statements, one has an obligation as a human being to back them up with one's actions. So I feel that it is poetry that has led me into political action and not political action which has caused me to write poems more overtly engaged than those I used to write, which is something that has happened to me, but that is just a natural happening. I've always written rather directly about my life and my concerns at any particular time.

EGB: What is it that happens to some writers who become so heavily involved in espousing causes that they become merely propagandists? What do you see as the reason for this?

DL: I think that that can happen when an artist is involved in some kind of political ideology that has a party line which he follows. I don't think that this happens in the peace movements in this country, where so many poets in the last two or three years have been increasingly writing poems overtly concerned with war, because the peace movement in this country is not an ideology, is not a monolithic organization with a party line, which a person enters and gives up his own conscience and thought and becomes subservient to that ideology. The peace movement in this country is just an agglomeration of individuals. Some people say that this is a weakness, that it would have more power or more efficiency if it were better organized. I think that would be only a very temporary and superficial advantage. I think its great underlying strength is that it is composed of individuals who do whatever they do—do their thing—because their own conscience leads them to it, and the proliferation of organizations within the peace movement is a reflection of that fact. I think it's basically a strength. And I think that artists who get involved with it are not affected in that way that you described, for that very reason.

EGB: The key might be—when issues touch the individual, then he can react authentically as an artist, but when those issues are on some . . .

DL: —theoretical—

EGB: . . . level, and don't really concern him as an individual, then he becomes simply a propagandist.

DL: Yes, I absolutely agree. I think there is no abrupt separation between so-called political poetry and so-called private poetry in an artist, who is in both cases writing out of his own inner life. It's like you were saying.

EGB: You spend a tremendous amount of time giving readings—and now, talking on behalf of this organization, do you wish on some occasions that this weren't so time-consuming?

DL: Well, I don't spend that much time doing it. Actually, last year I was teaching—I was teaching part-time at Vassar and I had two days a week that were taken up by that entirely, and I had some reading engagements during the year, which either were—you know—just a few bunched together so that I wasn't away more than five days, so that I could meet my schedule, or else I think a few of them were during periods when Vassar wasn't having classes, you know—a reading period or vacation or something like that. I didn't spend a great deal of time giving readings last year, and this year I am not teaching. It was going to be a year off. We were going to do some nice things, which we didn't get around to do, because it was obviously not the year to lead a sybaritic life on the beach somewhere. So in December I went on a tour like this, which was a poetry reading tour, basically, and, in each place I went, I made contact with peace groups and spoke with them, too, and sort of made myself a double schedule, and I've done that this time, too, and it is very time-consuming and takes up a tremendous amount of energy, but in December I was away only a little over two weeks, actually. This time I am going to be on the road the whole month of April, and I'm sure I will be exhausted by the time I am through, but then I don't have plans for going on doing it the rest of the year.

EGB: Have you noticed or detected any new attitudes arising from either audiences or the sponsors for some of your appearances, by the fact that you are involved in this extra-poetic—shall we say—activity?

DL: Well, I try to be—very . . . I've only been doing the extra-poetic activity this winter, you know. It's true that in my readings last year I read some poems about the war, and I made my position clear, but I didn't do the kind of thing that I did in December, and that I'm doing now; and I've been very careful to meet my English-department commitments satisfactorily—not to take time from them—and to do all that I was asked to—was being paid to do. So I haven't had anybody feel that I was using an invitation for other purposes. Some of the English-department people under whose care I have been at different places have been really very sympathetic to my point of view and have encouraged me to bring in the discussion of the war and the draft. At other places, they are neutral, but they have never been hostile. Some audiences that I have spoken to in the last week, not whole audiences but some people in some audiences, have been offended by my political point of view. I spoke to high-school teachers in Minneapolis on Saturday morning, sort of an "in-service" series course of readings and discussions like the one they have here in Detroit, which you probably have heard about. (They have poets come and talk to the high-school teachers, and they also have young poets come read in the schools.) And . . . there were some . . . I felt a certain coldness, perhaps hostility, from some members of *that* audience.

EGB: I can imagine that there are still individuals who feel that a poet shouldn't be involved in political or whatever kinds of activity. I think they're becoming fewer and fewer as the years go by.

DL: I think there are. Although, if one goes to . . . I was in Mankato College in Minnesota, and that place is full of hawks. It's largely apathetic, and it has a tiny number of anti-war people. It has an increasing number of McCarthy supporters, but they are liberal more than radical, you know, as many such are, and it has quite a sizable number of people who are quite hawkish, and there some people walked out on my reading, they didn't walk out noisily or make a big fuss or anything, but I think that they were antago-nized by the fact that I had dedicated my reading to the memory of Dr. King, and because I stopped and spoke about some of the issues in the course of talking about the poems.

EGB: Since you brought Dr. King into it and the fact that we have been going through a difficult period and I am sure we have more difficulties ahead of us, how do you feel all the racial problems and the urban problems in this country may conceivably affect the anti-war and draft resistance movements?

DL: It's very difficult for me to answer the question in the way that you framed it. It would be easier to say something about . . . you know, if you reversed the question and say, "What is the possible effect, what is the rela-tion of the anti-war movement to the racial question." I think I could give an answer to that one, but I'm not. . . .

EGB: Let's rephrase it.

DL: Well, I feel that as long as billions of dollars are being spent on war—I don't just *feel* this and I think we all *know* it. There are very many essential priorities here at home which are being increasingly neglected at a time when they should be increasingly attended to, and if all the money that is being put into this war—if these fantastic, *fantastic* sums of money were put into hous-ing, schools, health, non-military economic development, we would have a very different racial situation here. People say, "Even if you improve the economic situation of black people in this country, you've still got the white people with deep-rooted prejudices." True, but I think that a better educa-tional system in this country, one of the things that it would do—it would begin to educate white people, too, and work upon their prejudices, and so it's all part of one thing. One can't consider these things separately. The moral climate would be changed, and this would affect the prejudice, and even if it didn't affect it deeply (the prejudice of people who are now middle-aged), it would very much, I believe, affect the attitudes of *young* white people in communities where there is a lot of prejudice. They would begin to change. There would be a different generation.

Craft Interview with Denise Levertov
William Packard / 1971

From *New York Quarterly*, 7 (Summer 1971), 9–25. Reprinted in William Packard, *The Craft of Poetry*. (New York: Doubleday, 1974), pp. 79–100. Reprinted by permission of William Packard and *New York Quarterly*.

NYQ: What stories or poems from your childhood reading do you remember particularly? Which ones do you think may have had an influence on your development as a poet?

DL: Well, it's always difficult to know what did and what didn't affect your work later. My mother read aloud to me a great deal when I was a child, even after I was reading to myself. She read Beatrix Potter, whom I consider a great stylist, the Andrew Lang fairy books, Hans Anderson. She read aloud very well, and she read not only to me, but to the assembled family, consisting of my sister, my father, and myself—all of Dickens, all of Jane Austen, and most of George Eliot, most of the nineteenth century classics. It was a somewhat nineteenth century household, I think, in that in the evenings we would sit around listening to reading out loud.

NYQ: Your name is often linked with the names of the Black Mountain poets, with William Carlos Williams, Ezra Pound, and H. D. Who are some of the other poets, early or contemporary, whose work has significantly affected your own?

DL: As a child, when I started reading poetry, I read Keats and Tennyson and Wordsworth. Then I also read the younger poets, the kind of avant garde ones in England during my childhood—Auden and Spender and Eliot. I read lots of Elizabethan poetry as a child—lots. When I was growing up, people in England were really very ignorant of American poetry. I really did not know many writers, and the ones I did know were not reading Pound. I did not read him until about a year before I came to America. Williams was totally unknown to me until that time. H.D.—of course, one always saw the Imagists' stuff, but I didn't know the latest. There is a lot of H.D. which was published in England which has never been published here. Stevens I began to read in Paris, the year before I came to America. I read, you know, the English people who were just a little older than I was, and who were being published in England when I was first publishing. And well, I'd read some French poetry at that time—a little Rimbaud and Baudelaire, nothing much else, really.

NYQ: The words "dance," and "dancing" appear regularly in your poetry, but only in your most recent collection, *Relearning the Alphabet*, is there a poem about the experience of dancing itself. Are there ways, perhaps in the area of rhythm, where your having been a dancer is reflected in your work?

DL: I have come to feel that there definitely are. You see, I studied very strict ballet when I was intending to become a dancer. I was sort of pushed into that by my sister, and when I quit I had a revulsion against it and didn't even like to think about it for a number of years. Then I danced again, just for pleasure. I did some modern dance in New York with a friend, Midi Garth, who is a very fine dancer; and when we lived in Mexico I found a ballet class which I went to a couple of times a week for a year, and I got quite good again, and began to enjoy the dancing for itself. I had looked on it as something with such a rigid technique, as something that did not seem to connect at all with what I became interested in—in writing and the other arts. But I came to feel that my experience dancing had definitely given me some sense of internal rhythm, and of gesture as it translates itself into language, of pace, of energy, of things like that which possibly I wouldn't have felt if I'd never danced. So it was a rather obscure influence . . .

NYQ: What about the kind of self-discipline a dancer has to learn? Do you discipline yourself in your writing—write at certain regular times, in a particular place?

DL: No. I don't really believe in anything that rigid and that imposed from without. I feel that classic ballet with its rigid discipline is a very very narrow medium—it doesn't have a wide or deep range of expressiveness. It can be very beautiful, I enjoy seeing it, but I think of it as decorative and relatively superficial, among the art forms.

NYQ: Do you feel differently about modern dance?

DL: Well, theoretically. Actually, I have very rarely seen modern dance that seemed to reach the kind of depth and subtlety and have the range of language arts or music. The dancer I spoke of, Midi Garth—I've seen some performances of her solo works, her own choreography, that did seem to me to be very high art, but I've rarely seen modern dance that deeply satisfied me.

NYQ: You encourage your students to keep writing notebooks. Do you do that yourself?

DL: Yes, I do.

NYQ: What is the relationship between the look of your notebooks, and the collection of material in your "Notebook" poem?

DL: It's really something of a misnomer. That was just a sort of handle, to refer to the poem by. The part that you've seen, in *Relearning the Alphabet*, has been augmented, and it will be part of a book called *Staying Alive*.

NYQ: When will that be published?

DL: There's a slim chance that it may be out in the fall, if we have a lot of luck in getting it together and get a printer to do it in time, but otherwise it will be out next spring. New Directions doesn't have a winter list. I'd like very much to have this book out in the fall, if it's humanly possible, because I have a certain sense of urgency about it—both because of its nature, and because one feels urgent anyway, at this time. Everyone feels somewhat apocalyptic, I suppose—one feels in a hurry to get things done and to speak to one's brothers and sisters while there's still time.

NYQ: The new book continues the revolution theme?

DL: Yes.

NYQ: What effect has your teaching had on your writing?

DL: I think it's had a mixed effect. Often it definitely takes time and energy away from writing. On the other hand, it's had a profound effect on my life in bringing me into contact with the student generation, and with political activism on the various campuses. If I hadn't been teaching I might easily have found myself very isolated politically, and perhaps would not have developed. I feel I have learned a lot through teaching which I wouldn't have learned without it. And in some cases, like last year at MIT and the year before at Berkeley, especially, I experienced a marvelous sense of community with my students at times, and I'm glad not to have missed that. Of course I've always felt it with individual students, but I've twice felt it—not all the time, but some of the time—with a group of students. I think that was a very important human experience.

NYQ: Are there areas in which you have generally found American students to be well equipped when they come into a poetry writing class, or places where they are often deficient?

DL: Well, I can't compare them with, say, English students, because I was never a student in England myself, and I've never taught anywhere but in America. But I'd say that most American students are grossly deficient in their reading background and general knowledge. There are lots of people with lots of natural talent, and very very few with any sort of useful background.

NYQ: Do you partly blame television for that?

DL: I don't blame any single factor for it, but I certainly don't think that television has helped. It is definitely a generation of spectators, and I don't know that this affects student *poets* particularly, but it does affect students in the classroom. My students this year, for example, tend to want to be entertained, I think. They want me to put on a performance for them in which they can sit passively back and not participate. Of course, the more politically conscious students are, the more they really try to participate in discussion and in everything else that's going on in the class. They want to create their own education. The students I have this year are politically very backward, an economically elite group, I would say, and it's very difficult to get to each other. They don't have a sense of collective possibilities. Students, and people in general in this country, have less and less of a common culture. Even if you get a bunch of people aged about twenty together who have all read a fair amount and looked at some paintings and had other experiences in the arts, there is very little likelihood of their having read the same books or looked at the same paintings, and the only thing that they can count on for sure is usually certain TV programs, such as Captain Kangaroo, which they watched when they were little. And that's the common currency, which is a very low grade of common cultural currency, the only dependably shared element. I think that's a pretty sad state of affairs, to put it mildly. However, as far as poets are concerned, it's very hard to say what is good or bad for a person of real talent. It's such an individual matter.

NYQ: You've written about helping your students to experience a poem as a sonic entity, apart from its meaning. How do you go about that?

DL: By trying to get them to listen to the poem, to hear it a number of times over, before launching into discussion of it. A lot of students—I would say the majority of students—have somehow picked up the idea that a poem is a problem to be solved, and that one reads a poem efficiently by making a paraphrase of it while reading it, and by this process of paraphrasing you somehow *obtain* the poem. Then you can forget it, and go on to the next one.

But they don't listen to music that way. Of course, if a person is a serious student of music, he will learn about musical form, he will be interested in it, and he will recognize when a theme is transposed into another key, or when it recurs played by another instrument—all those little things that take place in the structure of a piece of music. But certainly the average person who cares to listen to a piece of music isn't constantly doing that, he doesn't regard that as the only way in which he can really get the music. It's a direct experience which is accepted as such by most people. Poetry presents complicated surfaces of denotative and connotative meaning as well as of sound-patterns, and it's natural that people want to feel that they have understood what has been said, and sometimes a certain degree of interpretive paraphrase may be necessary if you want to talk about a poem. But you can receive a poem, you can comprehend a poem, without talking about it. Teachers at all levels encourage the idea that you have to talk about things in order to understand them, because they wouldn't have jobs, otherwise. But it's phony, you know.

NYQ: Do you think the fact that memorization has gone out of fashion has anything to do with the modern reader's having trouble reacting to a poem as rhythmic sound? Poetic rhythms aren't established in his head, in his ear . . .

DL: I don't know. It's an interesting theory. I've never been able to memorize anything myself, but I think I have a strong sense of rhythmic structure. I remember a French teacher I went to when I was a kid being quite impressed with me because I read aloud a French poem in a metrically correct way, and she said she very rarely had a student who did that. I think that's because I picked up very quickly on the rhythmic structure of the poem, but it certainly wasn't through memorization, so I don't feel I'm in a position to pass judgment on that.

NYQ: You have done direct translation, knowing the other language well yourself, you have also translated using a linguist, as you did with the *In Praise of Krishna* poems. Do you find the experiences very different in the degree to which you are able to reach the heart of the original poem?

DL: There's certainly a degree of difference. However, in those Indian poems, my collaborator was himself so deeply into the poems and was able to give such fine explanations of any questions I had, and his own versions which I worked on were so good, that in some cases I really changed very few words. In others I changed quite a lot. The degree of difference was not as great as it can be when you have a less sensitive collaborator. I once did that, and it just didn't work out. The big difference is that translating from a language you don't know at all, you have actually no idea what it sounds like. With the French, although I didn't try any sort of elaborate imitations of sound and structure, I did of course know what it sounded like and was influenced in my versions by the sound of the original.

NYQ: Where, on a scale that ran from literal translation to adaptation, would you put your translations of the Guillevic poems?

DL: The Guillevic ones, with few exceptions, are very close to the original, I think. I noted the places where I knew that I had departed, and there are many places where I just goofed. With those exceptions, they're not adaptations. They are translations, but I tried to make them stand up as poems, and therefore it's not a line-by-line thing. You'll find some stanzas are longer, or possibly shorter, in mine than in the original because I broke the lines differently with the idea of English-American rhythms. With some translators, if a stanza has five lines in the original they have five lines, quite rigidly. I didn't stick that closely, but I never deliberately changed an image, added an adjective, except as noted in the text.

NYQ: There are clear similarities between your poetic style and Guillevic's style. Do you feel one poet can successfully translate the work of another whose interests and methods are radically different from his own?

DL: I would think it would be very difficult. I myself would not be very interested in attempting it. I have to feel a certain affinity to be drawn to translate something.

NYQ: Why do you do translations?

DL: It's to—to really get deeper into the poem. One of the things one is doing in writing poems at all is grasping one's own experience by transmuting it, one is translating experience into language, one is apperceiving, one is finding out what it is that one knows. So with poems in another language, I tend to feel that if I'm attracted to a poem I want to absorb it more deeply by the act of translation. It's already a verbal experience, but it isn't absolutely distinct from that basic impulse to grasp experience in language that a poet has anyway, I think. It's just an extension of it.

NYQ: You've said you try to help each of your students find his own voice. When you came to this country to live, what impact did meeting the American idiom have on your poetic voice?

DL: Well, it certainly made a difference. Of course, it's impossible to predict what my development might have been if I'd stayed in England. I have always felt that I would not have developed very far because it was not a good time for English poetry. It was really in the doldrums, and I think I might have found it stultifying. I presume that I would have gone on being a writer because I can't imagine being anything else; and you know I had started writing very young and had had a book published before I came here. I think it was very beneficial for me to come to America at a time when American poetry was in a very live period. But, although it seemed so at the time, in recent years I've come to realize that it wasn't a dramatic break. My early poems are very kind of wish-y romantic poems, the ones in my first book, but they have in them the seeds of everything that I've done since, actually. Hayden Carruth pointed out to me that in the poems about my sister, and in the ones in which I am writing about my childhood, my diction becomes quite British. It was an unconscious thing, but in fact my language has always moved back and forth between English and American usage. It leads to problems for the reader, because there are ways I have of saying things, if I'm saying them in an English kind of way, that the American reader doesn't pick up on. As for the English reader, the English reader doesn't know how to read American poetry anyway, because the whole pace of American speech is very different. Of course, this has changed somewhat in the last ten or fifteen years because there is much more interest in American literature now in England, and people have seen so many American movies they're probably getting the feel of the American idiom. I feel that I am genuinely of both places, and that has simply extended my usage. I'm glad to have a foot in more than one culture.

NYQ: To what extent do you feel a poet can use words in his writing that are not part of his normal vocabulary?

DL: He can, if he's not doing it for pretentious reasons, but because really, in looking for the accurate word, he comes upon a word which, in its meaning and sound, makes him say, "Aha! This is the word I need for this thing that I'm saying." At that moment that word becomes a natural part of his vocabulary. After all, the whole thing was once unknown territory to each of us. Our vocabulary grows as we grow. So I wouldn't exclude words that a person finds because he's looking for them. But the sort of deliberate showing off— occasionally you find somebody actually looking through the dictionary for abstruse words and sort of saving them to be used in some poem—I think that's just childish.

NYQ: When a new poem begins in your head, do you start writing immediately?

DL: It depends on what is coming into my head. If it is a sort of vague feeling that somewhere in the vicinity there is a poem, then no, I don't do anything about it, I wait. If a whole line, or phrase, comes into my head, I write it down, but without pushing it unless it immediately leads to another one. If it's an idea, then I don't do anything about it until that idea begins to crystallize into some phrases, some words, a rhythm, because if I try to push that into being by will before the intuition is really at work, then it's going to be a very bad beginning, and perhaps I'm going to lose the poem altogether. So there is some feeling of when to begin writing, but it's really rather hard to describe, especially since it's somewhat different with each poem. There is often a kind of preliminary feeling, a sort of aura—what is it? An early warning?—which alerts one to the possibility of a poem. You can smell the poem before you can see it. Like some animal . . . Hmmm, seems like a bear's around here . . .

NYQ: Do you usually hear a poem's rhythm from the beginning?

DL: Well, if it was the smell of a bear, you know, you might begin to hear it kind of going . . . pad . . . pad . . . pad around the house; but if, let's say, it was a kind of a rustle in the bushes, which might be a bird or a snake or a squirrel, it might start to go blipblipblipblip . . .

NYQ: Do you revise a good deal?

DL: That again depends on the individual poem. Of course, the longer the poem, the more revision. The kind of poem that comes out right the first time is almost always a very short poem. When poems emerge full-blown, I feel that there's been lots of preliminary work done on them, at a preconscious level.

NYQ: Since you write in nontraditional, free forms, what determines the physical shape a poem of yours will take? For example, what most often decides stanza divisions for you?

DL: I've written about this in an article called "Some Notes on Organic Form," which has been published in a number of places. It was first in *Poetry Magazine*, and then it was reprinted in a *New Directions Annual*, and it's been reprinted again in an anthology called *Naked Poetry* which Bob Mezey and Stephen Berg brought out about a year ago. I think of there being clusters of perceptions which determine the stanza. Of course, sometimes the stanza breaks in the middle of a sentence, syntactically, but the perception cluster, nevertheless, did pause there for a moment.

NYQ: What do you consider in deciding the length of a line?

DL: I regard the end of a line, the line break, as roughly equivalent to half a comma, but what that pause is doing is recording nonsyntactic hesitations, or waitings, that occur in the thinking-feeling process. This is where the dance comes into it. You can't get this onto your tape, but I can sort of demonstrate it for you (*stands, and moves to the center of the room*). You see, in the composition of a poem, thinking and feeling are really working together, as a kind of single thing, although they often get separate in other areas of one's life. We don't want to call the movement of that process thinking-feeling, it's too clumsy; and we don't want to call it thinking—it's more than thinking, and we don't want to call it feeling—it's more than feeling, so let's call it perception, as perhaps a not totally accurate, but usable, term. That process does not go on at a steady walking pace (*walking*). It doesn't constantly dance around, either, but it may kind of hurry forward (*little fast steps*), and then it will stop (*stops*), and then it will walk more slowly, and it has definitely an almost dance-like movement to it, not constantly skipping and jumping and running, but a varied motion. For instance, when one is simply conversing, with feeling, with a friend, even if one tends to think and speak in rather complete sentences, nevertheless there are pauses in one's speech which are expressive pauses—sometimes for emphasis, sometimes because one has rushed forward to a certain point (*demonstrating*), and one doesn't really know what the next word that one is going to say will be. These are not syntactic pauses. The sentence is there, in back of them. Sometimes the sentence becomes broken, sometimes the sentence is never finished, often the sentences are complete. But articulations—in the sense that our bones, our fingers, are articulated, right? They have joints, they can bend— occur. These occur within the rationale of the syntax, and the line break is a peculiarly sensitive means of recording those things. So that one can pick up all the rhythm of feeling, all the rhythm of experience, in ways which prose is perhaps not as well equipped to do. Of course, good prose is rhythmic, too, but it doesn't depend quite so heavily as poetry does on the finest adjustments of rhythm and even of typographically indicated intonation.

NYQ: There is a remarkable variation in the speed with which your lines can be read—sometimes there are several speed shifts within one short poem, such as "The Singer," and sometimes the change comes between sections of longer poems, as happens in the one called "Six Variations."

DL: It's never directly stated in that poem, but the six variations are about language and what it can do. You know, it mentions Gertrude Stein's dog Basket, and how she learned what a sentence was. The section with the long rhymes, with the ashcans and the children on the street, demonstrates the speed of polysyllabic lines—the lines are longer, but there are lots of polysyllables in them, and the movement is a sort of fast, rippling movement. And then there's a section with many monosyllables that moves very slow and is about ". . . heavy heart and/cold eye." So they are variations almost on how the syllable works, variations on the theme of the function of the syllable? That's not quite accurate, but . . .

NYQ: You control line speed, by the length of the lines, and the number of syllables, and—

DL: Not the number of syllables so much as the kind of syllables, and whether the consonants are sufficiently harder to enunciate so that they help to slow things down, too. However, when one talks about these matters, it tends to sound as if the poet were extremely deliberate and conscious, but in fact it is something that becomes second nature so that you're doing it instinctively. When you're revising you may find places where you've botched it, your instincts were not working well, and then you may deliberately try to achieve an effect by those means which you know will help to achieve it. But in the first instance one is working pretty unconsciously, I think.

NYQ: Can you say generally, in deciding between several words for a particular spot in a poem, if you put more importance on sound or on sense?

DL: Well, the sonic effect would be the more important, but it's never a factor entirely separable from other things about the word. If you wanted a word that had something sort of thick about it, let us say, you might find a word which had that sonic quality and yet the associations of that word, or the fact that it was a homonym and the associations with the word that it sounded like, were all wrong, would prevent your using it. Let's say you have a choice of adjectives, and one has an onomatopoeic quality which you want, but it also has a couple of "s's" in it, and the rest of the line, or the line just before it, is already pretty sibilant, but you feel that that line is right. You might have to forego the word that you've just found and keep on looking, because you can't have all those "s's" jammed up together. There's almost never just one factor to be considered. You always have to weigh the one against the other.

NYQ: In your more recent poems you seem to be indenting less than you did in the earlier ones. Is there a reason for this change?

DL: Lately I've been doing it quite a lot again, I think. When I indent, I'm trying to do two things. One is very obvious. If I have something that approximates a list, a number of things mentioned in succession, in different lines, which forms a kind of category, I sometimes like to indent them and line them up. They're like a subsidiary clause. And that's for reasons of clarity. But the other reason for indentation is that if the eye is going from the end of one line all the way back to the margin, it takes infinitesimally longer than if it goes only to the beginning of an indented line. Sometimes one feels that the next line *is* another line. It's not just part of the line before it, yet it is in some way intimately connected with that line in a manner which makes one desire to have that little extra speed for the eye, which transmits itself to the ear and the voice.

NYQ: It's a psychological adjustment.

DL: It's a psychological adjustment which, however, is also, I think, a neurological one. I don't know if they have instruments which measure that—I daresay they do—but it's something one feels, one doesn't need an instrument to measure it. I'm pretty sure that it works because I have had the satisfaction of hearing people read poems of mine aloud who are not simply imitating me, because they haven't heard me read them, and they've read them right. The way I've deployed them on the page has been an accurate indication of how they're supposed to be read. Now just Wednesday, I had a sort of argument with some students who were objecting to that much direction by the poet. I defend it, absolutely, because I feel that it's exactly like the writing down of music. When music is written, it allows a considerable amount of interpretation to the performer, and yet it is always definitely that piece of music and no other. You get twenty competent pianists playing a Beethoven piano sonata, and each performance will be different. But it is recognizably the same piece of music. One may take the whole thing faster than another, one may make the loud parts louder and the quiet parts quieter, but the composer has indicated that here it's allegro and here it's adagio, or here it's fortissimo and here it's pianissimo. That is his privilege, and although we don't have such a generally accepted system of notation for the nuance, I see no reason why the poet shouldn't have the same privilege, and by that means obtain as fine results as composers have done. I don't feel that it is an imposition on the reader. It still allows him lots of freedom, and without that much care about the structure of a poem, I think what you have is a lot of slop.

NYQ: How concerned are you about the way the entire poem looks on the page?

DL: What happens visually produces a certain psychological effect, there's no doubt about it. When you look at a piece of music and the score is very very black with notes, you get a kind of crowded, agitated, perhaps even busy feeling. And a poem that fills up a page has psychologically for some people, or perhaps for all people at some moments, a somewhat intimidating effect. You're not sure if you can get into it. A poem that has two-line stanzas and lots of space tends to attract the eye. But I think these are very secondary effects. They're not essential where one is considering the nature of the poetry. The written poem is the written notation of a sonic effect. Which doesn't mean that the best way to receive poetry is to hear it and not see it at all. I think it's a question of eye-ear coordination. I'm not fully satisfied with poems that I only hear at a reading or on a record and never get to look at. I have to look at them, too. But by the same token, I want to *hear* a written poem, and I will either read it aloud to myself if I can't hear the poet read it, or even if I'm not actually reading it aloud I'm sounding it out in my head. I think the two things are equally important. Sometimes a poem will look absolutely, delightfully decorative on the page, but I think when that *takes* over, it's a mistake. They were doing it, of course, in the seventeenth century—wings, and crosses, and things—and sometimes it works out, but I don't think it's really a main direction for poetry. To hell with what it looks like, you know. Some poems that do sort of get all over the page, like some of Olson, or some of Duncan, I've actually heard objected to because they looked so messy. That's not the point. Never mind if they do look messy! They're indicating rhythm and pace, and all sorts of sonic values.

NYQ: You often repeat words or themes in your poems. Do you have any theories about the value and effect of repetition?

DL: Do you mean, throughout all my poetry the same things come up, or within one poem?

NYQ: Within one poem.

DL: Oh, well, there is the impulse to tie things together. If one feels them to be at all tied together, one wants to get that into the structure, instead of things flowing along to the point where they slip out of your fingers. Maybe it sounds a little compulsive, but in other works of art which I value I often see echoes and correspondences. I see the curve of the bushes in the corner of that painting by Howard Fussiner, echoed by the curve going the opposite way of the armchair down in the lower left-hand corner. I see the uprights of the delphiniums out the window, there, and the trunk of a tree in the distance, and the vase—they're all related to each other as uprights in that picture. It's the compositional sense, it's the impulse to create pattern, or to reveal pattern. I say "reveal," because I have a thing about finding form rather than imposing it. I want to find correspondences and relationships which are there but hidden, and I think one of the things the artist does is to reveal. That's the principle on which I've worked.

NYQ: It's interesting that you mentioned Gertrude Stein earlier. Repetition was so important in her writing.

DL: Well, think of any work of art that you really value. Can you think of one in which there are not such things?

NYQ: But sometimes there is more repetition in one work than in another, sometimes the repetition is especially obvious, and its effect is easy to feel . . .

DL: Where there's more of it, in any particular artist's work, I think it indicates that that artist has a feeling for denseness of texture; and where you find it very little, he is perhaps after a kind of transparence, an almost water-like, flowing thinness of texture. For example, the very unstructured work of Gary Snyder, whose poetry I like very much. Read his statement in that anthology, *Naked Poetry*, and compare it with mine. You'll see two very different sensibilities, in regard to form, operating there, and I think the differences in our work run naturally out of that difference in the way we want things to be. What pleases him is something more loosely formed, spread out. I certainly seem to have inherent in my nervous system more of a liking for pattern, not exactly symmetry, but I want to gather things together and see them in their juxtapositions.

NYQ: Since your poems are such physical wholes, is the need to divide the longer ones up into pages a problem for you, when you put them into books?

DL: No, but I have had one typographical problem. Sometimes, if I have a long line, and it's wider than the page permits, then of course the last few words have to be sort of tucked under. And since I do so much indentation for structural reasons, it bugs me very much when I have to have a line broken up that way, because the reader might well think that that is an indentation. It's sometimes a little hard to make sure it looks like what it is. I have wished that poetry books could be different dimensions, as some published by small presses are, but my publisher tells me that it's very hard to change the dimensions of books. Bookshelves are designed to hold books of certain dimensions, booksellers don't like to handle books that are odd shapes, and distributors don't like to distribute them, so one is stuck . . .

NYQ: Many of your poems reflect an experience of reality and of the present moment that is extraordinarily clear and deep. In "The Coming Fall," for instance, you speak of "A sense of the present," and, ". . . a shiver, a delight / that what is passing / is here . . ." Are you able to maintain this awareness for long periods?

DL: Oh, that's a hard question to answer. Not very often, I would say, and perhaps rarely when not engaged in the writing of poems. But sometimes, as something distinct from writing, I've experienced it, too.

NYQ: You often use the word "joy" in describing these moments. Once you say "terrible joy," and in the poem called "Joy," you say, ". . . glad to the brink of fear." What is that fear?

DL: "Glad to the brink of fear," is actually a quote from Emerson, where he speaks of crossing either the Boston or the Cambridge Common on a cloudy, raw sort of evening (I'm paraphrasing now; because I can't remember the exact words) with nothing very special about it, and being seized with "joy to the brink of fear." Well, I suppose joy is a passion, and all passionate things are perhaps very close in nature to their opposites. Joy, pain, fear—there comes a point, perhaps, where one no longer knows which is which. I think that is what he was talking about, and I guess that is what I am talking about, too. What people call ecstasy is more like terror than it is like contentment, isn't it.

NYQ: Some poets today are using drugs to reach a state of heightened consciousness in which they then write poems. Have you any feeling about this practice?

DL: Well, I smoke grass—I smoke it as a social pleasure and in order to relax, but I don't use it in order to work up poems. In fact, I don't smoke very much. It's kind of hard to get! I like to drink, but it's not something that I use in relation to writing, and I haven't taken any other kinds of drugs such as acid, mescaline, any kind of psychedelic drug. I've had experiences without the benefit of any such thing that I feel have been so close to what people describe having with drugs that I feel I don't want to disturb the peculiar balance of my imagination and my associative language. I feel that if others need to loosen up this way or that, well, that's their way of doing it. And I have felt a certain amount of fear of spoiling what I have got. It would seem kind of greedy. But if I came to a point in my life where I felt dried up and out of touch with my unconscious, with my imagination, then I guess I would try whatever seemed to be a good way to shake myself up again.

NYQ: Your poems contain many religious words, such as "hymn," "psalm," "communion wine," "pilgrimage." You speak of ceremonies and rites. You often use the word "light" in a Quaker sense. There is a sense of joy like that of the Hassidim. In your love poems there is frequently a kind of devotional feeling along with a sensuous one. And, throughout your books, one recognizes themes that recall the Quaker, Jewish and Zen emphasis on the importance of the present moment. What does the word "religious" mean to you?

DL: The impulse to kneel in wonder. . . . The impulse to kiss the ground. . . . The sense of awe. The felt presence of some mysterious force, whether it be what one calls beauty, or perhaps just the sense of the unknown—I don't mean "unknown" in the sense of we don't know what the future will bring. I mean the sense of the numinous, whether it's in a small stone, or a large mountain. I think at this particular point, that sense of joy which you've mentioned in my poems, and which I think is very real to me, and has been, is at a very low ebb. I think of my poem called "Living," which says:

> The fire in leaf and grass
> so green it seems
> each summer the last summer.
>
> The wind blowing, the leaves
> shivering in the sun,
> each day the last day.
>
> A red salamander
> so cold and so
> easy to catch, dreamily
>
> moves his delicate feet
> and long tail. I hold
> my hand open for him to go.
>
> Each minute the last minute.

There's a certain apocalyptic sense in that, but there's also a kind of joy in the marvelousness of that green fire in the grass and leaves, and in the beauty of the little salamander. My feeling this winter, like many peoples', is so doom-filled, the sense of time running out is pretty much squashing my sense of the beauty of the ephemeral being ephemeral. I've always hated artificial flowers unless they were just flagrantly and beautifully, sort of brassily, artificial. But the good imitations, the ones that you think are real until you get up to them, and then there's that awful dead plastic, are really vile. And the reason why I think they're so vile is because so much of the beauty of a flower is in its very perishableness. One doesn't want it to last forever, and accumulate dust. And so there is joy in the very sense of mortality, in a way. But facing not just the mortality that we have always had with us, but the annihilation of all life, which is every day more and more a real possibility, one's feeling of anguish and despair certainly takes over.

NYQ: Speaking of social protest, W. H. Auden has said, "I do not think that writing poems will change anything." Many people disagree with him, and you are one of the poets who, over the last five years, have written many poems of protest against injustice, particularly against the Vietnam War. That situation is worse now than it has ever been. What do you feel, at this point, a poet can do?

DL: To confine it to America of the last five years, let us say, I think the poetry of protest, indignation, anger and so forth, that has been written by many, many poets has helped to awaken many people to the situation. There were the Vietnam Poetry Readings that Robert Bly and other people organized, where slides of Vietnam, of napalmed children, and also of beautiful, still untouched villages—sort of alternations of terrible destruction and of what the country looked like before it was blasted—were combined with the reading of poems. Those things, back in 1966, stirred up quite a lot of people to become active in the anti-war movement. And the anti-war movement itself has grown very much and is becoming a more revolutionary movement in which people no longer see stopping the war as a single issue which can be divorced from racism, imperialism, capitalism, male supremacy. There are increasing numbers of people who understand, or are beginning to understand, the connections between all these things. And the poets have played some part in this consciousness-raising. There's a lot more going on in the way of organizing and educative work in local communities than there was two years ago. A lot of people who were activists in college, who have now graduated or dropped out, instead of also dropping out of the movement (which is the way it used to be) have gone further into it, but you don't hear so much about them because they're working in very sort of unspectacular, local ways. This is something about which in itself I'm not despondent. I don't think that the movement is a failure, and hasn't achieved anything, and so forth; but the fact is that we're working against time. And the factors, including ecological ones, against which people on the revolutionary side are working are so tremendous, they're such tremendous, heavy forces, that one just doesn't know whether there's going to be *time* for this new kind of patient, consciousness-raising work to produce its effect before a disaster is brought about by the other forces.

NYQ: As for your own activities—do you feel differently now from the way you did in 1966 and 1967 about what you should be doing? Certainly you are now more concerned than you were then about time running out.

DL: Yes, well, all we could think of to do in 1966 was to have big, peaceful demonstrations, which got bigger and bigger. People as astute as, let us say, Chomsky, feel that those demonstrations did have a deterrent effect, that the United States might have gone further, might have used nuclear weapons by this time, if there had not been a strong, growing, anti-war movement in this country. So you don't measure the results of those demonstrations by positive results, you have to measure them by sort of negative ones, which is very hard to do. Now, most people feel mere demonstrations, mere massing of people, is no longer enough. There has to be definite civil disobedience action, and the spearhead of the movement is those people who have done sabotage, who have destroyed files—not only draft files, but the Dow Chemical files, and so forth—all those sorts of actions. If there are going to be more moratoriums, they're going to have to take a different form. I think there are a lot of people who are still back in 1966 in their political development, and they need to experience big demonstrations, which do have a radicalizing effect. When they get tear-gassed, and they see police beating up people with clubs at a demonstration, either they cop out and never go to another one (in which case they wouldn't have been very useful people anyway), or, step-by-step, it radicalizes them. What I personally am trying to do at this point is very, very mild, because I find myself teaching at a school which is back in 1954, I would say, and I'm trying to organize a teach-in. I think that the right speakers at a teach-in could stir those people up, and it would be a beginning for a lot of them, at least.

Denise Levertov: An Interview
Michael Andre / 1971/72

From *Little Magazine* 5:3,5 (Fall/Winter 1971/72), 42–55. Reprinted by permission of Michael Andre.

Michael Andre: According to the biographical notes in your books you were educated at home. I was wondering if you were inundated in the English literary tradition?

Denise Levertov: No, it wasn't exclusively English literature that I read. My mother read aloud a great deal to me and to the family at large, not as a formal part of my education, it was just a thing that we did. And during my childhood, up until I was grown up really, she went on doing that. She must have read just about all the nineteenth century classics of fiction, but not only the English ones, I mean, she also read *War and Peace,* and, let's see, some Scandinavian literature. I didn't really have a formal education after the age of twelve and it was not very formal before then. So . . . We had a houseful of books, everybody read. And I did lessons with my mother, but I never studied literature with her or with anybody else. I just read.

Andre: In one of your poems you said. "The artist must create himself/or be born again." Do you feel that in a way you sort of created your own literary background?

Levertov: No. I had the opportunity to browse, so that opportunity was created for me—very fortunately. Of course, if you have the opportunity to browse, you follow your own predilections. But to create your own literary world sounds more purposeful and planned than anything I did. I was and am very haphazard, I guess.

Andre: Was coming to America a kind of re-birth for you?

Levertov: It was a very important point for me because I had an obscure but nonetheless strong recognition that coming to a new country with the same language but used differently, and with a very different form and pace to my life, something had to happen in my work as a poet that was consonant with all those changes. William Carlos Williams was for me very much of a gateway to the American language as a literary language.

52

Andre: It interested me when I first came across Guillevic and the other French poets that they were so similar to Williams. Why are they so similar?

Levertov: Well, wait a minute; what other French poets? I saw a relationship between Guillevic and Williams but I've never seen that between Williams and other French poets.

Andre: Ponge was the . . .

Levertov: O.K. Ponge is interested in the object and in ordinary things newly seen but still his technique and his feeling about the things, I think, is pretty different from Williams.

Andre: Was this pure coincidence or was there something in the times, phenomenology for example, that contributed to both?

Levertov: I don't really think that Williams, probably, knew anything about phenomenology. In fact I was led to Guillevic through an article on phenomenology which quoted Gaston Bachelard whom I like very much (although by other phenomenologists he's looked on as too literary and romantic). He was a kind of phenomenologist and the article was mainly about him, but it quoted Guillevic. And then I found Guillevic quotes in Bachelard. And I started to translate those bits of Guillevic I found there. But I don't think that Williams—see, by the time the term "phenomenology" really started to be thrown around in this country, Williams was not reading anymore because, you know, he had had several strokes and he was not able to read and he depended on his wife reading to him. He certainly wasn't reading anything like that, I would say, in the last years of his life.

Andre: You characterized Guillevic's attitude to objects as a kind of exorcism which struck me as very different from your own attitude, which is a kind of delight, don't you think?

Levertov: Did I characterize it as exorcism?

Andre: Well, yeah; he's slightly afraid of the objects at times.

Levertov: Oh. Yeah? Well, he sees a kind of malevolence in some objects, it's true. I think of some of his poems about rocks where the rock is definitely seen as a potentially destructive force. I guess, a resentful force, and that may be the fact of having spent part of his childhood right near Carnac, with those tremendously powerful stones, those menhirs. I see any resemblances between Guillevic and Williams as sort of coincidental though.

Andre: Your own attitude, as in for example *O Taste and See,* is one of intense delight, wouldn't you say?

Levertov: It's more melancholic as I've started to get older and the state of the world keeps on being so incredibly bad. But there is that element definitely in Guillevic too, you know. Guillevic's relationship to nature is not a hostile one. He recognizes the autonomy of things and therefore he doesn't interpret them sentimentally. And he doesn't seem to feel anthropocentric at all. But that doesn't mean he regards all things in nature as malevolent. I mean, he has a very powerful love of place, of country, I mean of the country, the rural, you know. He has a very sharp eye and ear, I think.

Andre: You mentioned becoming increasingly melancholic because of the state of the world. What would you say would be the social role of the poet in difficult times? Has he a special role or is it the same as another citizen's?

Levertov: Well, see, I think it's very hard to make general statements about that, relating the present to the past, because there has certainly been times when many important, indubitably first-rate artists have been notably apolitical. But I don't think that has very much to do with the present because we've really come to something unprecedented in the history of man: a kind of power that man has found he has in the development of technology and weaponry plus the fact that he has found he has completely goofed in regard to the ecology. So the possibility of total annihilation that mankind faces as a real possibility in our time has never had a precedent. People have feared the end of the world. They've had all sorts of apocalyptic theories. They've had plagues, and they've had war, and various scourges and earthquakes and so forth. But they've never had to face what mankind is facing today. There's never been the pressure of time to change things fast before it becomes totally irreversible. You find that poets in this country in the last five years, the best poets, have almost without exception been writing poems which are political—engaged poetry of a certain kind. They've not been able to be ostriches with their heads buried in the sand. And I think the social role of the poet is not so much a matter of rhetoric but, because the poet is an articulate person, he does have some power of influencing people's way of looking at things. Because he has that, he has all the more responsibility to participate in, to share, any action which he may indirectly have contributed to. In other words, it isn't only if a person writes an overtly political poem, let's say an anti-war poem, which may have been a factor in sending some readers of this poem which is not about the war at all but which increases a person's feeling for life—which is what Wallace Stevens says a poem must do—I think that he also has a responsibility to be there as well on that picket line, at that demonstration. See, what I object to is people whether as writers or teachers, who think that to have used words in a way they feel is good, is enough, that they have fulfilled their function.

Andre: What have you been writing lately?

Levertov: Let's see: along with short poems, I've been working on a continuation of a long poem that I started back in 1968 sometime, some of which you've seen because it was in *Relearning the Alphabet.* There it was just called "From a Notebook." That was an open-ended poem and I've since written about twice the amount that is in that book. And the whole thing as it now stands will be the nucleus, in fact the larger part of a new book coming out in the fall. And the poem now has a real title, not just "Notebook"; it's called "Staying Alive". So it's now reached a certain fairly conclusive feeling for me, enough so I want to publish the whole thing as a book. I feel it hangs together. But I still feel that it has an open-ended quality which is the advantage of a long poem.

Andre: The "Notebook" poem in *Relearning the Alphabet* reminded me of a couple of different things. It reminded me of Lowell's *Notebook* poems, and it also reminded me of your husband, Mitchell Goodman's book *The Movement Towards a New America.*

Levertov: Certainly, structurally, it's very very different what I've been trying to do and what Lowell's been doing in his *Notebook* where all the sections have a similar form. It's the Lowell sonnet as distinct, you know, from the Petrarchan or the Shakespearean sonnet. It's a series of short poems with linked subject matter. The preoccupations with current events certainly are similar, and I think one finds this preoccupation in the work of very many contemporary poets, inevitably I would say. As far as Mitch's collage or compendium, that huge book of movement materials with its many sections linked by a few words in each case of, sort of, editorial comment—it's very much not just a jumble I think; he envisioned it as, and I think succeeded in making it, a coherent whole—even though it's so huge, it is of course dealing with the same materials. I would say that Mitch really does use Pound's ideogrammatic method. It's a question of presenting concepts not by description and analysis but by presenting the materials in juxtaposition so that the meaning comes clear by these juxtapositions to the intelligent reader. And I think that many contemporary poets, *come* to think of it, you know, though they're not doing it in collusion or as a school at all, are tending to do the same thing. I think that Pound and Williams and *The Cantos* and *Paterson* certainly paved the way for us to do that, for us to incorporate prose passages and quotations from other people in order to try to make a coherent whole— and Olson of course was doing it too—a coherent whole that would be more inclusive of the ramifications and complexity of our lives than the short lyric poem can be. It's the twentieth century impulse towards the epic I think.

Andre: One thing I noticed in your husband's book was that it didn't include Canada in the Movement very much.
Levertov: Oh Canada, hmm.

Andre: I was wondering, Canadian poetry, too, just seems to get left out. It's not considered British poetry or American poetry. I was wondering if you had any opinions on Canadian poetry. Read any?
Levertov: It's appropriate that Canadian poetry should not be considered British or American because it isn't, it's Canadian poetry. [Laughter] Well, of course, as far as leaving it out of the book, you know, the book was about the United States, it doesn't have material about any other country, except some allusions here or there. God knows, it had to confine itself somehow. It's so huge anyhow.

As far as Canadian poetry is concerned I must confess I haven't recently read very much Canadian poetry. There is one Canadian poet whom I consider one of the very finest of living poets. I've lost touch with her in the last couple of years, she's an old friend. And I think she's a really, really marvelous poet and that is Margaret Avison. You don't know her work?

Andre: I don't.
Levertov: Margaret Avison had at one time quite a wide reputation in Canada. I say "at one time" because I don't know what she's been doing lately. She won the Governor-General's Award, or whatever that is called, and she had a book published by the Oxford University Press, the Canadian one; and when I was an editor for Norton's, I did a book of hers there. And it just didn't take in this country; I don't know why, partly because Norton just didn't promote it properly. But she's an absolutely—one hesitates to use words such as "great," "major," all those sorts of things—but she's a first-rate and remarkable poet with quite a wide range. She's a woman in her fifties.

Andre: Well what do you think of Irving Layton? He was connected with Black Mountain which you were connected with.
Levertov: Yes, he was one of the people that published in *Origin* and I

think also in *Black Mountain Review*. And I think that the poems that he was writing back in the fifties . . . he wrote some very fine poems which I admired very much. I regret to say that the last time I encountered him and heard him read and talk, I felt that he had become a fascist. His work appeared to be deteriorating too. He's become a sort of Jewish fascist. I found his attitudes repulsive.

Andre: Speaking of other poets, part of the interest in the Black Mountain poetry and Williams poetry and your poetry was its return to clarity and the rejection of the obscurity and so forth of Eliot. But now people like John Ashbery are turning out a different kind of fairly obscure poetry. I wonder if you'd care to comment on that.

Levertov: Lots of people found lots of Black Mountain poetry obscure too. But I think the difference was that whatever has been obscure in the poetry of the so-called Black Mountain poets, hasn't been deliberate—well perhaps it's not fair to accuse Eliot of deliberate obscurity—but the people who followed, who thought at any rate that they were following Eliot's lead, I can't think of anyone in particular at the moment . . . let's leave Eliot out of it and just think of the academic poets of the forties and fifties who sort of looked askance at the Black Mountain people. They were sort of intention-ally symbolic, I think that's one of the things they were doing. They put a certain value on wit which my crowd, you know, has never put.

The New York school has had a sort of second wave. After all it started out with Frank O'Hara, who was a really fine poet, a lyric poet, and certainly not obscure. But what has developed among that group of poets has become more and more abstract. And so it's the obscurity of abstraction. And again a certain value, putting a value on wit, wit of another kind—the in-joke, you know. A kind of diluted Dada, I suppose. That sort of wit.

Andre: I'd be interested in asking you about your methods of composition. Your rhythms are amazing, the way the various sounds echo, and I was won-dering if this required immense labor on your part or if it was a kind of intuition?

Levertov: I think I have a good ear. I think that's something I was en-dowed with because even my early poems which came out in England about a hundred years ago—1946 actually—while they're the poems of a very im-mature person, I think that, read aloud, they are musical and at that time I certainly was very unconscious of what I was doing. I wasn't laboring, I was listening. And I've always listened. In those days certainly I had no idea of what made it sound right, what it was. I could just tell if it was wrong. And I could just push things around until it sounded right. So that I think it's rather more intuitive than otherwise, except that, you know, as one has spent one's life writing poetry, one, unless one is absolutely an idiot, couldn't remain totally unconscious. And so certainly I've learned things about craft, and I think that in the process of writing, the kind of things I think I am able to convey to a certain extent as a teacher, are operating for me as a writer too. But they're not operating on a highly, highly deliberate level; they're just working into what I'm doing; I'm half-conscious of what I'm doing. It's a matter of experience, you know. It's like any craft; I mean a handcraft your hand learns, I mean it learns what to do, so what one has learned about a language art operates, it is knowledge:—It begins as intuition, then one becomes conscious of what one has done intuitively, and then that consciousness itself becomes again intuition. Something like that.

Andre: How long does it take you to write a poem? Do you do it at a single sitting or do you keep it around for a long time?

Levertov: That varies very much from poem to poem. The only poems that get written at a single sitting would be very short poems, that's sure. But sometimes short poems take a long time too. One might be writing in a white heat or something, and write a longer poem in the time it took to write a shorter one, but I certainly don't think there's any kind of rule-of-thumb about it. And I think that this is something that varies very much from one writer to another. Some people I know of are very very prolific, they write an awful lot, but they also discard a lot. Some people are compulsive perfectionists and work for years on a single poem. I think for instance of William Burford who has written really very few poems, I guess, or at least published very few poems over many years, and some of them in his second book were the same poems that were in the first book, only they were heavily revised. Norton published a book of his poems—and during the production period I used to get a letter, or a telegram even, from him practically every day for months with little revisions in each one. I mean, you know. They are very finely crafted poems; he's very good but he's relatively unproductive because you know that's his method of working.

Andre: Hayden Carruth said in an article, he obviously disliked the term romantic, so he described your poetry as "pre-classical pastorals." Does that strike you as accurate in some way?

Levertov: I don't think the word "pastoral" would cover my poetry, no, although some of my poems are. I've written poems in the country about country kinds of things. But as far as terms like "classic," "preclassic," "romantic" and so forth, I don't really think it is for the poets themselves to help the critic define those kinds of things. I really don't.

Andre: George Hitchcock who's one of the leaders of West Coast poetry wrote a kind of parody of your kind of poetry and the gist or the point of it seems to be that there is a certain banality, a certain lack of what he considered poetry-ness in your poetry. I wonder if you would comment on the charge?

Levertov: [Mild Laughter] I haven't really seen that thing that you're referring to which I think is "found poems," in other words pieces of prose kind of chopped into lines and titled *Pioneers of Modern Poetry,* right? I have read poems of George Hitchcock but I don't have a clear idea of what his poetry is like. Now I know that his magazine, *kayak,* features a kind of surrealist poem, a certain kind of American surrealism which would take too long to get into talking about I think. If what he considers poetic is the surrealist image, and he finds my poetry, for example, deficient in surrealism, well then I suppose by his standards my poetry isn't poetic. On the other hand, I find lots of people's poetry sort of what I've thought of as the Midwestern common style. I find it banal. And I don't think I do what those people do. I'm not thinking of any famous poets, but if you read little magazines, they all seem to have been written by graduate students or, more often, youngish professors who sort of regret the fact that they have been through graduate school and are professors but are also very much settled into it. They drink a good deal of beer. And the poem begins with "*I* was driving down the highway to Joey's Lunch and *I* thought such and such, and such and such" and then it recounts some little anecdote of no particular importance. It's sort of a little elegy for themselves really. They think they're using the American idiom; they, alas, think that they are the descendants of William Carlos Williams, but they've misunderstood Williams, if they do so suppose. Because that wasn't what he was doing at all. Or intended. Or promoted. I find that banal. And I find the *kayak* type of surrealism contrived. It doesn't very often ring true to me. The poets I most admire—Robert Duncan, Galway Kinnell, Robert Creeley and a lot of other poets lesser known than they—they do not go in for surrealism. Well Duncan at some periods has, there has been some influence of surrealism, but I mean that is not what is typical of his poetry. It's not a sort of deliberate conscious surrealism which is a mockery of what surrealism is. Nor is it a poetry without music, concerned very deliberately with the most drab details of life with the apparent intention of being gutsy. The poetry which I care for is strongly musical, it's a very aural poetry; and it speaks of the inner life but it attempts a kind of honesty, not a deliberate "poetic quality." The poetry has to come out of the structure, out of the sense of the quality of the language and not by the selection of poetic subjects as in "the poetic style." Nor does it try to be deliberately banal as in what I call the Midwestern common style.

Andre: On the other hand, I read in one of your essays, an essay on Edith Sitwell, you describe her mind at certain times as vulgar. That sort of Jamesian word has always sort of puzzled me. I wonder if you could tell us what you mean by it?

Levertov: I don't remember the thing I wrote about Edith Sitwell very clearly at this point, but I think I do remember what I meant by that term. It was a review of an autobiography; I found her self-praise and her egocentricity vulgar, I found it offensive, cheap. I think that's what I meant. Lacking in humility, lacking in a sense of other people's qualities and needs. That's what I would call vulgar.

Andre: Kenneth Rexroth in one of his highly laudatory essays on your poetry praised it for precisely the opposite, its humanity and its wisdom.

I noticed in *The Jacob's Ladder* volume that you have a series of poems really on excellence and human fulfillment, that you quote rabbinical scholars a number of places. I wonder if you could tell us of your acquaintance with rabbinical scholars?

Levertov: Those were quotes from Hasidic rabbis. When I was a child my father used to sometimes tell the Hassidic anecdotes. You know Hassidism was sort of an oral tradition and these anecdotes were sort of passed from mouth to ear. My father came partly out of that background and sometimes he used to tell us some of those stories. Then for a number of years I wasn't particularly interested in that type of thing, although I had enjoyed those stories as a child. And in New York back in the fifties I guess, I re-discovered the oral tradition in Buber's collections, *Tales of the Hasidim.* At the time of writing those poems I was very immersed in those two volumes of Buber's where he collected, wrote down and published many of these Hassidic anecdotes. It's a wonderful wonderful book. I felt very drawn to it and also very mad at myself for not having taken the opportunity while my father was alive of asking him more about those traditions which he knew so much about.

But, you know, when one is a kid, one is not interested in what one's parents were interested in, until I came to an age where I was very interested. But he was old and sick and then he died, so I never had the opportunity to really discuss those matters with him. But I felt very much that it was part of my heritage because I'm descended from one of those rabbis. Of course I was brought up as a Christian; my father was a convert to Christianity and I didn't go to synagogue, I went to church as a child—but I was always also very conscious of being Jewish. It was not a contradiction to be both Jewish and Christian. And so the Buber books really revealed a whole area that was very congenial to me, that was a part of my Jewish inheritance.

Andre: I took one of the themes of those poems to be the desire for human perfection and the individual movement towards perfection. I was wondering if you could connect that to your political stand which I take to be more democratic?

Levertov: I don't know what poems you're thinking of that seem to be striving—or talking about striving—towards human perfection, because I'm not aware of ever having had illusions about human perfectibility, no.

Andre: I was referring to such poems as "The Part" in which you criticize everyman for being an everyman and not coming up to his dreams and visions and so forth.

Levertov: No no no; maybe the poem is not sufficiently clear, but I don't criticize him for being an everyman. I call the person in the poem Homer Da Vinci but I qualify by calling him "Homer Da Vinci/with freckles on your nose"; I call him "sad everyman." Now I meant he was both the most ordinary of people and he had all of human potential. And what I was criticizing was that he had sold out, been corrupted, that he was not living his own life; he'd gotten off the track it seemed to me into someone else's life. The quote, the epigraph is from a Rabbi who was a kabbalist in Prague in the—I forget which century—the seventeenth century I guess. He preceded the actual Hassidic movement, but he was a kabbalist. And it says:

> In some special way every person completes the universe. If he does not play "his part", he injures the pattern of all existence.

Now what this is talking about is not perfectibility, human perfectibility but, as I see it, that there is some pattern being fulfilled. That is what that statement seems to mean, that there is some pattern in which each individual has his part. And there is also the possibility of not playing his part; it says if he does not play his part, he injures the pattern of all existence. So I wasn't condemning him for being everyman, but for being corrupted by, in his case, money. I mean it was suggested to me by a man who had been an artist, a painter—I don't know if he was a good painter, but because of his wife's demands for security he'd given up painting and was doing a really lousy advertising job drawing ugly furniture for some nasty company. And he really hated it. I mean he had a certain modesty. He'd gotten into the habit of looking at small things through a microscope and at the dinner table, where I met him, there were some veronic flowers which are formed of small florets, you know, and he was sort of peering at them with a special interest, you know, and obviously wishing he could get them under a microscope. And there was something very moving and also very exasperating about this man's situation which seemed typical of many lives.

Andre: Another poem, which you wrote after that, called "Abel's Bride", which is from a section of poetry called *Abel's Bride,* portrays the man-woman role in a kind of eternal way. I was also wondering how you would relate that to certain aspects of the Movement?

Levertov: Well actually there are several poems which I've written which do seem to be dealing with the man-woman role in an archetypal fashion, and they were really written before many of the Women's Liberation ideas were formulated and before I became involved in that part of the Movement. I still feel that this is true about women and men.

Andre: Perhaps you could read it.

Levertov: Yes, perhaps I'll read it and then see if I have something to say about it.

Abel's Bride

> Woman fears for man, he goes
> out alone to his labors. No mirror
> nests in his pocket. His face
> opens and shuts with his hopes.
> His sex hangs unhidden
> or rises before him
> blind and questing.
>
> She thinks herself
> lucky. But sad. When she goes out

> she looks in the glass, she remembers
> herself. Stones, coal,
> the hiss of water upon the kindled
> branches—her being
> is a cave, there are bones at the hearth.

Despite all that I've come to realize about the oppression of women and the necessity for a women's liberation movement, I still feel that in the basic character of man as I know him, there is a certain vulnerability that is greater than woman's vulnerability. I'm sure a lot of people would argue with me about that but this is my experience of it. There is a certain unconsciousness about man, about men, in regard to themselves that makes me feel that they are without some defense that woman does have. On the other hand, women's self-consciousness is sort of exemplified in the poem by the fact that she looks in the glass before she goes out; she has that sort of continuing consciousness of herself. She rarely forgets herself. Now that is sort of, perhaps, brought on by the society's demands and images of femininity but it also, I think perhaps, represents something deeper than that. Man's consciousness has gone out so much towards the abstract, also formed very much that way by history and the kind of education man has gotten and so forth and woman hasn't gotten, but it has left the typical man, the archetypal man, very undeveloped and unconscious about himself and his emotions in comparison to a lot of women, to the archetypal woman I would say. Men seem to me often (sort of) transparent. Their motivations seem so obvious. Women have more the habit of inwardness. Then the part about

> Stones, coal
> the hiss of water upon the kindled
> branches—her being
> is a cave, there are bones at the hearth.

I was harking back to the times in the ancient world, let us say, oh Babylon, where woman was dominant and where Isis was worshipped, and any time in any society where women were not oppressed as they have been in most societies in the modern world. Where they were actually a sort of dominating figure. I was thinking of that as part of the unconscious layer of the woman's psyche too.

Andre: W. H. Auden said that poetry makes nothing happen. Do you disagree violently or just disagree with that?

Levertov: Well I'm not feeling very violent this morning. But I don't think that poetry designed specifically to make things happen would make things happen. Poetry written overtly as propaganda wouldn't be very good poetry, hasn't traditionally been very good poetry and therefore hasn't made things happen. But I think that poetry as it sets in motion parts of people's being that would not be set in motion without it indirectly must make things happen. If a person through reading poetry feels more alive and more aware of things, and just has been reading poetry, then goes out and walks down the street and sees things and feels things he would not otherwise have felt if the poems he's just been reading hadn't stirred them up. Well, you know, I don't need to say more, do I? Obviously this is happening all the time. There are a lot of people reading poetry and it does affect their sensibilities, their actions.

Andre: It seemed to me in general until the sixties, that though your poetry was very avant-garde stylistically, the themes were really eternal themes of seers. Do you feel that's the way poetry should be?

Levertov: I don't think that there's any way that one can say poetry *should* be. I think that, speaking for myself, my poetry has become, what should I say, more engaged, more politically aware in its themes because my life has become so. When my son was little, I was mostly at home, and I led a more retired domestic kind of life. I had always had some political consciousness; back in the days of ban-the-bomb and so forth, I used to go to demonstrations and so forth. But I didn't become more involved really until I started teaching and found myself spending a lot of time with students and, you know, just the circumstances of my life began to change in a more public direction. And so my poetry naturally reflected that because if one can, one wants to deal in one's poetry with every aspect of one's life. When I was a young girl and the war was on in London, bombs were falling and I was working as a hospital nurse and really there are about two poems that reflect anything that was going on, and that not very clearly. But that was because I was too immature to deal with those things. So my poetry was all about sort of wooshy, vaguely dreamy feelings; it was the poetry of a young girl. But now, if I were leading the life that I lead, teaching and participating in political meetings and going to demonstrations and speaking at rallies and being in sit-ins, and not a word about it got into any of my poems, and I was writing poems about leaves and frogs and skies exclusively, I think there would be a basic dishonesty, or at least a terrific admission of failure and weakness in that fact. That does not mean that one should only write about these events either; the trees, frogs, skies et cetera are also part of one's life and perhaps it would be equally dishonest not to write about that.

Andre: Prior to the sixties you suppressed the direct autobiographical allusions. But now you seem to be pulling in more actual facts. Would you say again this is related to movements in poetry, such as confessional poetry?

Levertov: I'm rather antagonistic on the whole to what is called confessional poetry which seems to exploit the private life. I've even felt that some young poets, students, feel that they have to make a suicide attempt, that they must spend some time in a mental hospital in order to be poets at all. I think that's rather a bad idea. I feel at this point in my life—I'm forty-seven, and I've been writing since I was five years old, and publishing since I was about 20—that I have maybe earned the right to write more personal poems if I feel like it. I'm often bored and impatient with poems by young poets who, before learning how to relate to language, to make a poem that has structure, has music, has some kind of autonomy, launch out into confessional poems. It seems to me something that you earn by a long apprenticeship. I think the first poem in which I was largely autobiographical was in a group called "The Olga Poems" about my sister and that will be re-printed in my new book. It seems to be a prelude to some of the later stuff and I want to get it all into one book. I've written an "Introduction" for that book:

> The justification then of including in a new volume poems which are available in other collections is aesthetic. It assimilates separated parts of a whole. And I'm given courage to do so by the hope that whole will be seen as having some value not as mere confessional autobiography but as a document of some historical value, a record of one person's inner and outer experience in America during the sixties and the beginnings of the seventies, an experience which is shared by so many and which transcends the peculiar details of each life, though it can only be expressed through those details.

Of course it's true that the poems of Robert Lowell, Anne Sexton, W.D. Snodgrass and Sylvia Plath that deal with the experience of madness and of attempted cures also express a very common part of our life, so I don't mean to just put them down. It's the way it is taken by young poets who feel that they must go then and experience the identical circumstances in order to qualify as poets, that I'm objecting to. In my case I feel particularly straddled between an English-European beginning and America and the American language and culture; that's one thing. And, then, I feel very close to a lot of people very much younger than myself so that in a sense I'm straddled between a person who really loves Henry James and nineteenth century fiction and old things and a person who yet in friendships and political loyalties is really with people who are twenty years old, you know, passionately so. This is perhaps not that common but enough so that I don't think I'm just writing chapters of my autobiography. It has a certain documentary value.

Andre: Another confessional writer is Norman Mailer, and Norman Mailer will write at his best when he is most public. For example, I thought *Armies of the Night* was his best confessional book. And the most public thing that happened in your life, so far as I know, is your husband's indictment with Doctor Spock, and yet I don't think you talk about that in any of your poetry.

Levertov: I have a poem about waiting for that trial. It's called "An Interim," and it was written between the indictment and the trial. No, there is nothing about the trial itself because in a sense it was a very mundane trial. It didn't have the dramatic qualities of subsequent trials. Mitch felt that if he had to do it over again, he would defend himself, and make it much more into a political trial.

Andre: There seems to be in general a sense of doom in the United States, a despair in the citizens, that really isn't found in Canada so much, I wonder if. . . .

Levertov: In the most politically conscious, the most aware and active young, there is not really a sense of doom. There is an amazing amount of optimism in a way. The people I'm thinking of are the people who live and work in political collectives, really getting down to brass tacks in trying to revolutionize their own lives as a basis for what they do. And also not simply working from crisis to crisis, organizing demonstrations, responding to crisis situations with demonstrations, but doing stuff like organizing food collectives, rent strikes, bookstores that are also kind of information centers and gathering places, and trying to work with high school kids to educate them politically. I sometimes worry that those people whom I admire very much are perhaps a little lacking in a sufficient sense of doom. In other words, I think they perhaps tend to neglect the ecological threats. Now it's true that some politicians tended to use ecology, perhaps, to distract people from the war. You know, it's been used like anything else they can seize on. And perhaps some biologists have tended to exaggerate the threats. But I think there is some danger among political people who are trying to stop the war, change racist attitudes, and really re-structure the society, not by reform but by radical means. I think they are not paying enough attention to that threat. Now, you know, it's ironic, maybe if they paid more attention to it, it would be so debilitating, so depressing that they wouldn't get anything else done. I don't know. Maybe it's out of sheer self-preservation. One can't think about everything all at once. You have to decide what it is you're going to concentrate your energies on, at least to some extent, but you can't wear blinders either.

"Everyman's Land": Ian Reid Interviews Denise Levertov

Ian Reid / 1972

From *Southern Review* [Adelaide, Australia], 5 (1972), 231–36. Reprinted by permission of Ian Reid.

Reid: There's a comment I find interesting in your autobiographical note for Donald Allen's anthology *The New American Poetry.* You say that without the stylistic influence of William Carlos Williams you "could not have developed from a British Romantic with almost Victorian background to an American poet of any vitality." To begin with, can you explain more fully what "Romantic" qualities you had to leave behind in becoming an American poet?

Levertov: Probably I remained something of a Romantic if one is thinking of the larger historical sense of the term, but I was referring specifically to the now half-forgotten forties movement in English poetry, documented by Kenneth Rexroth in his anthology *New British Poets* (New Directions, 1948) which called itself the New Romanticism. My first book, *The Double Image* (Cresset Press, London, 1946) reflected the mood of this movement.

Reading Williams helped me to deal more directly with my daily life experiences in my writing, in less literary, more concrete, and less vague language. He helped me to bridge the gap between the idiomatic language we all use and the more rarified language of my life as a somewhat solitary reader. (I had not gone to school at all and had spent a lot of my life reading.) He helped me deal with being a grown woman, with a husband and baby and very little money, in a strange country, a strange city (New York) and a language which, though ostensibly the same in which I had grown up, was in fact different in pace, rhythm, and nuance.

Reid: What I had in mind in asking that first question was that your mature work seems in some important respects to be very closely akin to that of the nineteenth-century English Romantics. Going beyond general resemblances such as the preference for personal monologues, it's noticeable for instance that many of your poems present dream-like states of mind and incorporate images or rhythms suggestive of dreaming. You often explore the less con-

68

scious, less rational areas of the psyche, especially the no-man's-land between dream and waking. Isn't this the territory of Keats, Wordsworth, Tennyson?

Levertov: Yes, but also of Whitman, Rimbaud, Blake, Rilke—and Valéry, who is supposed to be a Classicist rather than a Romantic. The fact is, these categories just do not stand up to scrutiny. English poets are inclined to provincialism to an astounding degree, and perhaps Australian poets have inherited (culturally) this habit of attributing certain characteristics, e.g. "images or rhythms suggestive of dreaming," to a particular period or school of *English* literary history as if it were exclusive to that period or school— whereas in fact it is often simply a characteristic of most poetry everywhere, anywhere.

Reid: Well, without being so provincial as to try and deny the taint of provincialism, I'd better explain myself—for the sake of clear definition rather than mere defensiveness. I confined the terms of my question to that particular period and that country because you yourself refer to a Romanticism which is "Victorian" and "British." And what I'm suggesting is that, while it would be absurd to deny that modern American poetry is culturally autonomous—Williams, more plainly than anyone else, established that—yet it also seems true that many American poets nowadays continue to be influenced—not exclusively, of course—by English Romantic writers. In reading Ginsberg, say, doesn't one feel that Blake is almost as important a precursor as Whitman? And if Duncan's work, to take another example, shows his indebtedness to Emerson (among many others), isn't there Carlyle, too, looking over Emerson's shoulder?

Levertov: Oh, certainly I agree, as to the influence of Blake on Ginsberg, Carlyle and Emerson on Duncan, and so on. As for myself, I had never even read any American poetry to speak of until I was twenty-three. I would go further than you and deny the cultural *autonomy* of American poetry—the term seems to me hyperbolic and I don't think Williams did establish the existence of such autonomy, but only of evolutionary divergences (which are most definitely not negligible: but divergence implies a common source).

One small point: I was not characterizing the particular Romanticism I referred to as "Victorian"—that term was intended to apply only to myself, as describing my own upbringing—the not going to school, there being lots of family reading-aloud, the fact that my parents were fairly old when I was born and so were culturally linked with the past in some respects, and so forth. . . .

But to get back to the role of dream and reverie, if I may: the borderline between the conscious and unconscious, the realm of the intuitive, the sensuous music that evokes, and the image that presents and synthesizes, in contrast to the paraphrasable arguments of expository prose, have always been the territory of poetry. Poetry can narrate, explain, argue, and meditate, but its home base is that borderland you call "no-man's land" and which I would call "everyman's land."

Moreover, dreams—as I tried to point out in a prose piece called "A Note on the Work of the Imagination" (*New Directions* 17, 1961)—exemplify in a useful way the poetic, or imaginative, process: while not identical with it, they nevertheless show us how the unconscious parallels our part-conscious, part-intuitive, movements towards the construction of autonomous created entities (poems, novels, paintings, etc.).

Reid: Related, apparently, to this interest in dream is the fact that moments of calm reverie and meditation occur often in your poetry. You appear to share Wordsworth's conviction of the need for "wise passiveness" and the value of emotion recollected—or tapped—in tranquillity.

Levertov: I've somewhere used the phrase "intense passivity" or "intense receptivity," a receptivity which imperceptibly—in the creative artist, though not in the rare genius-reader (or receiver)—passes over into active construction. And Keats's "Negative Capability" is, I believe, the same faculty.

My belief is that the phrase "emotion recollected in tranquillity" only makes sense if one fully understands what is meant by recollection. Recollection, in this context—and Wordsworth, as poet, knew this, whether or not he *knew* he knew it—means not mere remembrance, in the hazy light of intervening time, but vivid *re-experiencing*. The "tranquillity" does not, then, refer to the state of mind (and feeling, and spirit, or psyche) during the re-experiencing/recollection, but to the physically removed circumstances. The battle scene is hard to write of clearly while one is in its noise and dust and immediate physical danger but to write of it *accurately* in the quiet of a solitary room later one must expose oneself to the painful—and exciting—reliving of its terrors and its energies. This is "the work of the imagination"—an *activity,* kinetic, dynamic.

Reid: It's mainly in this connection, isn't it, that the motif of silence recurs in your work?

Levertov: In connection with the silent solitude of the distance in which that vivid recollection occurs? Yes, I suppose so. Perhaps silence is equated with listening. In order to listen intently one must oneself be silent. The poet is speaker, singer: but to find the words of the song the poet first must listen.

Reid: In remarks you've made at various times about poetry, you speak of the Imagination—"that breathing of life into the dust." Belief in the Imagination as a power through which one can intuit transcendental harmony is, I suppose, a central tenet of Romanticism. Is it central in that sense to your own poetic creed? Or do you mean something else by the term "Imagination"?

Levertov: One way in which I could define the imagination might be to say it is the power of perceiving analogies and of extending this power from the observed to the surmised. Where fancy supposes, imagination believes, however; and draws kinetic force from the fervor of belief. Rather than breathing life into the dust, though, I see it as perceiving the life inherent in the dust. The poet sees, and reveals in language, what is present but hidden— what Goethe in *Wilhelm Meister* (or was it Carlyle writing about Goethe?) called the *open secret.* But just as the painter or sculptor only really *does* see by *doing*—by painting or carving—so too the poet only sees *in the process of language.* There is no disembodied vision the poet then seeks words for: the vision is given *in the work process*—though it is true some idea may, or even must, precede the process; but it is not the vision itself. "If words be not an incarnation of the thought," says Wordsworth, "but only a clothing for it, then surely they will prove an ill gift."

Reid: I'd like to hark back to William Carlos Williams. Beyond what you said earlier, how would you sum up the nature and extent of his influence on your writing?

Levertov: Williams' interest in the ordinary, in the present, in local history as microcosm, in the lives and speech of ordinary people; and his unsentimental compassion, which illumined the marvellous in the apparently banal, so deeply affected my "sense of living, of being alive" (which effect is, according to Wallace Stevens [in *Adagia*], one of the main functions of poetry) that it is impossible for me to measure. His prosodic influence is evident in early American poems of mine, e.g. "Pure Products" (*Overland to the Islands,* Jargon, 1958) which even takes its title from Williams. Stylistically I don't think my later work is that obviously Williams-influenced but his spiritual influence changed my life profoundly, and the development of my own style has been in turn the result of that deeper sense of what it is to be a human being. His prosody has surely been absorbed to some extent by every contemporary American poet—one could find some signs of its influence, probably, even in the work of poets who are not enthusiastic about Williams. The many long poems—e.g. by Galway Kinnell, Wendell Berry, Robert Duncan, etc. etc. (including myself)—of the last few years probably owe a great deal more, structurally, to *Paterson* and *The Desert Music* than to the work of Crane, Olson, Zukofsky, or even to the *Cantos.*

Reid: The *Penguin Modern Poets* book in which you and Williams are represented has selections from Kenneth Rexroth also. Do you regard his aims and techniques as similar to your own?

Levertov: Technically Rexroth's influence on me has been negligible. I have always enjoyed reading him and have marveled at the natural voice he achieves by a prosody so seemingly mechanical as syllables. I have experienced joy and illumination from poems and translations of his, and it was a great pleasure to me to have both him and Williams as fellows in the Penguin volume—indeed, I felt greatly honored. I cannot speak with confidence of his—or indeed my own, or any other poet's—"aims," for I am not sure if it is a word appropriate at all to the poet's life. Or, if the poet has an aim—*as poet*—it is *to discover poems.* As once navigators aimed to discover continents, islands, passages of the oceans. (Rexroth, by the way, was *my* "discoverer," to descend to another level of meaning: I had been published in England but it was he who first circulated my name and poems in America and first brought my work to the notice of my publisher, James Laughlin of New Directions.)

Reid: And another of your American contemporaries, Robert Duncan: you've expressed on several occasions a deep admiration for his work. How closely do his literary attitudes relate to yours?

Levertov: Duncan has been a close friend and an influence since the early fifties—or even before, for I first read some of his poems before I ever came to America, in Florence in 1958. In the last year or so he has felt that my political activism is in some way erosive of my poetry (though he himself has written many poems of political/social content, and his is not the tiresome attitude that splits human concerns into compartments: on the contrary, from him as much as from Williams and Pound I learned that anything and everything is potentially germane to the poem). Some vital exchange which had constantly taken place between us for many years is at the time of writing in abeyance. In my last book, *To Stay Alive,* there is a reference to a poem of his; I say, "And meanwhile,/Robert sees me as Kali. No, I am not Kali, I can't sustain for a day/that anger." He in turn has referred to, and in fact quoted, sections of my poems in his recent work. All this sounds "in-groupy" I'm afraid, but I think that in both his and my poems these personal references are given some universality by their context, which justifies them and makes them accessible to the reader not personally acquainted with either poet. As with Williams, his influence has been present too long and been too deep for me to adequately define it. His poetry is not only—as it obviously is—rich in ideas, in suggestions, "food for thought," but has given me much music and sensuous experience. To think of his poetry at large is to evoke images of candlelight and torchlight on gold and on dark wood. He made me aware, over the years, of the richness of many *lores*. We share a love of fairytales. He never separates the world of magic, or lore, from the grievous world of daily history. He is a mythologist—and it is probable that our present unusual block in communication is due to his mythologizing me into a role I do not believe true of me.

Reid: Would you agree—here's my hobby-horse again—that he has strong and specific affinities with the nineteenth-century Romantics?

Levertov: Yes, I would say the nineteenth century—Blake, Whitman, Hugo, Shelley (see his version of the "Arethusa"), the MacDonald and William Morris prose romances, and much more, are very important to Duncan. But far from exclusively important as influences: indeed his scholarship and enthusiasms have always been unusually wide-ranging.

Reid: Looking back at what you've written over a quarter of a century or so, do you see it all as having developed through certain distinct phases? Do individual volumes seem in retrospect to differ much? Or has it rather been a matter of continuing to work within a field marked out fairly early?

Levertov: During my early years in America I was rather embarrassed by my first, English, book; but later I came to accept it as not only not bad as an unsophisticated young girl's work, but also as showing intuitive signs— structurally—of qualities that link it with what I tried to do as I grew more aware of craft and what must underlie it.

Various American volumes reflect preoccupations or places—*Here and Now* and *Overland to the Islands* both include many poems of Mexican landscape, *With Eyes at the Back of Our Heads* has a lot of dream material in it, much of *O Taste And See* was written in the country in Maine, and so has many trees and flowers and birds in it, and *To Stay Alive* purposely gathers older poems of related theme together with the long title poem to form a single mosaic of that part of my life—the struggle against war and towards radical social change—which has become more and more intense and demanding in the late 1960s and looks likely to continue to be so now in the seventies. But I do not feel that there is a marked difference between volume and volume, just as I feel that there is no essential difference between my "political" and "personal" poems (the political *is* personal—and vice versa) and just as I feel definite continuity between the self I remember with long corkscrew curls at age five and myself now. I have always—even in the muzzy adolescent vagueness of *The Double Image*—written out of my own experience as I grasped it, so that the field has grown larger as I walked through it, one might say, but yes, it is the same field.

Reid: Finally, what about this new book which is coming out soon, *Footprints?* Do you take any new directions in it?

Levertov: This will be out in September. Many of the poems in it were written concurrently with *To Stay Alive.* The long poem that is the core of the latter is more of a new departure for me than anything in the forthcoming *Footprints,* I think. In it, utilizing the elbowroom of a diary form, incorporating prose passages as Williams had done in *Paterson* (do not imagine I am making Patersonian claims for *To Stay Alive,* though, please!) and as Haniel Long had done in *Pittsburgh Memorandum,*—I enjoyed the freedom of a longer journey than I had been accustomed to make. I have not given up writing short, "lyric" poems, but I felt the need of a larger form. The new book includes the concurrently written poems that were not germane to that particular book, plus those written after it; and I think if readers are looking for change it may seem a step backward, for it is not innovative, formally. What I've been writing since it went to the printer is however rather different—some of it, at least. I've just finished a fairly long poem in which a conversation takes place between myself, four Russian men, and a woman interpreter who, though everything is said through her, does not speak for herself. It arose from a visit to Moscow last December. Then last week I finished a very *plain* poem about the distance between the anti-war movement here and the actual struggle for liberation in Viet Nam. By plain I mean it sticks—except in one image—to very simple, ordinary conversational language, in contrast to the more heightened language of, say, "Life at War" or "What Were They Like," two of my poems on the war theme that have been rather widely reprinted; or than "Advent 1966" which harked back to the imagery of Southwell's "Burning Babe." In style it is more like a poem called "Despair" which follows "At David's Grave" in *Relearning the Alphabet*. This poem will appear in the anti-war issue of *Poetry,* Chicago, some time this year. The Russian conversation poem represents for me a direction not entirely new—"Somebody Trying" (about Tolstoy) and "Dialogue" (both in *Relearning*) are also poems in which more than one voice is heard—but which I would like to explore further.

An Interview with Denise Levertov
Maureen Smith / 1973

From *Tradition et Engagement dans la Poésie de Denise Levertov* (Unpub. Ph.D. dissertation: Université de Poitiers, 1979). Reprinted by permission of Maureen Smith.

Smith: On reading *With Eyes at the Back of Our Heads,* I was interested to see this very fine Toltec poem. How did you come across it?

Levertov: It was when I was living in Oaxaca, and lying on the ground near the *Bellas Artes* department of Oaxaca University was a sheet of onion-skin paper, and I picked it up. And it was this poem in Spanish and Toltec, and it said which codex it was from, but it didn't say who had translated it into Spanish. I took it back to the house, and what Elvira helped me with was *this* word, the word for a vulture, a Mexican vulture. You can see it must be derived from *xolopihtli,* and in any case they had translated it into *torpe,* which would be torpid, or slack, or lazy, but the root of the word is *carrion,* that which battens on, and so she gave me that word essentially.

Smith: What is the origin of the title *With Eyes at the Back of Our Heads?*

Levertov: You've surely heard the idiom?

Smith: I've heard it used to children.

Levertov: Yes. When my mother was engaged in something which had attracted my attention, and I would point something out to her that was behind her, she would say "I can't see it now. Do you think I've got eyes at the back of my head?" So that was the title origin. But then I took it to mean the in-dreaming, actual sleeping dream, and also the process of imagining; certainly in sleeping dreams it sometimes happens that way. Let's say you're walking down the street in a dream, but you also have the vision of a huge cavern which is behind you or something. It's as if you could see all around you, not just in front of you . . . and that's like the inner eye.

Smith: It's a kind of inner vision.

Levertov: (Reads)

> With eyes at the back of our heads
> we see a mountain

76

not obstructed with woods but laced
here and there with feathery groves.

The doors before us in a façade
that perhaps has no house in back of it
are too narrow, and one is set high
with no doorsill. The architect sees

the imperfect proposition and
turns eagerly to the knitter.
Set it to rights!
The knitter begins to knit.

For we want
to enter the house, if there is a house,
to pass through the doors at least
into whatever lies beyond them.

we want to enter the arms
of the knitted garment; As one
is re-formed, so the other,
in proportion.

When the doors widen
when the sleeves admit us
the way to the mountain will clear,

the mountains we see with
eyes at the back of our heads, mountain
green, mountain
cut of limestone, echoing
with hidden rivers, mountain
of short grass and subtle shadows.

Smith: You see a mountain. Would you say this was something like the Delectable Mountain, an object of desire?

Levertov: Yes, I think the mountain in this dream means something like the one in *The Pilgrim's Progress:* it is a place, a desirable place to go . . . it's a place one wants to attain.

Smith: So the images in the poem are dream images: the façade with the doors, and . . . ?

Levertov: Yes. Many of the poems in *With Eyes at the Back of Our Heads* contain dream images. One is looking so straight at the façade so that it seems as if perhaps there is nothing behind it; it's so flat that you don't get any sense of depth. You have seen pictures of old Hollywood sets for street scenes, that are just façades; and sometimes in the country, in New England for instance, there are farmhouses where the front door is never used . . . everybody goes in by the back or side doors, and the steps up to the door have never been put in, so that there's just this door, so that's why it's set high and doesn't have a sill to reach it by.

Smith: Then there is the knitter and the architect.

Levertov: I would say that this is a dream in which the personages are elements of oneself, and these are two sorts of creative elements. The architect is the one who has the ideas and makes the plan, and the knitter is the kind of craft-worker element that actually carries it out. In the dream there was this craft relationship between knitting and architecture, so that like in a fairy tale, if the knitter kept knitting and knitted right, the house would change as the garment was made. Dreams about houses can be dreams about one's own mind. One wants to develop the house of one's life and of one's art.

However, in this dream I'm outside the house, not in it. It is something which I am making, but I am there as a dreamer who is observing the architect and the knitter. We are outside it, all those three elements, and so there's a certain distance between us and the house, although we still want to get through the doors, and into whatever lies beyond those doors.

There is a sort of "as" implied here: as we want to enter the arms of the knitted garment, as one is re-formed, so the other. And now the curious thing is that although the mountain is behind one, by this rite of passage one knows that one is going to find out, one knows that one is going to see the way to the mountain by passing through that door.

Smith: It's like a door of initiation . . .

Levertov: Evidently.

Smith: It reminded me of a phrase by Jacques Maritain, who uses the image of the door; he says the poet's essential need is to create; but he cannot do so without going through the door of the knowledge of his own subjectivity.

Levertov: Where does he say that?

Smith: In *Creative Intuition in Art and Poetry.*

Levertov: I'm rather fond of that book.

Smith: In this poem you have the image of the door and the façade, but also that of "hidden rivers, mountain /of short grass and subtle shadows."

Levertov: I love the kind of place that you find in Wales and Yorkshire and places like that, where there's mountain grass—it's very short and there are little tiny flowers in this kind of place on the edge of the moors, lady slippers and so on; and then the "subtle shadows," and every hummock has its own shadow. I love that kind of place. So that is really descriptive of the desirability of the mountain.

Smith: You use the mountain image a good deal in the early poems, the early American poems.

Levertov: I was among mountains when many of these, this one for instance, was written in Oaxaca, and those ("The Dead Butterfly") are the mountains around it. This is a perfectly factual poem. In this other poem, I don't have them there in this particular case because I like mountains, but because I'm talking about a quality of love: a landscape that the mountains *define,* but not like a sort of *wall* of mountains, but like mountains that also have gaps and valleys, so that there's a connection between the landscape defined by the mountains and the landscape beyond the mountains. It's not a claustrophobic, sort of shut-in valley.

Smith: It's an open landscape, like many of those that you describe. Some of those in *With Eyes at the Back of Our Heads* are similar to the one in "Revolutionary."

The idea of the artist as craftsman is something which has been cropping up in your work all the time, and you use the image of an artist working a fabric over the years. Some of the themes of your poetry have changed, and some have remained constant. Would you say that your attitude to life has changed radically since you wrote your early poems?

Levertov: Well, my *life* has changed; I don't know that my attitude to life has changed very much. There have been many kinds of changes in my life, and therefore the content of my poems has reflected those changes, because the content has always more or less dealt with what was happening to me. With of course the exception of my first book, the English book, you know . . .

Smith: *The Double Image . . .*

Levertov: [One would never] deduce that there was a war on when those poems were written. I wasn't capable of dealing with that material—they're about my adolescent inner feelings, essentially, you know. I wasn't mature enough to be writing anything more beyond that, I guess, at that time, but I don't think that my attitude to life or my methods of writing have changed, except in ways perhaps imperceptible to myself.

Smith: Could you say something about the mission of the poet in society?

Levertov: Well, I wouldn't phrase it that way, but I think that the poet can have a function within society, yes, and I think that any poetry, all good poetry has the . . . what's the word I want? Well Wallace Stevens says in his *Adagia* that poetry should increase the sense of living, or being alive, something like that. And I think it does so. It enlarges and increases one's experience, whatever the subject matter, if it's a good poem. And so it sensitizes the reader just that infinitesimal little bit more: one is not the same after one has met a work of art as one was before it. It's a kind of chemical change— it's an experience that one has lived through, even if one forgets it afterwards. Just as one forgets what has happened to one's body but one's body doesn't forget, and it's the same with the mind. So willy-nilly, poetry has a social function, on that level, and then beyond that if it deals with, let's say, politics, history, etc., it can have an influence on other people, over the readers' attitudes, if it's good poetry.

Smith: Would you in that case consider poetry as a tool for social commitment?

Levertov: Yes, I would regard it as a tool for social commitment as long as the artist, the poet, recognizes that for it to be a good tool, it has to be good art. So one has to sacrifice to the gods of art first and foremost; otherwise, however greatly you desire for it to be a tool of your social commitment, it won't, because it will be lacking as art. Poetry can only be socially useful if it's aesthetically sound.

Smith: So good literature has an essentially educative role.

Levertov: One of the social functions of poetry, indirectly, is that it develops the imagination, and it seems to me that if more people read and wrote and just experienced poetry, it wouldn't necessarily make more virtuous people of them, but it would sensitize them to the point where, if they found themselves doing something like bombing, they would be more likely in imagination to follow the bomb down or try to picture to themselves what the result was going to be . . . whereas the people who have grown up never hearing stories read to them, going to awful elementary and high schools and technical colleges, where they got the absolute minimum of humanities and television programs that are just completely remote from the imagination—they're such garbage that they don't awaken the imagination—then as a result their feelings are numb, not towards the people who are close to them, but there is this terrible divorce between what they do, and its effects. All they're conscious of is pulling a lever or pressing a button, and they don't make the connection.

Smith: Many of your poems are anti-war poems.

Levertov: Well, I've always written about what I was living. When I've been in the country, I've written about the country, when I've been in love I've written about being in love, and when I've been on demonstrations, I've written about that. So poetry is all about one thing. One big influence has been teaching, because in teaching I got more involved in a more day-to-day level with the student resistance movement, and I've learned a lot from my students, particularly at Berkeley and M.I.T.—very radical students who had done a lot of radical political thinking. There was plenty of exchange, and I shared their lives to some extent. It influenced my life and therefore of course it influenced my poetry. It's just as simple as that; you write about what you live. If one is what one eats, one's poems are what one does, I think.

Smith: So there is a direct relationship between art and reality . . .

Levertov: It has always seemed to me that most of the art that interested me, that I loved and was stimulated by, was directly related to what we call *reality,* ordinary life, and was not all that rarified. I mean, I have been very much influenced by William Carlos Williams, and his art as a poet is so rooted in life. He says in his autobiography that being a doctor all his life, and not an expensive family specialist, but a G.P. in Rutherford, New Jersey and in Paterson, and living a very full doctor's life, his life as a doctor just fell into his life as a poet, and gave it strength. He picked up on speech rhythms. He would often go out on the tracks on night calls, and not just sit in a comfortable office all the time.

Smith: When did you first meet Williams?

Levertov: Well, I can't remember the exact date. It was in the fifties.*

Smith: Did he have a great impact on your thinking about poetry?

Levertov: Yes, tremendous. What was this impact? Well, I felt some inner

---

*Since 1951, Denise Levertov and William Carlos Williams had exchanged letters. They met in 1953.

need for change in my way of writing that would correspond to the change in my way of life in coming to America—this whole new thing I couldn't deal with in the melodious romantic language of my English poems, and Williams kind of pointed a way for me. I think he's one of those poets that . . . you know, there are poets who are very great poets from whom there is very little to be learned as a writer, because they are so idiosyncratic. One can go in some ways beyond the idiosyncracies of their style, but stylistically there is very little to learn, for example from Gerard Manley Hopkins (whom I adore), because anybody who has been reading a lot of Hopkins and is susceptible to influence, is going to come out with imitation Hopkins, and it's just ghastly. You can immediately tell if a student has been reading e. e. cummings; you can tell if somebody has been reading Dylan Thomas. These are poets of the kind you can't learn much from. Then there are poets who are much less idiosyncratic, and have a much plainer, more transparent style, who have method rather than style.

Williams, you see, based his poetry mainly on speech rhythms and common speech, and from that base he moved out into a lot of other places. He didn't stay there, but he was founded on that. And he was a person who had a very strong capacity for perceiving and illuminating the ordinary, for revealing the wonder of the ordinary. So that a person reading Williams can learn two things: reading him just as a reader certainly increases one's capacity for seeing the ordinary as not ordinary at all, and as a poet can learn also to base oneself in a language that is natural to oneself, and move out from that base. One can learn not to be "literary," you know, but to start plain and only get fancy if the development of what you're doing naturally takes you in that direction. So this is method rather than manner, right? Because your common language, your ordinary idiomatic speech, may be different from his.

Smith: You had come from Europe, and were learning to use different speech rhythms. Yet the language you were using was English. Do you think that anyone coming from another country, say France or Spain or Italy, could be positively influenced by Williams?

Levertov: A poet from another country could learn to do the same thing. Someone whose language was a dialect, and they were resolved to write in that dialect, could learn from Williams as much as a person who shared his language and diction, who had also been born in the 1880s, grown up on the eastern seaboard of the United States, had the kind of education and social milieu that he had—such a person might absolutely share his base, but a person from somewhere completely different, you see, could learn to do the same, not imitating him, but in their own terms.

That's why he was, not just for me, but for countless people, such a truly useful influence, not just someone whose influence one can see because it comes out in imitation.

Smith: What other poets have been important for you?

Levertov: Well, Rilke's letters have been extremely important for me, ever since I was about 22. The edition I have is just choc-a-bloc with things that are essential statements about the vocation of the artist. I think Rilke has been a great influence, but not really so much as a poet because my German is not adequate to reading anybody without a crib, and a dictionary, in fact, and it's certainly not adequate to reading Rilke without those helps, so although I've read many of Rilke's poems that way, reading the translation and then going over the original, I can usually, if the translation is really bad, detect it, but I wouldn't feel that I had been influenced by Rilke's poetry to any degree, but by his letters very much, I think.

Well, I mentioned Stevens, and of course Williams. I translated some Antonio Machado, and I love Machado; he is certainly one of the poets that I really look up to. As a child, I used to read the short poems of Tennyson a lot, because they were sort of melodious, and I think I had a good ear, and maybe some of that musical quality may have rubbed off on me. But, well, I real lots of Wordsworth and Keats when I was quite young—you know I never went to school. Then I read the young poets of my childhood: Auden, Spender, Day Lewis, MacNeice, but those were poets I read a lot so long ago, that I don't think there's much sign of their presence. And I read a good deal of Eliot many years ago, but I really got turned off Eliot after I came to America and began to read Williams, not because Williams didn't like Eliot, but because there seemed such a lack of vitality in Eliot's diction and rhythm comparatively, and it began to bore me. And then I've read Pound's criticism and taken a lot of it to heart.

Smith: You appear to have some connection with Robert Duncan. Have you in some way a common attitude to poetry?

Levertov: Yes. I've been close to Duncan for years, and he's certainly been an influence for me. At present, and in the last two years I guess, we've really rather drifted apart . . . but for many years I felt a real dependence on him. No matter what anybody else said and however much praise and approval I got from other quarters, if I didn't have his, it didn't mean much to me. He was like my touchstone. I no longer feel like that; I just grew up to the point of not needing that seal and approval.

Smith: Are you familiar with the poems of Federico García Lorca and Juan Ramon Jiménez?

Levertov: Not really with Jiménez, but with Lorca, yes.

Smith: Do you like him?

Levertov: Yes, very much. I used to read a lot of Lorca. In fact I taught myself Spanish through reading Lorca. But I read very little Jiménez; he seemed kind of vaporous to me.

Smith: Sometimes the rhythm of some of your poems reminds me very much of Lorca, especially in the occasional verbless phrase: "el barco sobre la mar / y el caballo en la montana," and your "the emblems torn from the walls / and the black plumes."

Levertov: I could well have been, in fact I'm sure I was, influenced by my reading of Lorca, when I was really into him, which was mainly when I was living in Mexico, and for a year or two afterwards, when I was in a sort of dry period, I used to work myself up by reading Lorca, and occasionally trying a translation or two, but I never seriously worked at Lorca translations, because for one thing there are quite a few good ones—he's been better served I think than some poets—and so just for my own edification I would try and translate a poem to get into it more deeply, and I'm sure he was an influence.

Smith: You have expressed a kind of affinity with Guillevic.

Levertov: Well, I think I say in the introduction that I would never attempt to translate the work of a poet if I did not feel some kind of affinity with him. And also Guillevic of course reminds me very much of Williams.

Smith: There is the Guillevic poem which you translate by "I dwelt in the blackbird, I lived in the flower," and Guillevic's attitude to granite when he says "J'ai besoin d'être dur avec toi." Do you consciously try to live within things?

Levertov: No, I don't think I consciously try to, but I've always had a sort of empathic projection into things. I suppose it's true of most poets . . . well, some poets are more abstract than others, but I think it's true of many poets at any rate.

Smith: Claudel seems to have considered the object as a messenger of absolute joy; he said absolute joy exists, and visible objects are its messengers.

Levertov: That's beautiful; yes, marvellous. But I don't think I know what absolute means. I don't think as a human being one *can* know what absolute means. I think one can have an experience of joy so intense that one doesn't know how it could be more so, but only moments, I think . . . yet I often seem to be seized with exhilaration for no good reason!

Smith: You often talk about joy . . .

Levertov: Yes. And yet I'm very conscious of so many wrongs and oppressions in this country, and in other countries, that often what I express is anger. And also intolerance. I've come to be more and more intolerant of people whom I can't respect politically, and to feel in fact that there are situations in which tolerance is not a virtue. I have a poem about it. It says "O tolerance, what crimes have been committed in thy name." Elridge Cleaver coined a phrase which said "If you are not part of the solution you are part of the problem." It's a modern version of "He who is not with me is against me," and there are a lot of people too timid, too cowardly, too generally uncommitted in this country; there are countless people who have not done all they could have done to struggle against the war and the evils of the social system; they haven't tried.

Smith: Poet-prophet, poet-priest . . . I notice that you sometimes use the altar image in your work. Do you in fact conceive of the world as a temple, and the poet as priest at the altar?

Levertov: Somewhat, yes; I think of poetry as something beyond the poet, of which the poet is a servant, and I think of it as a power, a force beyond oneself. I was brought up, as you can imagine, in quite a religious atmosphere, although not really a conventional one; I think that the amount of religious imagery that comes up in my poems is certainly accounted for largely by my background . . . the terminology of religion and myth has always been very natural to me.

Smith: Political themes appear more and more frequently in your work. What constitutes a stimulus for your writing?

Levertov: Well, in the case of *To Stay Alive,* the whole experience of the war, my involvement in the anti-war movement, a history of actions and feelings during that experience and then, as I said in the preface, you know,

I reprinted those earlier poems because I began to see them as steps towards this larger poem that would deal with these political-social-ethical involvements . . . And, of course, I have always written about what I was experiencing at any particular moment.

Smith: The poet's role in all this stems from the fact . . .

Levertov: That he has received a gift, the gift of poetry, and he is obliged to serve his gift, to be a voice.

Denise Levertov
Sybil Estess / 1977, 1978

From *American Poetry Observed: Poets on Their Work,* ed. Joe David Bellamy (Urbana: University of Illinois Press, 1984), 155–67. Reprinted by permission of Joe David Bellamy and the University of Illinois Press.

The interview was conducted at Tufts University in Boston and at Ms. Levertov's home in Somerville, Massachusetts, in October 1977; and in Houston, Texas, in March 1978.

Estess: What first led you to writing?

Levertov: Well, I lived in a house full of books, and everybody in my family did some kind of writing. My earliest memories of my father seem to picture him swathed in galleys. It seemed natural for me to be writing something. I wrote poems from an early age, and stories. I began to keep diaries and journals when I was a little older.

Estess: What were the circumstances of your being educated by your parents rather than in schools?

Levertov: There weren't any schools in the neighborhood which my parents thought were much good. My mother had taught school, and was a great reader. So from year to year it just seemed to work out better for me to do lessons at home, Victorian style. My mother gave me daily lessons from age five to twelve. I also listened to the BBC school programs. After that I began daily professional ballet classes and went to private French, art, and music lessons. I used to wander around the V and A a lot, and go to art exhibitions and to the British Museum and so on. It has always been intended that I should eventually go to school, perhaps to the university; but between my ballet mania and the war it just didn't happen.

Estess: Could you say more about what effect the war years in England had on you?

Levertov: First of all, the career that I had been working toward as a ballet dancer did not materialize; the war had some effect on my giving that up. To avoid the draft, which in England conscripted women as well as men, I joined the "land army," and worked for a while on a dairy farm and in a market garden. Then I began an intensive program of nurses' training, called "Civil Nursing Reserve." After a while I decided that I might as well be really training professionally to get something out of my wartime work, and I enrolled in a regular training hospital. I continued until I had become what is equivalent to a Licensed Practical Nurse, but I did not go on to become a Registered Nurse because I didn't like the strain of taking even the one and only examination that I ever took in my life, and I didn't like the way in which one's personal life was regulated. (I was always crawling in and out of windows to avoid curfews!)

Estess: How old were you during these years? Were you writing even then?

Levertov: I was nineteen, twenty, twenty-one; and yes, I was writing. I began publishing during that period, actually, although my very first poem had been printed when I was sixteen.

Estess: What are your memories of your artistic development during the war?

Levertov: One significant thing that happened during that time was quite coincidental. When I was nineteen and entered the Civil Nursing Reserve Program, the hospital to which I was sent was in a little town in Essex— Billericay. When I first arrived there, I was walking down the main street and I saw a sign which said "Grey Walls Press." I said to myself, "Those are the people that put out *Poetry Quarterly* where my [first] poem ["Listening to Distant Guns"] was published." I went in there three days later and introduced myself to the man who by this time had become the editor of the magazine, Wrey Gardiner. He began reading my poetry and eventually publishing it. He also introduced me to several poets, there and in London.

Estess: Who were some of these poets?

Levertov: Tambimuttu, Alex Comfort (who nowadays is famous for *The Joy of Sex,* but was then known as a young poet), Nicholas Moore, Dannie Abse.

Estess: Did you meet regularly with any of these writers to discuss your work?

Levertov: No, but I developed some contacts. Much of the poetry in England at that time was not very good, including my own adolescent writing which appeared in my first book in 1946. But the sentimentality and lushness of what was known as the "New Romanticism" then was a reaction, partly, to the daily life of wartime—the drabness and grayness of England in the early 1940s.

Estess: Concerning the political conditions of the time then, how well do you remember the bombing in England?

Levertov: I was in London and the environs throughout the entire war, and I remember it very vividly. You wouldn't think so—to read my poems at that time—because there is very little reference to it. I think that this is simply because I was too immature as an artist and as a person to deal with it.

Estess: Did you realize what was going on historically?

Levertov: Well, I knew more than the average English person. I surely knew what Hitler represented, because I had grown up with refugees right in my home. I knew what went on in concentration camps more than most people did until the war was over.

Estess: Your family was in contact with Jewish people on the continent?

Levertov: Yes. From the time I was nine years old when Hitler came to power my family was involved with saving people from Germany and Austria. Perhaps because my mother was Gentile and my father a Jew who had been converted to Christianity, they specialized in refugees who had one Jewish parent, people who had possibly been brought up as Christians and only recognized the fact that they were Jewish when they were forced to wear a yellow star.

Estess: How did you, at such a young age, assimilate such horrible political (and human) realities into your consciousness?

Levertov: There had always been a good deal of political consciousness in my family, which I absorbed. The issue of Nazism was not the only issue with which my family concerned itself. During the Italian fascist invasion of Abyssinia, now Ethiopia, I remember my father speaking on the street on a soapbox about that. And in the Spanish Civil War, when I was eleven, I think, I was an ardent partisan of the left-wing elected government. I recall that I listened to news broadcasts all the time. I grew up in an atmosphere where such issues were discussed.

Estess: As you grew up, did you develop a distinctive sense of being Jewish?

Levertov: Oh yes. Even though my father had become had become a Christian, and of course an Anglican priest, he always emphasized that he was a "Jewish Christian." He emphasized the fact that Jesus and the disciples were Jews. To him Christianity was really a fulfillment of the messianic hope. He and my mother, who was Welsh, certainly instilled in me and my sister a great deal of pride in being Jewish, although the Jewish community did not consider us so. We were apostates in their eyes. They thought of my father as either a traitor or just crazy.

Estess: How aware were you of the ugliness of anti-Semitism in *your* life? Did you yourself ever feel discriminated against because you were part Jewish?

Levertov: I never felt myself discriminated against, but I surely knew what anti-Semitism is. I used to get into big arguments with people if I sensed some prejudice in their remarks. I remember that when I was about ten I used to lecture my good friend Jean, who was non-Jewish, on the subject. (I was always lecturing her about *something!*)

Estess: How did your father happen to be converted to Christianity?

Levertov: Well, his father, who was an Orthodox rabbi of Hasidic ancestry and also a man of general culture, wanted my father to get a general education as well as a purely Jewish one. So after my father had been to the theological seminary at Valójine, he went at the age of eighteen to the University of Königsberg, in Prussia. (He couldn't go to the university in Russia at that time, because he was Jewish.) While he was at Königsberg he read the New Testament and became convinced that Jesus had, in fact, been the Messiah.

Estess: So it was really an intellectual conversion for him?

Levertov: Yes.

Estess: That's a fascinating story, and quite a remarkable personal history. I would like to shift the subject, if I may, to your life after you came to America. Was it during your early years here in this country that you began to have a sense of the political role that an artist can have in society?

Levertov: My sense of the social role that the poet, specifically, can play came gradually, I think. I could not put a date to it, although I would say that the first really political poem that I wrote was about the Eichmann trial, from *The Jacob's Ladder.*

Estess: Could you characterize how you have changed, or evolved, politically during the last twenty or twenty-five years?

Levertov: Well, during the days of the Korean War, for example, like a lot of other people I was really unaware and unconcerned, I think. You will remember that there was actually no antiwar movement during the Korean War comparable to the one against the war in Vietnam. I shared that apathy, I'm afraid. But I began to participate in antinuclear demonstrations back in New York in the "ban the bomb" period. I was a convinced pacifist for a number of those years. Then I became more and more politically involved with the antiwar movement concerning Vietnam, and I began to feel that being a pacifist was an unbearably smug position to take. I felt it was self-righteous. I realized that there was a connection between the Vietnamese people who were struggling for self-preservation and between people's struggle for self-determination in all places, and with racism. So I gave up my pacifism at that point and became more revolutionary.

Estess: Would you make your political stances normative for any artist? Do you make judgments against persons who do not choose to live such a public and political life as you do?

Levertov: No. I don't think that one should make that judgment. I feel that if a person is just coldly, cynically unconcerned, that his or her art will suffer from this. But I also think that many people are concerned with the fate of their fellow beings but are just constitutionally not capable of giving their time and energy to activism. I think it would be wrong to judge them; people's own consciences should judge them, not another person.

Estess: You have spoken a great deal about American writers, such as those within the Black Mountain school of poets, who became your friends and who influenced you after you married Mitchell Goodman and moved to the United States. I wonder if you would care to rename any American writers who influenced you other than these.

Levertov: William Carlos Williams and Wallace Stevens.

Estess: You have written more of your being influenced by Williams than you have about Steven's influence on you. What drew you to Stevens's poetry?

Levertov: Stevens is a very musical poet, and it's really the sensuous aspects of his poetry which I have always liked. I am fascinated with his use of language for its own sake.

Estess: Do you think that perhaps your poems are often like his in this way?

Levertov: I think that there are poems of mine which show Stevens's influence, but influences do not stick out as if they were bumps. You absorb them; you cannot really talk about them directly. I can speak a bit more concretely about Williams's influence on me because certainly, coming from England, as I did, the manner in which he incorporated the rhythms and diction of common speech into his poetry gave me a shot in the arm and a way in which to deal with coming to live in America.

Estess: What caused you to make pilgrimages to see Williams? What was the nature of your visits to his home in Rutherford?

Levertov: I suppose that my first visit to Williams *was* somewhat of a pilgrimage. I had been reading his work for a few years before I went to see him. I had even written him a letter and had a reply from him two or three years before my first visit. On my first trip I went out to Rutherford on the bus, with either Bob Creeley or Cid Corman, possibly even both. I think that Mitch came too. Then I began going out about twice a year, for some years.

Estess: Would you read *your* poetry while you were there?

Levertov: Yes. He would ask me to read my poems, and sometimes he would hand me one of his poems which he wanted to have read to him. When I met him he had already had the first of his series of strokes and it was difficult for him to read to himself. We would talk about poetry, or about people. I always had a *marvelous* time; but unfortunately, like a fool, I did not make a record of those conversations. They always seemed so vivid in my mind as I left there that I could not imagine I was going to forget them. I do remember that often they would ask me to come out for lunch—or as early in the afternoon as I could make it. I would perhaps get out there about 2:30, and stay until about 6:30 or 7:00.

Estess: Do you think that Williams had the sense that he was fulfilling some mission by helping younger writers?

Levertov: No. He was a most unpompous man; I don't think that he thought of himself as a "missionary" to younger writers. But I do think that he not only enjoyed these occasions but needed them. He wanted the assurance that he was in touch with younger writers and that his ideas about poetry were influencing other poets.

Estess: Did he ever ask you your reactions to any part of *Paterson?* He had completed it by then, right?

Levertov: I last visited him only weeks before his death, so he had published all of his books. I don't remember that he asked me anything about *Paterson.* But unfortunately I just can't recall.

Estess: You have mentioned in another interview that the poets of your generation "owed Pound a great deal." What were some of the things that you owed him?

Levertov: One thing we all owed him was an awareness of the need for precision in poetry, and also an awareness of the dangers of self-indulgent sentimentalism. I really learned more about these things from his criticism than from his poetry. In *The ABC of Reading* he emphasizes really standing by your word. This became very important to me—taking responsibility for the precision of what you say. This seems to me the most basic thing that one can learn from Pound. His poetry is fascinating in some ways too, however. For example, its Cubist influence, and the idea he projects that the relationship of objects changes as you yourself move. Some of Pound's apparently mosaic method combines elements so that you get a new perspective on them. But he brings this about by causing the perceiver to move—to look at things now from here and now from there.

Estess: Would this kind of sensibility be able to effect some kind of "revelation"?

Levertov: Yes. I think so. But for me revelation in poetry always concerns the movement of the mind as it thinks and feels, and does so *in language.* For a poet, the thinking-feeling process is not merely immediately transposed into language. Rather, it *takes place in language.* For example, the way that a poem is written on the page is a score for the way that it should be read aloud, and the way that it will be experienced. Such concrete manifestations of perception are crucial aspects of the way that poetry can "reveal." I believe strongly that the line itself is expressive of patterns of seeing. I have never really understood the breath theory that Olson talks about; but I think that line-breaks are determined not just by physiological breathing demands, but by the sequences of your perceptions.

Estess: In regard to the matter of lines and line-breaks being a record of the sequence of perceptions, is this different from "enjambment"?

Levertov: Definitely. When writing in open forms, "enjambment" is irrelevant, although some people don't realize this. Some poets break their lines in places which throw a quite undesired, heavy accent onto a word that commences the next line, for example. But this practice of enjambment in nonmetrical forms is really a useless practice. In tight metrics it provides relief from the monotony of metrical patterns, but when one is writing in nonmetrical forms, then the line takes on a more intense function that it ever did before. So the whole concept of "enjambment" just gets in the way of the real function of the line.

Estess: Do you think, also, that traditional forms in poetry are largely passé?

Levertov: I think that the kind of closures imposed by traditional forms relate to the sense of life within the periods which gave rise to them. After Einstein, the certainty about the future that people used to have was changed. The universe has turned out to be much less defined than we had thought— with hell below and heaven above—and we obviously live in a time of uncertainty. Forms in poetry, then, have become in my opinion anachronistic. Nevertheless, if an individual's basic sensibility is generally in tune with those kinds of underlying conceptions which gave rise to the form in the first place, a couplet, for instance, or a sonnet, then maybe he or she can use them successfully. But I think that the use of traditional forms in a sort of wishful-wistful way—to give order where we have apparently little of it—is not poetry. I think that we should acknowledge the chaos we live in and deal with it; open forms can allow one to explore chaos and see what can be discovered there.

Estess: In addition to a sense of line-breaks, what else constitutes either a "good ear" or a "bad ear" for poetry?

Levertov: There are two ways that I characterize either a good ear or what I term a "tin ear." The first is the sense of line-breaks, that I have discussed. The second is a person's ear for the mimetic in sound. If a poet is deficient in this, he or she does not have a feeling for combining sounds well, noticing the quality of sounds insofar as they are smooth, rough, heavy, or light. These people tend to combine content and sound textures inappropriately. They will use really heavy, thick, dense, sticky sounds when they are dealing with material which is light, airy, or ethereal.

Estess: Can a tin ear be improved?

Levertov: I think that a good ear for poetry, like a good ear for music, is something that one is either endowed with or is not. But a poor ear can be improved by trying—if that person allows himself or herself to listen enough. So many people end up only reading poetry silently. Some poets don't even read aloud to themselves as they write. So poetry remains to many people abstract, deprived of a large measure of its sensuousness.

Estess: Speaking of the auditory sensuousness of poetry, I would like to tell you that I think that you are one of the best readers of poetry that I have ever heard. It seems to me that you have wonderful breath control. It is almost as if you were trained as a singer. I notice that when you read you inhale and then exhale slightly before you begin to speak. It's as if the inhalation gathers energy, and then as you begin to exhale you build up to a momentum which enables you to sound the words effectively. Is this process conscious with you?

Levertov: No. I don't think that the process itself is conscious. I think that this habit probably comes from having been reared in a family that had a certain tradition of being eloquent, of being able to speak in public. I grew up hearing my mother read prose aloud, and read it extremely well. When my son was little I read aloud to him a great deal and loved it. And I have a strong voice—that helps.

Estess: Isn't it true, then, that you might read another poet's poems in a more animated manner, perhaps a quite different manner, than that person would read them? Is this fair to the other poet?

Levertov: I regard the way that the poem is written on the page as a notation, and one should be able to follow the score and come out with a pretty close approximation of the way it is intended to be read. Some poets, though, have the ability to write beautiful scores but not to play them. It is as if they don't have the confidence to do the performance properly. Many poets are just really bad at reading their own or anyone's poems.

Estess: To get back to your own writing, you have said that in composing poems you do not begin until you have an entire line, or at least a phrase, perhaps a rhythm, in mind. You say that you do not start to write when you just have a vague feeling about something you might want to say or write about. In other words, you don't push. You wait until a line or a phrase crystallizes in your head, or your ear. How would you teach students to cultivate this process of waiting, and knowing when to begin to write and when not to begin?

Levertov: Well, it's certainly a hard thing to try to teach if a person has not experienced it. But one way that I try to teach that process, which I think is extremely important, is that when a student has a poem that has been discussed in a workshop, and it has become clear that revision, more work, is necessary, or that a certain word or words are just not the right ones, I tell them: do not try to search for the nearest synonym. I try to encourage them, rather, to return their attention to the experience which gave rise to the poem, to revisualize what they then saw, to refeel what they then felt. In other words, to go back to the source of the poem.

Estess: This is really sort of beginning again, isn't it?

Levertov: Yes. And if they can learn to revise in this way, then I think it teaches them something about that necessary waiting for crystallization. It teaches them to reattempt to unearth the experience.

Estess: Sometimes if the student has typed this poem already, does it help them to go back to handwriting when they begin to revise in this manner, in order to go back to the original experience?

Levertov: Probably. But whether or not they do that, I try to instill in them the idea of not trying to "patch up" what already exists, if they think that it isn't quite right. They do better when they ignore their draft, and return to the source. I encourage them to explore what they see when they go back. I ask them, "What do you *see* when you return to this experience in your memory and imagination?" I encourage them to recall it, recollect it.

Estess: What if a student comes to you, though, and says "I haven't begun to write the poem yet, but I have had this experience that I want to write about. How do I begin?"

Levertov: I would say something like "Go on thinking about it. Go on feeling it. But begin to write only when the words themselves begin to come."

Estess: You have said that writing poetry in "organic form" arises out of faithful attention to the object, and yet that it is really a presence of "the unexpected," or "the muse," which transforms that attention into poetry. You have referred to this process as a kind of "alchemy." Could you comment further on how this unpredictable "x" factor may come about?

Levertov: It is the reward that sometimes happens from having paid careful and faithful attention. If you do *not* give the experience your patient attention, you may be working solely by will and intelligence, and then you have to manipulate the experience. If you are very skillful, you may do some good things this way; but they are relatively superficial. But if you give to your material a kind of humble devotion, or attention, you will, if you have got any native talent to help you along, be *given* a good deal. And if you *persist,* then sometimes you are given the poet's special reward of the absolutely unpredictable. No amount of faithful attention can guarantee this, but sometimes you may be whirled right off your feet and taken into some areas of experience which you had never considered possible. This, indeed, is a gift. You cannot will it to happen. But you can place yourself in a relationship to your art to be able to receive it if it should happen; this relationship is "faithful attention."

Estess: Do you feel that when you are given this gift that you have had a "religious" experience, or do you shy away from that term?

Levertov: No, I don't object to the word religious, although it is hard to use the word without getting into some kind of definition of it. But I would say that for me writing poetry, receiving it, is a religious experience. At least if one means by this that it is experiencing something that is deeper, different from, anything that your own thought and intelligence can experience in themselves. Writing itself can be a religious act, if one allows oneself to be put at its service. I don't mean to make a religion of poetry, no. But certainly we can assume what poetry is *not*—it is definitely not just an anthropocentric act.

Estess: Before we conclude this interview, I would like to ask you how real you think that the apparent revival of poetry in America is?

Levertov: The proliferation of little magazines, the publication of many books of poems, and the sales of some books of poems prove that there is some kind of renaissance going on. But even though there are more people reading poetry today than there were, say, thirty years ago, the number of people who read poetry is still small in relation to the total population. There are a lot more people who *write* poetry, too, than who *read* it, since some people are only interested in "self-expression," which of course is not necessarily art.

Estess: Speaking of self-expression, would you care to define what the term "confessional poetry" means to you. Do you consider yourself a confessional poet?

Levertov: Confessional poetry to me means not just poetry with autobiographical elements clearly present in it but poetry which utilizes the poem as a place in which to confess parts of one's life which are troublesome—the kinds of things which require the act of confession. Although I write many poems of a personal nature, I don't consider myself a confessional writer in these terms.

Estess: You said in another interview that confessional poetry is "a poetry that isn't interested in sound or philosophical ideas, or in images as such, but in psychology." I wonder if it is possible to have good poetry which is interested *only* in psychology?

Levertov: No. I don't think that a lot of confessional poetry *is* good poetry. Sometimes poets writing in confessional modes are gifted poets, if their language instinct is good. But I think that this is the exception rather than the rule. As I understand it, the confessional poem has as its motivational force the desire to *unburden* the poet of something which he or she finds oppressive. But the danger here is reducing a work of art simply into a process of *excretion.* A poem is not *vomit!* It is not even tears. It is something very different from a bodily purge.

Estess: Does confession imply guilt? If a woman, say, writes a "Confessional" poem about having had an abortion, for instance, would that not imply that she has some predisposition against abortion? Why else would she have to "confess" the abortion?

Levertov: A poem about an abortion could be confessional without being about guilt. It could simply be about pain. Or it could be exhibitionistic, since sometimes the impulse to tell the world about one's private life includes exhibitionism. On the other hand, a woman might write a poem about abortion from a highly ideological point of view; she could want to tell the world what it's like to undergo this. There are many different ways that one might write such a poem, none of which would involve guilt.

Estess: But would most of these rally be confessional in the way we use the term for much of contemporary poetry?

Levertov: It's a very subtle, tricky point, really. Does the way in which "confessional" is used today imply guilt? I tend to think that it doesn't have to. It can just be the need to get something off your chest. Confessional in this sense is just telling a personal story and feeling better for having told it. But it could be true that when this becomes exhibitionistic, then guilt is involved. I don't know about what psychologists would say about this.

Estess: Do you think that the best confessional poetry is that which creates a myth of the self, and thus universalizes the experience. Lowell's poetry, for instance?

Levertov: Yes. Then confessional poetry transcends the merely self-therapeutic; it attains some kind of universality. And I should conclude this topic by emphasizing that what I object to most in some so-called confessional poetry is that the impulse for the works is so exclusively related to the need for the poets to unburden themselves that the aesthetic considerations are disregarded.

Estess: I wonder if you find that writing poems is particularly painful?

Levertov: Dealing with pain is not a primary function of poetry for me; that's why I say that I am not "confessional." The act of writing poetry is, to me, extremely pleasurable. I think that the whole myth of the sufferings of the poet is vanity—vanity in the biblical sense even. The sufferings of the poet are not greater than those of any other person. Perhaps some people who are poets may be said to be more aware of some things than a lot of people are, and in that awareness they may suffer a little more than average. But I think that there are so many other people who are just as sensitive but who don't have anything creative to *do* with their sensitivity. Since they have not found a way to incorporate their sensitivity into action, they actually suffer a great deal more than anyone who is able to create out of sensitivity.

Estess: My question concerning pain involves, partly, just what you brought up: the sense that people do suffer according to their level of consciousness, of sensitivity. Especially sensitivity concerning their own self-consciousness. The question sometimes becomes "how much sensitivity or self-consciousness can one stand?" Obviously poets such as Sylvia Plath and John Berryman felt that they could not stand any more.

Levertov: Yes. But it was not as poets that they suffered. It was as individuals who happened to have a very low threshold of suffering, of pain, that they despaired. One can say that if they had not been poets they would have suffered just as much—or more. Yes, more. And they might not have lasted as long as they did.

Estess: Berryman remarked in the last interview that he granted, published in the *Paris Review,* that he wanted to be pushed to suffer. He wanted God, as he said, to push him toward suffering in order to be able to write. His words were, "My idea is this: the artist is extremely lucky who is presented with the worst possible ordeal that will not kill him. I think that what happens to my poetic work in the future will depend upon being knocked in the face, thrown flat, given cancer, or other things of that kind. I hope to be nearly crucified." What would you remark about such an attitude?

Levertov: I would remark that there do exist in the world masochists, and that some masochists happen to be poets. It has nothing to do with the nature of the poet per se.

Estess: In what direction was Sylvia Plath developing when she died? We tend to think of her as a confessional poet.

Levertov: I think that she was fantastically gifted in her images; she was indeed an inspired image-maker. This saved her poems from being just therapeutic.

Estess: How much is sheer loneliness and isolation essential for the artist, if not pain?

Levertov: Loneliness is different from solitude. I think that solitude is essential, in varying degrees, for any artist. I happen to need a lot of it. And since I lead a very busy life, and am also quite sociable, I really enjoy living alone now that I do so. Because if I did not live alone, I wold have an inadequate degree of solitude.

Estess: Did you have an inadequate degree when you were married?

Levertov: Well, sometimes. But I was married for twenty-five years, and I expect that most of that time I needed to be. I have no regrets about that part of my life, and I don't think that writing and coordinating family life was all that difficult to do, as some people say it is. But people change; their needs become different.

Estess: You have said in an essay entitled "A Sense of Pilgrimage," which you incorporated into *The Poet in the World,* that you consider your own life myth as that of a pilgrim or voyager. Does such a sense of your exploratory life path have within it loneliness, or merely solitude?

Levertov: Both! Pilgrims go through trials and tribulations; that is part of pilgrimage, isn't it? Even in fairy tales, there are always all sorts of dragons and dark woods to be encountered on one's way to where one is finally going.

Estess: Is there any specific myth that you would use to characterize where you are now in your life?

Levertov: Ah, where am I in my life. . . . Well, I am certainly in a different time period from the one I was in, say, four or five years ago. Perhaps it began with buying my house, or perhaps it began with deciding, definitively deciding, to end my marriage. I am not at all sure where to put the beginnings of it. But I know that I am in a phase of life which has to do with living alone, and with having a lot of freedom. All of my decisions now have to be my own decisions. I alone decide whom to see, whom to love, whom to spend time with, what time to get up, what time to eat. Of course I realize that many decisions which one thinks one is making are actually already made for one by life itself.

But in any case, I am sure that there must be a myth which is about a person having come to a new country or a new mode of living. There is always a myth to express practically anything—all phases of life, all attitudes, all stances; so I would bet that if I really searched among the world's literature I could find one. But I haven't got one to present you with, though it is an interesting thought.

An Interview with Denise Levertov
Kenneth John Atchity / 1979

From *San Francisco Review of Books* (March 1979), 5–8. Reprinted by permission of *San Francisco Review of Books.*

Levertov has read her poems at many colleges, as well as at the Poetry Centers of New York and San Francisco. During 1961 and again from 1963 to 1965 she served as Poetry Editor of *The Nation.* She has been a Guggenheim Fellow, a Scholar of the Radcliffe Institute for Independent Study, and the recipient of a National Institute of Arts and Letters grant. She presently teaches at Tufts University and is active and effective, in both voice and person, in the anti-nuclear power movement.

KJA: Do you think the general public today is more or less sensitive to language?

DL: Unfortunately, I feel from my teaching experience that people's vocabularies and their general knowledge have been steadily shrinking in the last fifteen years and are at a pretty low point right now. There are individuals who are born with an innate feeling for language, just as there are people who are born with an innate feeling for color or for music, and so forth. This has to be developed, though, and it's an historical, or sociological, fact that people's relationship to language in this time is undeveloped so that poets who are called elitist sometimes are simply using the resources of their own vocabulary. Since that vocabulary is larger than that of the people who are reading them they are labeled elitist. They are not being elitist, they are just tapping their own reservoirs.

KJA: Tapping reservoirs that other people are not tapping any more?

DL: Right. And if they don't tap them they are doing a great disservice to the people and to the future, if there is a future, because they are going to let the language deteriorate. I think that writers have an *obligation* to be what is called elitist, even—the way that the monks in the dark ages kept alive some aspects of learning and culture.

KJA: You said "if there is a future . . . ," and last night you talked about cultural and political revolution being necessary if we want to survive.

DL: Yes, when I said "if there is a future" I was thinking especially of the

101

nuclear threat, and I feel that the highest priority, which of course must not be an exclusive one, because there are all sorts of other things which are intimately connected with it, but the *highest* priority I feel is to struggle against the arms race and against nuclear power. Those are the things that are going to do us in.

It is corporate capitalism that is the biggest, even if not the only, purveyor of nuclear power and arms; and the socialist countries that either have or want to have comparable nuclear technology are absolutely blind and misguided in desiring that kind of technology, to my mind. Anybody that calls himself a radical or revolutionary is wearing blinders if he doesn't participate in *that* struggle (the anti-nuclear movement), as well as trying to work for social change in all sorts of other aspects ranging from getting US investments out of South Africa, to working against racism in this country, to whatever you like.

KJA: Ray Bradbury was quoted last week as saying that he loved the atom bomb because it made us safe and brought us peace in our time and it should be above the crucifix in churches, and last night you read your poem about the smart bomb—I wonder what you think about . . .

DL: What I think about Ray Bradbury is that he sounds like Rip van Winkle. He seems to have been asleep since about 1945 and *where has he been?!*

KJA: I was talking to Yoram Kaniuk, the Israeli novelist, a couple of months ago [SFRB, May 1978]. He was talking about American writers, contrasting their situation with his country as being very important to his writing. He felt American writers really have no deep relationship to the United States. They have a hate relationship, but that alone is insufficient: you have to have an equally great love relationship. As someone who has emigrated to his country and who is very cosmopolitan in your origins, I wonder if you could talk about your relationship to America and its past and future?

DL: One of the things that I noticed about Americans and America when I first came here and which has gone on seeming true to me, is that Americans, much more than any Europeans, are self-conscious about being American. And when I first heard that kind of conversation about what is American, what is it to be American, I was intrigued and surprised, because I had never heard English people talking about what is England, or French people talking about what it is to be French. They *know,* right?

KJA: Right.

DL: My own relationship to America—I came as a rather enthusiastic immigrant, having married an American, and fell enthusiastically into the arms of an American poetry that was in a phase of vitality so very much greater than anything that was going on in England at the time, so I felt it a fortunate, and still feel it a fortunate thing for my own development that I came to America. I don't know what would have happened to me if I had not done so—if I had stayed in England—it's hard to imagine how my poetry would have turned out. So, I became known as an American poet, but I never have fully assimilated as an American. In the more recent years when I've visited England, I've felt my British and European roots reassert themselves and I know that my diction and even my accent is perhaps more English than American. But I've spent a good deal more than half of my life in this country and yet I don't feel identified with America.

KJA: Do you feel identified with the English language?

DL: I do feel identified with the English language and yet I certainly don't feel English. In fact, my mother was Welsh, which is quite distinct. I feel a great love for the English countryside and for English literature, but I feel a love for American literature too, and . . . I don't know—I feel rootless. I don't feel that I am a parasite, I feel I am more like an airplant—you know, one of those things—it doesn't suck blood out of whatever it lives on, but it doesn't actually have roots—that doesn't really describe my feeling either, because I do feel that I have deep roots in the culture and experiences that I obtained as a child. Perhaps you could say I am a child of the London streets, I am a child of the Victoria and Albert Museum, I am a child of my mother's girlhood memories of Wales, I am a child of my father's Hasidic tales, I am a child of the Christian upbringing that I had.

KJA: It seems to me, though, that insofar as your poems are observations about society, they are observations about American society. Maybe your relationship with America has helped you assume a poetic voice in American society—that you're not exactly rooted in it.

DL: I'm not exactly rooted in it, but I certainly have thrown in my lot with it. I've not attempted to go and live elsewhere. I have felt an obligation to stick around and try to go on participating in the amorphous American Left, the non-party American Left—the somewhat anarchic American Left. I have felt that it would be a copout to leave that. That's why I'm coming back from England to go to Seabrook in June.

KJA: I'd like to discuss the business of poetry readings—I always wonder what the poet thinks about the audience's uneasiness at a poetry reading. I wonder whether the poets also are uneasy when the audience doesn't seem to know whether they are allowed to clap or whether they should clap— whether the poet wants them to clap.

DL: I find audiences—it's an obvious statement—audiences vary. Sometimes there is an electric atmosphere from the audience which transmits itself to the reader and helps you to read better. Sometimes an audience appears extremely impassive yet at the end of a reading they give tremendous applause. Sometimes there's an audience that one thinks is very simpatico and you feel that things are going well, and then somebody will come up to you afterwards and say, "Well, that was quite nice," and you feel very let down. I don't know. I feel that I am at a disadvantage with audiences because I'm very nearsighted and I cannot really see their faces.

One of the worst things that can happen with an audience is if they clap politely. If they clap one poem spontaneously, that's just fine, but then sometimes having done so they feel somehow obligated to clap every poem and it becomes quite meaningless. I don't like that. If an audience claps an occasional poem then one feels that it is a spontaneous expression and that makes you feel good and you feel more at ease with the audience, because you feel that they are really listening and that they are having different feelings about different poems.

KJA: Do you expect anything from the audience?

DL: I expect attention. I mean expect in the sense of hope. It's nice when there is an intimate enough atmosphere that people can call up to you, "Would you read such and such?," you know. Then there's the kind of reading where I have occasionally had the nerve to read each poem twice. It *takes* a certain nerve because I am afraid of boring people by doing it.

KJA: A lot of poets and audiences seem confused about the public versus private nature of poetry. I'd like to know how you feel as a public poet—even though as you say you don't even see your audience—that they are a blur. You obviously are involved in a public situation.

DL: My theory has long, long been that although yes, the arts do communicate and as an artist I *want* to communicate and I feel it's esthetically a poor show to be deliberately obscure—one should always be as clear as one can be—nevertheless the way in which to communicate is not to think directly of your readers, or of any reader, or of any class of readers because you immediately limit yourself by doing so. What you have to do, I believe, is to believe that there is a reader, a listener, a needer, within yourself, who corresponds closely to those readers out there, and you have to satisfy that element of yourself which needs the poem that nobody else has written and that the active artist part of you, the writer, is writing. And that needer part of you has to be demanding and require precision and the best; and at some point during the writing of the poem, at various points in fact during the making of the poem, you have to move into that aspect of yourself and read it with that kind of objectivity—not cold objectivity—and then you have to move back into the active artist aspect and do some work on it when needed, and so on. And that if you do this you will come out, with some work and some luck, with a poem that is finely crafted enough to communicate to others. Even though its subject matter may be personal you will have wrought out of that subject matter something which corresponds to the experience of others, because we are not that different from one another at the deepest levels. In fact, it is precisely at the deepest levels that we are most alike. So that's in the *writing* of a poem.

Now, in the *performance* of a poem, the reading of it to a live audience, I think that you have to bring in some other aspects. There are undoubtedly poets, and always have been, who are not very good performers. Their voices don't carry, they mumble, they don't have good enunciation and so forth. They have no presence on a platform, but I think as far as one can one owes it not to oneself, but to poetry, the art which one serves, and to the people who have come to listen to that art (even if they think they have "come to see the poet," as they always say, one hopes that they will come away having heard poetry.) To learn to read aloud as well as one can, and project one's voice as well as one can to *serve the poem* rather than to project one's personality.

I would always sooner hear a poet read his or her own poems than I would hear most actors perform them because actors don't understand the service of the poem for the most part; they tend to use the poem as a vehicle for their own personality in a very egotistic way and they tend to ignore the structure of the poem, just as if a musician were to play from a written score ignoring the time signature and transposing it into another key at will and doing things like that to it. At least the poet himself or herself, if their craft is properly developed, will have some sense of how they want the poem to sound and although their voice tone and elocution may not be good, yet they are going to give a more faithful rendering than most actors. I've heard exceptions.

Albert Finney reading D. H. Lawrence years ago on a BBC tape was wonderful, for example.

KJA: I think audiences sometimes forget that when they hear a poet reading a work it's no more the definitive reading than having the poet or someone else read it on another occasion.

DL: Yes, but it seems to me that the poet will observe the score. If they understand about what line breaks are, they're not going to change the line breaks. If they observe the spaces between stanzas as pauses, if they regard them sonically and not only from some other point of view, most things are going to remain fixed just as similar things in a piece of written music would remain fixed. Of course, you know, let's say Beethoven playing or Mozart playing one of his own compositions on one occasion and on another occasion—well, they might give a better performance one time and a worse performance another. They might take the whole thing a little faster one time than another—a few things like that, but they wouldn't have made major changes.

KJA: People ask why should we write poetry rather than writing songs, for example, because everyone listens to songs and buys songs.

DL: (Laughs).

KJA: And you can influence a lot of people that way and they have this direct feeling that the more people they influence the more important their message is.

DL: Well, what is completely left out is that which I think artists who really *are* artists experience, and that is the overriding interest of *doing your art,* actually being engaged in doing it. Cezanne was not interested in *having painted* apples or the Mont St. Victoire and having them hang in exhibitions and what effect that was going to have on people's heads; he was interested in actually taking his paints and his brush and *doing* that work.

KJA: In Joyce Carol Oates' latest collection of stories, *Nightside,* one of the stories talks about immortality and the artist. I think, after reading this particular story by Oates, the immortal is something any poet or artist experiences precisely in the moment of doing the art because the doing takes you outside time.

DL: This brings us back to part of your question about the social obligation of the writer to the people, the audience, the potential audience. I feel that that obligation resides in the utmost devotion to art. The first loyalty of the artist must be to the art. Through the exercise of that loyalty she can serve the people; and as a political animal, as a social being, an artist may have a profound desire to serve the people; but I think that the artist must recognize that the best way of doing so is in a sense indirectly, not by the deliberate effort to serve the people but by the deliberate effort to serve the art.

KJA: The question is audience again. Who are you trying to influence?
DL: I'm not trying to influence.

KJA: You're trying to do your art and to do it well, to be true to your art and you're assuming . . .
DL: I trust that the art is going to live its own life and I know from my own experience that art does it. What does it influence? It influences, it awakens, the imagination. If people's imaginations are already awake, it gives them further nourishment. If their imaginations are sleepy it may awaken them. It puts the cells of the imaginative faculty into action, which otherwise might atrophy, and that's part of its social function.

KJA: One of the most admirable things about your career, and I think unusual, is that you have, over a long period of time now, continued writing poetry and coming out with new books. Your style seems to be evolving, it seems to be constantly changing, and you don't seem to have reached a plateau that people speak of when they look at other contemporary poets and say, "he hasn't been writing anything new for the last 10 years."
DL: That's a relief. I'm glad to hear it!

KJA: How do you feel about your development? Is it something that you're conscious of after a while—of going through the same thing again?
DL: In some ways I see myself thematically repeating, not that I realize I'm doing it while I'm doing it, but when I look back I see that there are certain recurrent themes. I feel two strains in two directions going on in my poetry currently. One is a development of a fairly tight, not I hope hermetic, but still, rather—not introspective, that's not the word either—but a lyric poem that derives much of its imagery from somewhere close to the unconscious, a kind of dream level of image. And the other is a longer lined, more discursive poem, with a fictive or narrative element. Part of my new book is going to be called *Homage to Pavese,* because I very much admire his poems in that vein—in *Laborare Stanca*—which I think are absolutely marvelous. So those are two very different lines. They seem to be simultaneous needs in me at present, and I want to push them both a lot further than I have yet.

KJA: So you haven't felt yet a sense of the limitations of form in the sense that there's no sense in experimenting or going into new directions because there are only a limited number of forms. I've talked to poets who feel there are only a limited number of forms; you learn them soon and then you repeat them over and over again, and there's no sense in trying to find new things.

DL: No, I don't feel that. I mean, life is continuously surprising one with its events and its people and you know the unforeseeable is constantly occurring in life. So why not in poetry?

An Interview with Denise Levertov
Fay Zwicky / 1979

From *Westerly: A Quarterly Review* [Nedlands, Western Australia], 24:2 (July 1979), 119–26. Reprinted in Fay Zwicky, *The Lyre in the Pawnshop: Essays on Literature and Survival 1974–1984* (Nedlands: University of Western Australia Press, 1986). Reprinted by permission of Fay Zwicky and the University of Western Australia Press.

Zwicky: What first induced you to write poetry?

Levertov: I started very young, too long ago to remember actually. I know that I used to have a manuscript of a poem dictated to my sister. A long ramble about a fairy ball. And the reason I was dictating to my sister was that I had not yet learned to write. I know I had learned to write by the time I was six so presumably I was five. I was read aloud to a lot. I lived in a pretty literary household and it sort of came naturally.

Zwicky: Did you hear much music as well as the spoken word?

Levertov: Well, my sister, who was nine years older, was a very fine pianist; my mother, who was Welsh, had a fine singing voice. Then there was the BBC although I don't think we had a radio till I was about seven.

Zwicky: Did you play an instrument yourself?

Levertov: I had piano lessons and I still have a piano. But I seem to be playing the same things that I was playing when I was about twelve. Cleminti sonatinas and so on. I never got beyond a certain point: my technique never improved sufficiently to allow me to venture further.

Zwicky: Were you still writing poetry as an adolescent?

Levertov: Yes, I was also studying ballet very seriously at that time.

Zwicky: I notice you have a strong rhythmical sense—this came out when you gave your readings. Did your earlier affiliation with Robert Duncan and Robert Creeley have any bearing on the development of movement and rhythm in your work?

Levertov: They were the first American poets that I came to know. I had corresponded with Kenneth Rexroth because he was editing an anthology called *New British Poets* in the two years preceding my coming to America so he was the first American poet I met—not, actually, in the flesh, only by letter. Then when I came to America the first poet I met was Creeley, and a few years later I met Robert Duncan. They became very close friends. I'm still very close friends with Robert Creeley, but Duncan and I had a sort of "falling out" some years ago. Our friendship, of almost 20 years, was conducted mostly by letter because he was on the West Coast and I was on the East. Finally, not too long ago, he wrote and apologized for something he'd said and had allowed to be printed which had upset me very much. He offered a sort of apology but I don't think that, alas, our friendship will ever be quite restored to what it was. Too much time went by between the offence and the apology.

Zwicky: Were you influenced particularly by his work on metrics, his rhythmical experiments?

Levertov: No. I don't know that I was particularly affected by that. We shared a lot; I learned things from him but I don't know that I can put my finger on what they were. I have written a long essay for a collection of pieces on Duncan which is "in the works." It's being edited by two people, one of them Australian—Ian Reid and Robert Bertholf. My piece on Duncan was written about four years ago and is really an account of his letters to me. Wonderful letters about poetry. I was reflecting on the kind of thing that I'd learnt from him and found it hard to sum up. He certainly introduced me to some ideas and writers, and we shared a love of fairy tales and certain children's books.

Zwicky: Did you feel he was putting you in touch with your own unconscious sources? He showed the way to a number of poets who were perhaps overly-intellectual—would you consider yourself to have been of this kind?

Levertov: No, I never would. You see, I have never been through an academic experience. I didn't go to school. Ever.

Zwicky: You were privately taught?

Levertov: Yes. I didn't do lessons even after I was about twelve because I began to study ballet. I did lessons at home (my mother, who had been a teacher, teaching me), and I listened to some of the BBC Schools' programmes. But those were not very heavy learning experiences—rather, delightful dramatizations of episodes in history and things like that. My sister sort of nudged me into ballet although I was put on my honour to continue reading some serious books, which I used to do in the train every day. I used to go to the Victoria and Albert Museum for pleasure. My formal education essentially stopped when I was between twelve and thirteen. I'm consequently a mathematical moron and I had virtually no scientific education except the little bit that I got when I was a student nurse later on.

Zwicky: Did you feel the lack of socialization when you were at that age? Did that colour your future relationships in a way?

Levertov: I've been asked that before. No, I don't think so. Next door was a girl three years older than I who was a friend and there was another in the next street. I used to go to a beautiful big park in the London suburb I lived in. It was huge and had a little stream in it—a wonderful place to play. I just used to pick up kids, mostly kind of slum kids from the other end of the town. And we'd fish for sticklebacks and things—I never felt lonely.

Zwicky: You turned to literature after you gave up the ballet at 17?

Levertov: Well, I'd never turned away from it. I had sufficient *hubris* to imagine I was going to be able to do everything. I painted too.

Zwicky: In a poem you read the other night you referred to a meeting in you of the "Celt and the Semite." Are these your mother's and father's sides of the family?

Levertov: Yes. My mother was Welsh, and my father was a Russian Jew. When he was a student at the University of Königsberg in Prussia (to which he was sent because a Jew couldn't go to the University in Tzarist Russia), he read the New Testament and became convinced that Jesus had indeed been the Messiah. He then rushed home to give the people at home the Gospel. They thought he was crazy, locked him up in his room, but he climbed out of the window and escaped. He eventually became an Anglican Clergyman not long before I was born. So I am a mix, racial and religious. I was brought up as an Anglican clergyman's daughter but with a strong sense of pride in being Jewish too. My father always referred to himself as a Jewish Christian.

Zwicky: Well, it's an attractive bonus, for you seem to have a strong bardic strain as well as the moral intensity. You and Robert Creeley are both committed to a sense of personal and political liberty. Have you any comment to make on the paradox, as I see it, of wanting freedom in principle, yet proposing its constraints in poetry? You reject unrestrained anarchy yet you demand the right to speak in your own voice—how do you reconcile these opposing currents?

Levertov: Because of my peculiar upbringing and various kinds of professional good fortune, I've always had a lot of liberty and therefore I don't tend to think of freedom as being the great priority; I've tended to take it for granted. During the 60's and earlier 70's when I was involved in the anti-war movement, I went to Hanoi and read some of Ho Chi Min's statements. One that is always quoted by the Vietnamese people is: "Nothing is more precious than freedom," and I have often thought that too. But I've come to believe that peace and mercy are more important. A lot of people would query this: "What kind of freedom would that be? What kind of peace?" When freedom becomes the primary goal, so much justice and mercy goes out the window. As for peace, it becomes only something you attain later, if you're lucky. Freedom can mean pretty instant death and bloody-mindedness. By the time you emerge with the supposed freedom you've been fighting for, you've become so much like your enemy that you have, in fact, lost everything. When one talks about freedom as a top priority, one also tends to feel that the end justifies the means, and that's fatal to the quality of freedom attained.

Zwicky: Are you, then, a pacifist?

Levertov: There was a period when I defined myself as a pacifist. Then I began to feel, in the face of the heroic struggle of the Vietnamese people against vicious attack by the United States, that it was priggish to maintain this position. I still feel this with regard to Vietnam and all guerrilla movements and movements of national liberation. At the same time, I have come back to a more pacifist position because I feel that it's almost impossible to avoid acting like those whom you're struggling against. I don't know what the answer to this dilemma is. I think the spirit of the non-violent movement that I am now involved in is a very beautiful one, and that people grow in it to kinds of personal strength that I didn't see among my comrades in the anti-war struggle. I don't condemn people defending their lives and ideologies with arms although I'm completely against terrorism—a bugger of a paradox!

Zwicky: Perhaps this is what Yeats had in mind when he had Parnell say: "Ireland shall get her freedom and you still break stone." The poor peasant would become a hard master to the next generation of peasants.

Levertov: I thought you were going to quote the other line—"The best lack all conviction, while the worst are full of passionate intensity." People trot that out as if it were a political formula that fits all times and places. The best people are surely full of passionate intensity?

Zwicky: Yeats was talking about the abuse of language and the debasement of feeling, wasn't he? "Bellows full of angry wind" etc.

Levertov: But do you feel that the best people you know lack all conviction?

Zwicky: I'm not prepared to speak in terms of "worst" and "best" unless with irony. Yeats was surely being ironic in implying that the "best" refuse to act because they are sceptical of action based on too-passionately held conviction in case it should lead them into dangerous, supra-rational waters.
Levertov: Well, then, they are not the best because they don't have any guts.

Zwicky: Guts in that sense may amount to little more than blind impulse from which good may come but also evil. Surely some scepticism is appropriate?
Levertov: But he *used* the term "the best." I suppose I'm thinking of people I come into contact with teaching in the University—those bland academics, the old-time Liberal without any convictions. They've had some of the best opportunities but they are not the best people. They are pleasant enough but when it really comes down to brass tacks, the fact that they do lack all conviction makes them, to me, sadly lacking. You know the typical academic fence-sitter.

Zwicky: But lots of people sit on fences, academic or otherwise. Most people are scared, politically, morally and spiritually. Isn't it unfair to single out academics as the offending tribe?
Levertov: They are in a position to commit themselves at no great cost to themselves—they're an élite, they've had a lot of privileges. They have the opportunity to influence the course of history in minor ways. Over and over this opportunity comes to them and they don't use it. Someone who works in a factory all day is exhausted by evening and spends that free time he has watching t.v. or going to the disco or falling asleep over the newspaper; you can't blame that person in the same way you can blame someone with the advantages of an easier work schedule. We are a privileged group, and we are supposed to be leading "the examined life" and developing some convictions.

Zwicky: You feel a sense of moral obligation both as a teacher and a poet?
Levertov: Yes. Every privilege brings with it some obligation, doesn't it?

Zwicky: To change direction for a moment (or maybe not): you were involved in a controversy in 1973 over the poet, Joseph Brodsky who defected from the Soviet Union to come and live in America. What, precisely, was the nature of your objection? Was it connected with his employment at Michigan State, or what was it?

Levertov: No. There were several things I felt about Brodsky. One was that, although I didn't feel critical of people, especially Jewish people, leaving Russia, I did feel critical of such people coming to America at a time when America was engaged in a particularly heinous war. Their doing so, aside from the war, was always used by professional anti-communists, even anti-socialists, as an opportunity for sounding off. I felt that if people wanted to leave Russia (which is sometimes quite understandable) they should try to go to some neutral kind of country. Especially educated people. Some people don't understand that coming to America at that time was a political act. I felt that a sophisticated literary person like Brodsky couldn't be excused from knowing that it was a political act. Then, on top of that, Brodsky made more statements admiring Richard Nixon. Then he made some sort of broad generalizations about American poetry in which he totally ignored a poet like William Carlos Williams and claimed, I think, Robert Frost as *the* Great American poet. And I felt that he was being darned ignorant in doing that.

Zwicky: Did you feel that he took too much upon himself as a foreigner to pontificate on the state of American poetry?

Levertov: Definitely. And, taken together with his attitude towards Vietnam, his praise of Nixon—these things all revolted me. They all seemed to be interconnected.

Zwicky: I notice in your essay on William Carlos Williams written in 1972 you said: "How different Williams, re-explored, is from the stereotype in which he has been cursorily presented to many minds, assuming him to be essentially prosaic, a putter-together of scraps of reportage merely, the best of his potential ongoing audience—the young poets in their early twenties, the fervent and intense readers who, consciously or not, are looking for magic, illumination, the Dionysian, the incantatory word, the numinous song—turn aside from him to look elsewhere." Would you like to comment on this? Clearly, William Carlos Williams means a great deal to you.

Levertov: Yes, he did. I meant that many of those things that I say people consciously or unconsciously were looking for *can,* in fact, be found in Williams. But that fact seems to have gone unnoticed and the other aspect of Williams has been made into a stereotype. I stand by what I said there but I'm not sure what else to say about it.

Zwicky: Yet another guru undone by his followers, which reminds me of something I want to ask you about Pound. In an essay you wrote in 1972 you said: "Racist and rightest views are abhorrent to me—but I look on these when they occur in Pound as an aberration; and who among us does not have some kind of aberration? And all the evidence points to Ezra Pound's personal dealings with whoever came into contact with him as being marked by kindness and probity." In view of your belief in the moral responsibility of the articulate, do you still defend Pound's political views as an "aberration"? What would you say had Pound supported the U.S. government against the North Vietnamese?

Levertov: I do believe that Pound was mentally deranged and became increasingly so; if you read his letters you see his funny spellings and his obsessions increasing steadily over the years. What in very early letters and essays is a kind of conscious generosity (he was always trying to educate and promote friends and acquaintances), that cheerful sort of Tiggerish aspect of him, becomes later incredibly overblown arrogance. I think that is one of the first signs of something really pathological in his psychology. The anti-Semitism begins as just the attitude common to virtually all non-Jewish people of his epoch. I mean, you find it *everywhere!* It was something "received" in his social world, and it was the rare person that recognized that there was something wrong about that, and escaped from it. You know how people used to use expressions like "To Jew him down" or something like that?

Zwicky: But Pound was surely, by your definition, just such a "rare person" with all the concomitant privilege and responsibility that this entails. Do you still feel he can be exonerated for having expressed views identical with those of any concentration camp attendant?

Levertov: As I said, I think his anti-Semitism started as the common, unintense sort of received anti-Semitism of his time and place. But then it grew as he begins to get interested in economics. And he begins to attach all his anger—perfectly reasonable anger—about banks, usury and so forth, in an absolutely mediaeval style, to Jews. I have been told by those who knew him well that he was certainly encouraged in this kind of intensification of prejudice by both his wife, Dorothy, and by his other wife, Olga Rudge. So he did not develop these prejudices all alone, but they were reinforced by people around him. He gets more and more obsessive and ignores the fact that there are bankers and arms dealers and all kinds of international racketeers whose actions he deplores who are not Jewish at all. He attaches all kinds of wrongdoing to Jewishness to a point where it becomes absolutely wacky—a kind of personal "I-know-best" wackiness. He ignores his own unconscious, something you see in other aspects of his writing. Even his valuable criticism (and it *is* valuable) is always on the side of the intellectual, the rational. It suppresses the intuitive. It ignores it, in fact, and I think that he did this in his own life. He ignored his own dark side and it ultimately overwhelmed him, because what you ignore in yourself comes up and bites you. It would be quite impossible to defend him if one didn't feel he was, in certain respects, crazy; you can't hold him to the same kind of responsibility. I mean, it's as simple as that.

Someone told me an interesting thing, someone who had gone to meet e. e. cummings who was coming as a guest to some University. Cummings had just been visiting Ezra Pound at St. Elizabeth's at the time. Now Cummings's own politics were not really very Kosher—he was pretty nasty, politically speaking. I mean, he talks a lot about freedom, but I think he was pretty fascistic and anti-Semitic, especially as he grew older. And, having just visited Pound, he was preoccupied with him, and was talking as much to himself as to this man who I think was a stranger to him. The man who told me the story asked him: "Well, what did you think of his mental condition?" He (cummings) said: "What struck me was that we conversed about all sorts of matters, and there was absolutely nothing to indicate that he was not as sane or saner than anybody else. And I began to feel more keenly what an outrage it was that this great man should be shut up in this mental asylum with all these crazy people. Until suddenly he began to talk about economics—and then it seemed to me that he was completely insane. He was completely bonkers when he began talking about that," or some words to that effect. And this, coming from cummings whose own politics were not so different from Pound's, seems to me rather important additional evidence to support the idea that Pound really was in a pathological condition.

[Zwicky's note in original: *Further discussion took place about Pound and the poet's responsibility which, for reasons of space, had to be cut.*]

Zwicky: How would you define the areas of a writer's responsibility?

Levertov: The basic responsibility is that the writer should recognize he is a social being, that he really lives in a world with other people, and that his words and deeds may have some weight with others. The person who is actually irresponsible is the one who has no convictions, who is purely self-serving or is a-political in a callous way. That is irresponsible. But the person who is responsible, and who attaches his or her high ideals to what I or you may consider grossly wrong is not being irresponsible. He or she is just being perhaps mistaken. I don't think there have been any great writers with Fascist convictions. Let's put Pound out of this for the moment because, in the first place, when he was relatively sane, he mistook the nature of Fascism. That was lack of political astuteness, and clear analysis, but it wasn't actually a lack of responsibility. Take Yeats who I think was always pretty sane. I think his support of a Fascist group didn't really mean that he was a Fascist (even if his ideas about the obligations and style of the aristocracy led him to write those not-very-good examples of his poetry, those marching-songs for Duffy, the blue-shirt Irish Fascist). I think he was doing something more like what Pound did in the 20's before Mussolini actually came to power when he supposed that Mussolini represented a Confucian attitude. The paternalistic but noble ideal (*noblesse oblige*) that Yeats attached to Duffy for a while was not represented by the Blueshirts at all—it was another gross mistake. My God, if we were all to be condemned for every mistake that we made, we would all be very much in the soup, wouldn't we? There *is* a difference between making mistakes and being irresponsible.

Zwicky: I'd like to go briefly to the subject of the woman writer. Since the Women's Movement is politically powerful in America, have you yourself had any connection with it?

Levertov: I haven't really had an active connection with the Women's Movement. Of course, my life has been affected by it. Everyone's has. And I have supported some Women's Movement things at different times. As far as the poetry goes that has emerged from the movement, some of this is very bad poetry. I think it's written by people who are feminists first, and possibly not poets even second. They are feminists who decide to write poetry because they think of poetry as a vehicle for their feminism. So some of the anthologies of feminist poetry are filled with extraordinarily bad poems. And I object to the term and the concept, "Women's Poetry." I think there is poetry by women, but "Women's Poetry" is used by some of the feminist groups to mean poetry by women for women. It limits the readership. I feel that the Arts always have transcended and must transcend gender. If it's a good work of art, then it's for anyone that wants it.

Zwicky: What would your criteria be for bad poetry as such?

Levertov: Well, I think at the moment it's often free form doggerel. And it's not written with any concern for language or music, it *utilizes* an art, and one should not utilize an art. One should *serve* an art. The art is greater than oneself, something sacred—not something to be just manipulated. A poem is not a vehicle for ideas. A poem should be an autonomous thing—it should have a life of its own. I think the attitude of the people I'm thinking of towards poetry is essentially disrespectful. It is the people who latch on to poetry as a form of journalism that I object to.

Zwicky: I think our Women's Movement is not as forceful nor as militant as yours in the States.

Levertov: No, I wondered about that. I was going to ask you, actually.

Zwicky: It has its spurts and surges but only a few brave souls around. On the other hand, I observed in America (and this can only be a superficial observation) that, although women seemed much more dedicated and committed to the pursuit of their rights, they were also much angrier than I had anticipated.

Levertov: Yes, well one of the things that rather alienated me from the Women's Movement in the beginning was that, while the anti-War movement was still in full force, a lot of women, justly antagonized by the *machismo* of some of the male leadership in the movement, not only separated themselves from anti-War organizations (which I could well have understood if they had gone on working against the war), but they gave up on the anti-War movement and began proclaiming that the first priority was Women's Liberation. It was at a time when Vietnamese children were being Napalmed, and defoliants were being dumped over a huge section of that country. It seems to be extraordinarily white-middle-class-privilege-type thinking to suddenly drop your attempts to stop that, and say that the immediate priority is Women's Liberation. I felt those women should have gone on doing anti-War work, ignoring those *macho* males who were bugging them, instead of dropping out of it altogether. This weakened the movement and slowed up the eventual end of the war. The other thing is that, in a lot of places in America (it tends to vary from city to city) the radical Lesbians have tended to dominate. I find that offensive because a Women's Movement has to be for *all* women, and there shouldn't be some attitude that says you are not a feminist if you are not a Lesbian. I mean, if you are a Lesbian, you are a Lesbian. O.K. But don't make heterosexual women feel they *ought* to be Lesbians. Don't make them feel they aren't feminists *unless* they are Lesbians. I mean, I really like men (and they are half the human race after all). That doesn't mean I believe in their continued dominance of society.

Zwicky: Your own poetry is often about love, and has forceful and passionate life which is intensified when one hears you read. I notice, in your essays, you are very attached to Lorca's concept of *duende* which you defined somewhere as "soul." Would you make some comment about its importance to you?

Levertov: Well, I was casting around for some English term that would be an equivalent of *duende*. Really, the American black use of the word "soul" seemed to be about the closest thing. Once, at a demonstration in Berkeley, I had just said something at this rally into the mike in Sproule Plaza, and a black man (whom I'd never seen before or since) came up to me, hugged me and said: "You've got soul, baby." And it was one of the most wonderful things anyone could ever have said to me. I shall always remember it.

Zwicky: Well, I'm sure that people who have been fortunate enough to hear you read in Perth, and who have been moved by your poems will agree that you do indeed have "soul." I thank you very much for sharing it with us.

Levertov: Thank you, Fay.

Levertov: A Poet Heeds the Socio-political Call

Penelope Moffet / 1982

From *Los Angeles Times* (June 6, 1982), BKS-3-1-P. Reprinted by permission of Penelope Moffet.

Denise Levertov says the ability to create does not exempt the artist from social action. Her concerns about the world and her adopted country, America, stimulate Levertov's physical participation in demonstrations and impel some of her most powerful essays and poems. Now established as a major American poet, splitting the academic year between two coasts by teaching at both Stanford and Brandeis, she continues to voice outrage at many aspects of life on Spaceship Earth, circa 1982.

Emcees have a way of eulogizing this poet when they introduce her to an audience. They say such things as, "She has put her person in jeopardy for her convictions." They mention her peace activism during the Vietnam War, her anti-nuclear stance and participation in the Seabrook protests of 1978, her current protests of U.S. aid to El Salvador.

While her actions have been a large and necessary part of her life, she says, they are "no big deal"; "I mean, one does what one can do, and what is offered to one, I've been in lots and lots of demonstrations and sit-ins," she goes on, but, "People speaking of that kind of thing tend to elevate it to more importance than it really had. It's what thousands of other people have done—and I certainly have not spent as much time in jail, or provided such loyal services, as (have) many activists."

In 1968, when then-husband Mitch Goodman faced trial on charges of "conspiring to aid and abet young persons to avoid the draft," well-meaning friends wrote to express sympathy and found themselves incorporated into the long Levertov poem, "An Interim," later published in *Relearning the Alphabet.* "Something like a cramp/of fury begins to form," she wrote, "a cramp of fury at the mild,/saddened people whose hearts ache/not for the crimes of war/ . . . but for us."

"Sure," says the Levertov of 1982. "People who don't give a damn will suddenly express a lot of concern because someone of their own class whom

120

they meet at a dinner party or otherwise know socially is involved in something like that. It's the only thing that seems to hit them sometimes. And I find that rather—contemptible."

The writer's own involvement in politics dates back to childhood. Born in England to politically aware parents, she was "passionately interested in the Spanish Civil War and desolated at the outcome of it." She knew about the Nazis because her parents aided refugees, and at age 9 she spent Saturday mornings selling the *Daily Worker.*

Then came "growing up and getting married and having a child and having culture shock in coming to America, although there wasn't a word for culture shock at the time." Her politics submerged until the 1950s, with the Ban the Bomb movement and her first participation in demonstrations.

Levertov is somewhat reluctant to spell out the full extent of her involvement in political protest. Although some of her action—Vietnam sit-ins and teach-ins, a 1972 trip to Hanoi, the Seabrook protests—is described in her two collections of essays, there are gaps, gaps the writer is not inclined to fill at the drop of a question. That would be "blowing my own horn," she says.

What she will do is "keep trying to raise people's consciousness" by bringing up current issues whenever the chance arises. At the moment her priorities are El Salvador, nuclear disarmament and nuclear power.

Over the years, as Levertov's interest and involvement in politics has grown, her poetry has become increasingly political. Later books are filled with pieces on a variety of issues, in contrast to the *Collected Earlier Poems 1940–1960,* without a single political note. Some of the 1940s pieces are shadowed by a young woman's fear of living in World War II England, but they are the work of someone merely "Listening to Distant Guns," not protesting their firing.

These days, when she protests the firing of guns and nuclear generators, Levertov attempts to "fuse the lyrical and the polemical or didactic." Sometimes it works, sometimes it doesn't. Still, "some (poems) are better and some are worse, but I don't think I'd disown (any of) them," she says.

Writing a good political poem is not easy and Levertov does not consider poetry a mandatory activity for everyone with a social conscience. "It is very important for people who write and who teach and who are able in their writing and their teaching to articulate their consciousness" to do so, just as it is important for them to take other kinds of action, she says. However, "there's absolutely no sense in trying to write a poem out of a sense of obligation, because it's not going to be a good poem. It's going to be doggerel. Perhaps sophisticated doggerel, but still doggerel."

The poet probably would not go so far as to describe any of her own political work as "doggerel," but she does acknowledge that some pieces are only "sort-of" poems. One anti-draft "speech" written for a 1980 rally is included in her 14th book, *Candles in Babylon,* due this May.

"It (the anti-draft speech) is some sort of writing," says Levertov, "but it's not the kind of poetry I'm most interested in" and "I'm sure it's not going to help my reputation any. If any reviewer wants to criticize that book when it comes out, they've got an obvious place to begin—'well, it's not poetry, this ranting and roaring and speech-making.' It *was* a speech."

She makes no apologies for some of her more recent work, however. One still-unpublished piece, "Thinking About El Salvador, 1982," is as good, she says, as anything she's ever written. Ironically, it is a poem about impotence, about her own wordlessness in the face of the rape, torture and murder of countless people in Central America. By describing her inability to work words in the face of that horror ("thoughts/think themselves worthless"), she creates a powerful poem, a statement of power.

Levertov, 30 years later, is still clearly a "poet in the world." She seems surprised that anyone would comment upon or question her about her reasons for social action ("What else? How not?"), just as she is puzzled why so many of her fellow activists from the 1960s have dropped from political sight. An anarcho-socialist who "would like to see a very decentralized kind of socialist society" with "a lot of local decision-making, not a centralized, state socialism," she continues to speak out, to write and act upon her concerns.

"How," she asked, before she read for the "Visions of Peace" conference at Cal State Long Beach, "can people take time out, when the nuclear clock is ticking ever closer to midnight?"

Poetic Justice in El Salvador: Denise Levertov Brings Her Poetry and Politics to the Oratorio Form

Janet Tassel / 1983

From *Boston Globe Magazine* (May 15, 1983), 14, 34, 36, 38, 42, 44, 46, 48, 56. Reprinted by permission of Janet Tassel.

It hardly seems possible. This year the young radical poet Denise Levertov will be 60. But after all, what are years? Diminishing units relative to the past, say the physicists. To the poet herself, they are an illusion, "the blink of an eyelid."

Indeed it does seem but an eyelid's blink, and not fourteen years ago this month, that Denise Levertov was in Berkeley, shoulder to shoulder with the kids at People's Park, facing down the police and National Guard. Perhaps our reluctance to grant the poet her years is based on the time-telescoping continuity of her activities: Denise Levertov, though "stumbling, falling, / getting up, going on," has been treading a consistent and defiant political path for the more than three decades since she arrived here from England.

From the early ban-the-bomb sit-ins through the Vietnam War protests, from Seabrook, New Hampshire, to the nuclear freeze rally in New York last June, Levertov was there, up front with bullhorn in hand or encamped anonymously among the protesters. She has journeyed to Bulgaria and North Vietnam on peace missions, and in this country she has been jailed several times—four or five, she can't remember. The years may not be altogether illusory: by 1978, when she demonstrated with the Seabrook Natural Guard in Washington, jail was becoming more difficult for her. In *Light Up the Cave* she wrote that her "fifty-four-year-old body seemed to develop aching knobs and knots all over."

But though the autumn years beckon, Denise Levertov shows few signs of gently mellowing. While other antiwar activists have settled into lucrative midlives of stockbroking, fitness entrepreneurship, and networking, Denise Levertov slogs on, indignation unabated, thundering her jeremiads against nuclear power, the draft, ecological mismanagement, racial inequity, abridgement of prisoners' rights, military spending—still flogging the Establishment up against the wall as if she were twenty.

123

And now the poet has embarked on a new venture. She has written the libretto, her debut in this genre, for the oratorio *El Salvador,* with music by W. Newell Hendricks. *El Salvador* will premiere next Saturday, May 21, at Sanders Theatre in Cambridge, with Larry Hill conducting the Pro Arte Chamber Orchestra of Boston, the Back Bay Chorale, and soloists.

"I was the one who suggested the subject of El Salvador to Newell," Levertov said recently. "Pro Arte got a grant from the Massachusetts Council [on the Arts and Humanities] and commissioned him to write an oratorio, with no text specified. My friends Karen and Tom Henry introduced me to Newell, and after we talked, we agreed that I would do the libretto. Of course I checked out his music first. It's been an interesting challenge for me. Something new.

"Why El Salvador? El Salvador was—is—very much in my mind and in anyone else's mind who thinks at all politically. Archbishop Romero had been murdered at the altar as he was saying mass, and the four churchwomen had been murdered. Whatever the outcome in El Salvador, the subject has already passed into timelessness. The murder of an archbishop never loses its significance—think of *Murder in the Cathedral.* El Salvador has become a paradigm of oppression and the struggle against oppression. Romero and the four sisters say it in the oratorio: 'We ask that our story be known not as a story of Salvador only: everywhere, greed exploits the people, everywhere, greed gives birth to violence.'

"At first I thought of modeling my text after Gerard Manley Hopkins' *The Wreck of the Deutschland,* but I gave that idea up, not only because it was so presumptuous of me, but also because after I started work, I realized I wasn't writing a poem. This was something to be used by a composer, that he could alter—to *some* degree, that is—where I wasn't going to be able to be possessive about every comma and line break, as I am with a poem.

"The real model would be the Bach Passions. We have a narrator, parts for Romero and the four Catholic women, and a large chorus, divided antiphonally. The chorus is basically the people of El Salvador, whose homes and bodies and lands have been systematically defiled ever since the first Spanish conquistador set foot in that unfortunate country."

She is in the kitchen of her West Somerville home, ironing. Her gray-flecked dark hair is "wild, isn't it? Got to get a new perm, but where's the time?" Her teaching—the fall term at Brandeis, winter at Stanford—her libretto, her writing, and "truckloads of mail" are just about doing her in, she says. Looking younger than her years, she leans on the ironing board as she talks, often neglecting her ironing to pursue her arguments. With hoots of laughter, she allows her visitor to spell her with the ironing so she can read from the libretto. In evidence are the vestigial Londoner's inflection and the famous gap-toothed smile—"gat-toothed," she called it, echoing Chaucer, in one of her poems in *To Stay Alive.* "They say it's lucky," she wrote, "and means you will journey / very far."

What "they" say must be at least partially true; though good luck has often dodged out of her path, Denise Levertov has traveled very far indeed. She described her starting point to an interviewer some years ago:

"My mother was descended from the Welsh tailor and mystic Angel Jones of Mold, my father from the noted Hasid, Schneour Zalman, 'the Rav of Northern White Russia.' My father had experienced conversion to Christianity as a student at Königsberg in the 1890s. His life-long hope was towards the unification of Judaism and Christianity. He was a priest of the Anglican Church (having settled in England not long before I was born), author of a life of Saint Paul in Hebrew, part translator of the *Zohar,* etc. I was born in October 1923 at Ilford, Essex. I did lessons at home, and never attended any school or college, except for some years at a ballet school. However, we had a house full of books, and everyone in the family engaged in some literary activity. Jewish booksellers, German theologians, Russian priests from Paris, and Viennese opera singers visited . . . and perhaps my earliest memory is of being dandled by the ill-fated son of Theodore Herzl, the great Zionist."

(Quoted in *Alone with America,* by Richard Howard.)

This autobiographical recollection stops short of her years as a nurse in London during World War II, and it omits to mention that in addition to being a dancer she was a talented painter. But the most important unstated fact is that she had been composing poems since childhood. When her first book of poetry was published in 1946, it immediately attracted the attention of important critics. Poet Kenneth Rexroth, one of her earliest American advocates, wrote that in the post-war years she was considered "the baby of the New Romanticism. Her poetry had about it a wistful *Schwarmerei* unlike anything in England except perhaps Matthew Arnold's 'Dover Beach.' "

That growing-up sketch may explain why, despite the absence of any formal schooling, she "knows far more" and is "more civilized" than most poets, according to Rexroth. Her formidable intellectual scope embraces several languages, mostly self-taught, and she has translated poetry from Spanish and French. Above all, her unconventional upbringing was doubtless the source of her expansive humanism.

From her parents, both scholarly writers, from the wide assortment of types who thronged her London home and her father's hostel for refugees, from her intense sister Olga, nine years her senior and also a poet, Denise Levertov absorbed influences that were to shape her poetry as well as her vision of the poet as a politically engaged being. There was first of all the dual religious legacy, an immeasurable gift to the poet. "The Jew on the Day of Atonement," she wrote in *The Poet in the World*, "the Christian on Good Friday or Easter Day, experience a profound crisis of which the religiously unattached poet is deprived." The two mystical strains she inherited from her father's Hasidic forebears and from her mother's ancestor, Angel Jones of Mold, compete to heighten her alertness. Hasidism alone, she has written, "has given me since childhood a sense of marvels, of wonder." In the Hasidim, as in the Franciscans, "there was a recognition and joy in the physical world. And a sense of wonder at creation. . . . I think that's what poems are all about."

Schneour Zalman—together with Dionysus, whom she claims as her name patron—must also have been seminal to her affirmation of dance in life and in poetry: When her father lay dying, she—an ocean away—performed a wild dance of mourning and praise, unaware that he, perhaps at the same moment, had risen from his deathbed at the last to perform a Hasidic dance as well. (A dancer all her life, she is prevented from strenuous exertion now by a mild form of Sjogren's syndrome, a connective tissue disorder producing extreme dryness of the eyes and mouth.)

The "recognition and joy in the physical world" she gleaned from Hasidism was reinforced by her mother, her principal tutor in all things, as a poem in *Life in the Forest* records:

> It was she
> who taught me to look;
> to name the flowers when I
> was still close to the
> ground,
> my face level with theirs;

and Levertov is still an astute bird- and plant-identifier.

With her sister Olga, whose life was ended by cancer when she was 49, Denise Levertov sharpened the political perceptions absorbed from the refugees and wanderers who filled her parents' house with talk of the sorrows of Europe. Her memorial tribute to her sister in the "Olga Poems" *(To Stay Alive)* reveals much about the two impulses that eventually converged in herself—outrage at inequity and admiration of artistic excellence:

> You wanted
> to shout the world to its senses,
> did you?—to browbeat
>
> the poor into joy's
> socialist republic—
> What rage
>
> and human shame swept you
> when you were nine and saw
> the Ley Street houses,
>
> grasping their meaning as *slum.*
> Where I, reaching that age,
> teased you, admiring
>
> architectural probity, circa
> eighteen-fifty, and noted
> pride in the whitened doorsteps.

At about the time Levertov's first book, *The Double Image,* was published in 1946, Olga also published a book of poetry. Concerned that readers would confuse the two sisters, Denise changed her name to Levertov from the family name of Levertoff. "That was a silly reason, wasn't it?" she asks. "I've regretted it many times since. I get mail and airplane tickets and all sorts of things spelled 'Leverton.' Now isn't that commonplace? People wouldn't be making mistakes like that if my name still had those two long tails hanging down."

Her travels beyond England began after the war when she worked as a sort of *au pair* girl in Switzerland, Holland, and France. In Switzerland she met Mitchell Goodman, then a Harvard student traveling under the GI Bill, destined to become an author and to be one of the co-defendants in the 1967 trial of Dr. Benjamin Spock. After their marriage in 1947, they lived in Italy, France, Mexico, and New York, where their son Nikolai was born in 1949.

Levertov and Goodman were divorced in 1974. He now lives in Maine with his second wife and their son, Matthew. There is a picture of 2-year-old

Matthew on Levertov's refrigerator. "See that toy turtle he's sitting on?" she asks. "I bought him that. Divorce doesn't have to be acrimonious, you know. We're still good friends. When you live with a person so much of your life, you're always attached to him. What does he do? He still writes, chops wood, grows his own vegetables, lives off the land. Mitch and I sort of switched our relationship to nature; he didn't used to care what the names of flowers or trees were. He was a real city person. Now he's the country boy, and here I am in Somerville."

West Somerville, actually. She stresses the "West" because of a wonderful childhood dream—of Somerset, in England's West Country—that she treasures, as she does all her dreams current and past, many of which have dictated poems to her. It is no irritable reach for toniness but the *sound* of "West Somerville" that she likes, for it bonds her to that dream. Though she is a fully acculturated American with an American's point of view and mastery of the idiom—acquired after many years of "picking up fragments of New World slowly"—she still shares with all native Britons the nostalgia for the mother country that always makes them feel a little like transplants, undone by "time and the straddled ocean."

But Levertov has not only traveled the voyager's miles; more important, she sees herself as a pilgrim in the country of art, repeatedly introducing in her work the theme of life as a pilgrimage. She jauntily begins "Overland to the Islands" with "Let's go—much as that dog goes, / intently haphazard." A good deal of her poetry is characterized by this movement, this "haphazard" journey for its own sake, "every step an arrival." But the traveler in the province of art must begin and often perhaps come to rest within himself. "The Runes" (a work given her in a dream) concludes: "In city, in suburb, in forest, no way to stretch out the arms—so if you would grow, go straight up or deep down" *(O Taste and See).*

This is not to imply a solipsistic view of art as some sort of exercise in narcissism or therapy for the artist. On the contrary, Levertov has no patience with that "Midwestern Graduate School school." She speaks of "self-indulgent spittle-dribblings" and the "vomit-it-all-out" concept of writing, dismissing such emetic theories as "totally alien to my belief in the poet as both 'maker' and 'instrument' and of poetry (not poets) as a *power,* something held in sacred trust" *(The Poet in the World).*

She does hold, however, that the poet must savor the "honey of man," which "has no analogue but itself." And the poet must be alert to the simplest phenomena of the surrounding world: Only in such homely, everyday details will the authentic be found. "Marvelous Truth," she tells us in "Matins" *(The Jacob's Ladder)* will "confront us / at every turn,"

> dwell
> in our crowded hearts
> our steaming bathrooms, kitchens full of
> things to be done, the
> ordinary street.

Critics have called the subject matter of certain of her poems banal (even perhaps gratuitously so, as in, for example, her "rising from the toilet seat" in "Matins"), but she has written that, like Thoreau, she does not believe in the "intrinsic banality of any existence." If there is banality in poetry, she says, it is there because poets do not bring to their material—the self and its environment—"the attention, the intensity," the ecstasy "that would penetrate to its reality."

The word "ecstasy," she has written, is the key here. Again we may perceive the line between the poet and her ancestors, "The Rav of Northern White Russia," who "prayed / with the bench and the floor," and the Welsh mystic tailor "whose meditations / were sewn into coats and britches" *(The Jacob's Ladder)*. The childlike quality of this ecstasy aroused by the most mundane of *things* is another factor belying her approaching senior citizenhood; but here again (as in her poem "Joy," where the woman of 80 finally grasps at the "joyfulness of joy") years are nothing, a chimera.

And how grateful she is for this extraordinary receptivity: "to be a person to whom miraculous birds, or caverns measureless to man, *do* appear—isn't that the most astounding good fortune?" *(The Poet in the World)*. She delights in all creation, from the snow moon to a scroungy dog, including its fleas. Her poetry is an amiable bestiary of creatures from the antelope to the serpent. There is room in it, as in Whitman's, for all things born or made. But above all, like Whitman, she is a singer of humankind, in all its stubbly crudeness (and her frank naming of parts has raised a few eyebrows). God, she writes, can be "replaced awhile,"

> awhile I can turn from that slow embrace
> to worship *mortal,* the summoned
> god who has speech, who has wit
> to wreathe all words, who laughs
> wrapped in sad pelt and without hope of heaven. . .

"Earth Psalm,"
O Taste and See

Ultimately, the worship of mortal [life] leads her, as it did Emerson, to an unreconstructed optimism. Evil, she has written, is potential, but not inevitable. She continues: "Man's capacity for evil . . . is less a positive capacity, for all its horrendous activity, than a failure to develop man's most human function, the imagination, to its fullness, and consequently a failure to develop compassion" ("Origins of a Poem," *The Poet in the World*).

It is a short step from such Emersonian theorizing to activist commitment, and Levertov long ago took the step—a move not universally appreciated by her readers. Translated polemically, her theory is, roughly, that evil, as we know it in the world, is the inescapable corollary of capitalism, the ultimate "failure to develop compassion." Applying this etiology, for example, to prisoners in American jails, she believes that these people are in a real sense political prisoners, because they are victims of an inequitable society that breeds a wholly justifiable anger. The question of the sadistic killer and the atrocious act she prefers—in the Emersonian tradition—to leave to heaven. Conceding that there are wrongdoers among us who are "very, very sick" and who should be "separated" from those they have harmed, she nonetheless contrasts this "antisocial behavior" with what she calls the "real plague, the Nestle's executives and Nixons of the world; if you're looking for evil, that's where to look."

She has written that politics is "the word I use to mean / striving for justice and for / mercy" *(Life in the Forest).* Her detractors have objected that her politics is not a striving but a naive and pharisaical anger directed at the usual constellation of bogies of the Left—the white, the Western, and the well-to-do—while tending to romanticize those she perceives as dispossessed. As one example, they would point to her essay in *Light Up the Cave,* "Solzhenitsyn Reconsidered," in which she writes, "No one, so far as I know, has proved that conditions in Soviet prisons and camps today, however bad, are such that it could be claimed they are worse than those in US jails," which are "brutal and racist" and feature "terrifying mind-control programs." She compares Solzhenitsyn's "martyr complex" with the "continuing martyrdom" of many minority prisoners in American jails, particularly "hell-holes" like Walpole.

May we be allowed to construe this as a form of bias? She reflects, then muses, "Yeah, I suppose that's true. Frankly, it isn't something I've ever thought about. But I think it's inevitable that one feels more responsible for things that are done by, you know, one's own kind. Oh, yes, I definitely still feel the same way about Solzhenitsyn. I think he's an absolute creep. He's *terribly* reactionary; he'd like to see the *Czar* back, for God's sake! I do wish people wouldn't go around moaning about what goes on in Russia, when the forms of torture used in places like South Africa and South Korea—places the US supports, of course—are *infinitely* worse."

The inclination toward self-reproach, toward punishing "one's own kind," often leads to a facile dualism, as in her glimpses of Vietnamese life and much of her political poetry. "Greetings to the Vietnamese Delegates to the UN," in *Life in the Forest,* is a series of such dichotomies:

> Our large hands
> Your small hands
>
> Our country's power
> Our powerlessness against it
>
> Your country's poverty
> The power of your convictions
>
> Our corrupted democracy
> The integrity of your revolution
>
> Our technology and its barbarity
> Your ingenuity and simple solutions
>
> Our bombers
> Your bicycles. . . .

Her poetry during the Vietnam War period was on occasion so graphic that it estranged even her friend and mentor, poet Robert Duncan, who was moved to write, "What is going on?" He was reacting to some of the imagery, for example, in her poem "Life at War" in *The Sorrow Dance* (imagery she later conceded she had "elaborated . . . for harsh language-sounds"); "delicate Man," she had written,

> still turns without surprise, with mere regret
> to the scheduled breaking open of breasts whose milk
> runs out over the entrails of still-alive babies,
> transformations of witnessing eyes to pulp-fragments
> implosion of skinned penises into carcass-gulleys.

What about the situation in postwar Vietnam? Is she disillusioned? "Not at all," she says. "I think there are a tremendous lot of falsehoods being spread in the general press about North Vietnam. The publications *I* get don't make me feel at all discouraged. I think things would have gone better in Vietnam if America had not been so vengeful, doing everything it possibly could to prevent the economic recovery of a country that it ruined. Those economic difficulties always make it very hard for a society to fulfill its best philosophical intentions.

"No, I'm not a Marxist. I'm a Christian anarcho-socialist. I would never call myself a Marxist because I've never read the boring stuff. Did you ever read Kropotkin? What? Never read Kropotkin? Well, there, you see, I didn't read Marx and you didn't read Kropotkin."

In the late sixties and early seventies, when she spelled America with a "k"—as in "Amerikan polizei / and tight-assed DAR's"—she called for revolution. However, today she recants somewhat—59 being perhaps less furious, or quixotic, than 50. "As long as the Vietnam War was on," she says, "there was a feeling in the antiwar movement and the Left generally, I think, that we were on the brink of a revolution; but that was childish of us, because we were a long way from it. As to whether I consider revolution necessary, I would answer that *if* we survive the nuclear threat, there must be *many* revolutions, because there is such terrible injustice in the world. The world's resources must be distributed more fairly, but I would have to say that violence is not the way. I've come back to a nonviolent position—but that doesn't mean passive! People are going to have to learn creative nonviolence."

Beyond the content of her poetry, some readers have a larger problem with the poet as agitator. Such critics detect a general coarsening of the fiber, a dulling of the customary sharpness of perception when the poet turns propagandist. They lament a tendency to neglect the fresh image for the cliché of the moment, to substitute stridency for subtlety, hectoring for radiance. A poet of Levertov's capabilities, says one Boston professor, should devote her fire to her muse and stop wasting her substance on "politbabble and libergibberish."

Such criticism does not bother Levertov; it's old news, she says. She delivers herself of an exasperated one-syllable expletive and flaps her arms at her sides, reminding us it was she who termed the artist the "All-Day Bird." "My politics and my muse happen to get along very well together," she says. "Sometimes I'm annoyed at the time-consuming business of politics for taking me away from my poetry, particularly now when I'm so overworked, but otherwise the two are in harmony.

"Look. An artist is only an artist when he or she lives and works in the world, not in a 'whited sepulchre.' If artists, with their finely tuned receptors and their gift of reaching people, don't act on their deepest moral commandments, who on Earth should? They won't write bad poetry unless they're bad poets; good poets don't use poetry, poetry uses them. My didactic poetry should be judged by the same criteria as my lyric poetry; in my opinion, it won't be found wanting."

Levertov's writing of the libretto for *El Salvador* represents a confluence of her politics and her muse to a degree beyond their fusion in her poetry. It requires that she don "singing robes" and make of her deeply felt ideas— music. Particularly now, the need is urgent.

> We breathe an ill wind,
> nevertheless our kind
> in mushroom multitudes
> jostles for elbow-room
> moonwards
>
> an equalization of
> hazards
> bringing the poet
> back to song
> as before
>
> to sing of death
> as before
> and life, while he
> has it, energy
> being in him a singing
> a beating of gongs, efficacious
> to drive away devils.
>   "Three Meditations,"
>   *The Jacob's Ladder*

Then, too, the excursion into libretto writing fits happily with her lifelong, loving relationship to classical music. Her poetry contains numerous references to technical music terms and composers. Asked about her desert-island luggage, she replies, "How many do I get? Let's see . . . I'd need some Beethoven quartets, some Schubert lieder and Bach cantatas, Haydn's trios,

a Byrd mass, some Palestrina or Monteverdi, and *The Magic Flute.* Or maybe
Der Rosenkavalier. Every older woman identifies with the Marschallin."

El Salvador composer Newell Hendricks is impressed with Levertov's musical savvy. "Generally," he says, "she left the music to me and I left the
text to her. But she was *very* concerned about the melodic integrity of her
words. The few times she crossed into my territory were with the sorts of
suggestions a musician might make. For instance, when Romero reads off the
names of the dead (as he did every week), she suggested we use a snare
drum. And that gave me an idea of what kind of tone she was after. Or where
the narrator and chorus say that Romero and the Catholic women have been
killed, she has put in parentheses that she thinks this should be quiet, that
'more auditory tumult' would be inappropriate.

"She also made suggestions about orchestral interludes. For example, after
the narrator and chorus tell how the sacred land is given over to money
crops—rum, indigo, coffee—the chorus repeats, 'Hungry, hungry, hungry,
hungry, hungry,' and the narrator sings that this is the century that has made
'the whole world into a marketplace.' At this place her note to me says, 'Here
we might have an interlude, and the music might be slightly jazzy with a
coffee upbeat.' I must say I've grown to admire her more and more. I'm
really struck with the care she gives to each phrase. She's a poet of great skill
and craft."

Denise Levertov would appreciate that. For ultimately true art, carefully
honed and crafted, will outlive this world's cruelty and nonsense.

> The gods die every day
> but sovereign poems go on breathing
> in a counter-rhythm that mocks
> the frenzy of weapons, their impudent power.
> "Art,"
> *Collected Earlier Poems*

In the meantime, head high and chanting, she continues her pilgrimage into
the indifferent darkness. In one of the poems from *Life in the Forest,* she sees
herself, years away.

> an old wine-drinking woman, who knows,
> the old roads, grass-grown, and laughs to herself.

An Interview with Denise Levertov
Lorrie Smith / 1984

From *Michigan Quarterly Review* 24:5 (1985), 596–604. Reprinted by permission of *Michigan Quarterly Review.*

LS: You were a social activist before political topics showed up in your poems of the mid-sixties. Could you talk a little about that and about what impelled you to include more public themes in your poetry.

DL: The Ban the Bomb demonstrations in New York started in the fifties and I had begun to participate in them. I did not participate in the Civil Rights movement. I come from a family that had a strong social conscience, but I was still pretty new in America, and my son was little, and I had not yet reached an understanding of the relationship of public and personal lives in a radical way, not until later in the sixties. I certainly admired what people were doing with voter registration and all that, but I felt detached from it. I was not assimilated into America enough to feel impelled to do that kind of thing myself. My husband, who was American, did not participate in Civil Rights demonstrations, but our sympathies were with the movement. I kind of felt, well, some people do one thing and some people do another, a feeling I later revised, because I think you have to do a little bit of everything, although you have to have some kind of focus, obviously. By 1964 or '65, the Vietnam war was underway and I began to be very much involved with the anti-war movement, and not just as a follower, but as an organizer. I think that the only poems up to then you could really describe as political were the "Eichmann" poems. And there's one poem from that period—the one which says, "We go on testing new ways of dying"—that was a political poem, but it was very oblique, and I don't think many people recognized it.

So how did I come to start writing more specifically political poems? As a natural process of becoming more politically involved. You would not have been able to deduce from my early poems that I was a nurse, that there was a terrible war on. "Christmas 1944" talks about war, and there are a lot of images about death and all that.

> The wind has tales to tell of sea and city,
> a plague on many houses, fear knocking on the doors;

> how venom trickles from the open mouth of death,
> and trees are white with rage of alien battles.

I know that a lot of that stuff is false romantic. I wasn't going around in a constant state of fear. I wrote a sequence of poems called "Images of Fear" or something. "Fear" was a buzz-word, an adolescent buzz-word. And that being so, one might well ask, "Why did you reprint them, then?" I think that for what they were and for the age that I was, and in the context of the British New Romanticism, they have a certain adolescent romantic charm. They're musical. I'm not ashamed of them. So when New Directions wanted to reprint my early poems, I selected those that seemed not bad. I mean, it's interesting for students to see what poets were doing when they were the same age. I wasn't ever thinking of them being given heavy critical treatment, really. It's sort of ridiculous. It really embarrasses me. I don't mean to say that they are riotously funny, but they should not be taken more seriously than they deserve to be.

At any rate, at that period I was not writing out of my daily life, and I don't think I was techically or emotionally capable of doing so. But once I became able to, my poetry has always sprung from my experiences, so if my experience was a political one, it was bound to happen that I would write poems out of that. After the event, I was criticized for not writing purely, recognizably lyric poems, but the people who criticized me were most often people who disagreed with my politics, anyway. Because there is a lot of prejudice about political poetry, I began to theorize about it and tried to determine what was wrong with political poetry—a lot of it—and what can be right with it. There is no reason why a poetry of political and social engagement can't be as good as any other poetry. It very often isn't, and that applies to some of my own, too. But the hope of writing poems which were both politically engaged and have the qualities of lyricism I found very challenging and very exciting. I would like to write poems of such a character that people wouldn't be able to say, this is a political poem, and this is a lyric poem.

LS: In your essay "On the Edge of Darkness: What is Political Poetry?" you say this is a "probably unattainable goal."

DL: Well, I think it's hard to attain and it is hard to *sus*tain in a long poem. I don't think it's an unattainable goal, actually. I think it has been done, and I think that among others, I have done it from time to time. Even some of my early poems—"Advent, 1966"—I think that one does both things, for example.

LS: I think in each volume there are enduring political poems.

DL: In *Candles* there's "A Speech: For Antidraft Rally, D.C., March 22, 1980." I know it's not a poem. Some people say it is, but I don't consider it a poem. It was written as a speech. I could have put it in my prose book, but I felt it would, politically, be of more service in a book of poems. So I was ready to sacrifice my reputation to that degree, to stick it in there, with its own language of open exhortation:

> My dear
> fellow-humans, friends, strangers, who would be friends
> if there were time—
> let us *make* time, let us unite to say
> NO to the drift to war, the drift
> to take care of little disasters by making a
> big disaster and then
> the last disaster,
>   from which
> no witness will rise,
> no seeds.

LS: Do critics still get angry because you insist on sticking explicitly political sections in your volumes?

DL: Oh sure. I haven't had too many reviews that have really slammed hard at me, but it does often happen that a reviewer will praise the lyric ones at the expense of the others: "On the other hand, when she . . ."

LS: Are there other poets currently writing political poetry whom you admire?

DL: Well, Carolyn Forché shows real promise. *The Country Between Us* is an important book, though perhaps more problematic than it seemed on first reading. Later, maybe a year later, I read that book with my students at Brandeis, and under that kind of close scrutiny, although she's very gifted and there's a lot of interesting stuff in the book, the poems were not as good as I first thought they were. The best thing in the book is the prose poem about the ears ("The Colonel"), which is amazing. There is a lot of confusion, a lot of muddle, which she is humbly aware of. I had a conversation with her because I wanted to ask some of the questions that the students had asked and that had puzzled me, too. She was very nondefensive. She still suffers from what I call, when I'm teaching, unconsciously withheld information. She knew what she meant, but she hadn't seen that it wasn't really in the poem for others to find. But she's still very young. She was thirty-two when it came out, so she was probably thirty-one or so when they were written. It's her second book. The first book I didn't like very much. I hadn't met her yet, and I thought the book was slightly phony. It all seemed more tribal than I could really believe it was. But I may have been wrong about that. Anyway, this one was only her second book. She has lots of possiblities; she's very gifted. But what has happened since that book? She keeps dashing manically around the world doing this, that, and the other, and she never seems to be in one place long enough to sit down and write a poem, almost. She's neglected her health—she collapsed on a platform somewhere. I mean, I really want her to go on writing and developing. I think she could be wonderful.

LS: Do you think it's hard for American poets to be political?

DL: It's certainly harder for American poets, or any English-speaking poets, to write engaged poetry than it is for Hispanic poets, for the simple reason that there isn't an accepted tradition. If you look for it in the past, you can't find it. There never was a strong accepted tradition. That probably makes it harder. Perhaps American poets are more self-conscious about it.

LS: In "On the Edge of Darkness" you discuss the breakdown in English-language poetry of a public voice and an engaged sensibility. The first Romantic poets were very political—Blake, Wordsworth, and Shelley—so it's not Romantic subjectivity or lyricism *per se*. It's something, perhaps, in our culture or literary history.

DL: Blake, Shelley, and Wordsworth all dealt with politics in one way or another. Wordsworth had certainly confronted issues. There isn't as much politics in Shelley's poetry as one might think there would be, is there? You find a poem like, "I met murder on the way/He wore a mask like Castlereigh." "The Masque of Anarchy." But most of the Shelley canon doesn't have much political poetry.

LS: In American poetry, of course, there's Whitman.

DL: There's Whitman, but Whitman did not establish a tradition until Allen Ginsberg. You know, there was the occasional poem on some issue. I guess there was a good deal of not very good poetry on slavery and so forth that is now forgotten except by specialists. There's a poem by Bryant that has a political subject. There isn't really very much.

LS: There isn't, although there is a real tradition in America of speaking on behalf of the culture.

DL: Again, though, not in the poetry. Mainly in the prose. Think of Thoreau and Emerson.

LS: I think the modernists had a lot to do with it, too—separating lyric and didactic, or complicating the relations between them.

DL: In this century you get Williams making lots of social and sometimes very political statements and allusions. And Stevens writing about war, and Pound making valuable points, usually, but also so mixed up with his odd politics. It's very hard to separate. Olson makes *cultural* statements which obviously have a social aspect and political implications, but I don't think he's really a poet who deals with politics head on.

LS: Speaking of Williams, I was wondering if the triadic lines in some of your recent poems are from late Williams. Are there certain types of poems that are better suited to this form?

DL: Yes. In the "Pig Dreams," the one about the cow is in that shape, and there's also one in *Candles in Babylon* in the first section. I personally find it has a kind of adagio effect, though I don't think that's always true in Williams' own case. When I was writing the one about the Jersey cow, I couldn't get it right at first until I hit upon the triadic variable foot structure in which each segment has the same duration in time, at least roughly speaking.

> Kaya, my gentle
> Jersey cowfriend,
> you are no pig,
> you are slow to think,
> your moods
> are like rounded clouds
> drifting over the pasture,
> casting
> pleasant shadows.

I found that in the case of the cow poem that absolutely to me evokes a stately walking cow.

LS: It *is* dignified. In "The Cry" it works that way, also.

DL: In "The Cry" it has an adagio effect. I think anybody with any sensibility trying to read that poem aloud would find themselves reading it at a slower pace than if it were lineated differently—I mean, if the triadic lines were written as straight lines. This slows you down. You'd have to be very stupid, very lacking in sensitivity, not to be slowed down. So although it doesn't say, like a piece of music at the beginning, adagio, allegro, or whatever it's going to be, I think the structure itself implies something which is subliminally effective. Actually, there are some late Williams triadic line poems whose subjects don't seem to call for that adagio pace, but I haven't really thought that through. It really is a question of content. For instance, what about the one called "The Drunken Sailor"? It's hard to read with the proper attention to the duration of the segments. And the first line and a half doesn't really seem related to the rest of the poem. I think the slight confusion of mind after his strokes might have affected him. I like it a lot, but I think it needs a certain speed. I don't think it needed that slowing down.

LS: One thing I'm interested in is your movement toward explicit religious and spiritual concerns in the latest volumes.

DL: I found a really wonderful thing in Ruskin the other day which, had I come across it before *Oblique Prayers* went to press, I would have been very much tempted to use as a little preface to the last section, "Of God And Of The Gods." In fact, since I've been speaking these poems at readings, I've found myself giving a little preface to that section. I now wish that I had put it in. It's sort of an incomplete section—I mean, it's overloaded in the direction of trees! I wanted to write more poems for that section, but I wasn't sure that any more were going to come that really fit into it, and I wanted to get the book out of my way. Here is the passage from Ruskin. He's been speaking of someone dancing: "Real dancing—not jumping, or whirling, or trotting, or jigging, but dancing, like . . . winning applause from men and gods." Then he has a long section:

> I must here once for all explain distinctly for the most matter-of-fact reader the sense in which throughout all my earnest writing of the last twenty years I use the plural word, "gods." I mean by it the totality of spiritual powers delegated by the lord of the universe to do, in their several heights or offices, parts of his will respecting men or the world that man is imprisoned in. Not as myself knowing or insecurely believing that there are such, but innately accepting the testimony and belief of all ages to the presence in heaven and earth of angels, principalities, powers, thrones, and the like, with genii, fairies, or spirits ministering and guarding, or destroying or tempting, or aiding good work and inspiring the mightiest. For all these, I pick the general word "gods" as the best

understood in all languages and the truest and widest in meaning, including the minor ones of seraph, cherub, ghost, wraith, and the like, and myself knowing for an indisputable fact that no true happiness exists nor was any good work ever done by human creatures but in the sense or imagination of such presences.

Isn't that fantastic? I mean, that's exactly what I mean, really.

LS: But you're very careful to distinguish "God" from "the gods."

DL: Yes, and I was also very careful to avoid using sexist language simply by avoiding pronouns: "The Task" starts by saying, *"As if* God were an old man," but then it says, "No, God is . . ." And then in the whole passage that says what God is doing, there is no pronoun.

LS: Mary Daly would be proud of you!

DL: Well, I'm not proud of Mary Daly! It's not Mary Daly. Actually, I think it's perfectly appropriate that some people imagine God as a woman. I didn't want to lend lip service to that concept, but at the same time I didn't want to cut others off from the poem by saying "He" so I used syntactic avoidance strategies.

LS: Was the "Mass for the Day of St. Thomas Didymus" [*Candles in Babylon*] commissioned?

DL: No. My initial idea was just to use those forms which had been so nourishing as a structure for composers through so many centuries and see what I could do with them in poetry. So it started off, paradoxically, as an agnostic mass. In the process of writing it, I moved somewhere.

LS: It's interesting, because it's not Christian, in an orthodox sense.

DL: Well, it gets to the Incarnation. I now define myself as a Christian, but not a very orthodox one, and I think that there is a way of looking at Christian faith as involving the cooperation of man. I think that's part of the meaning of the Incarnation.

LS: It seems to me to be very fundamentally political, even though you don't need to be as explicit about issues and events. You keep reminding the reader that what is valuable is now so threatened. Maybe that's where the merging of lyricism and didacticism comes in, with renewed, or continued, celebrations of nature . . . all those trees!

DL: I think that the sense of urgency and of all life being threatened is something which has grown so much. That knowledge has been there since Hiroshima, though it's not been in everybody's heads since Hiroshima. At the time of Hiroshima, there were a lot of people like myself who were *grown up* enough to know what was happening, but not *mature* enough to know what was happening. It registered with some people, but the vast majority of people didn't register at all the enormity—the enormousness—of it. Certainly by the fifties that worry was there, but one's moral energies during the Vietnam War were directed exclusively to ending the horror of the war, and then one became more and more aware of racism and social injustice. It wasn't until the anti-war movement had come to an end and after a period of about two years of total apathy, that the anti-nuclear movement, in the form of a movement against nuclear power, took the place of the anti-war movement—not on such a scale, but some of the same people found themselves in Clamshell or the Catfish Alliance, or whatever. And then all of a sudden that seemed to be curiously parochial.

LS: Where do you think the movement is now?

DL: Well, I think that after the initial discouragement of the election and the general disarray during the campaign, I get the sense that people are starting to rally their energies again, because the threat of nuclear armament is a focal point and the way in which people keep on getting poorer is another focal point. And I think that maybe in a funny way Reagan having been reelected, in the course of these four years, will galvanize people. Did you know that yesterday—perhaps you heard it on the news—Weinberger spoke to the National Press Club. One thing he said gave a lot of encouragement to us. He said, "We will not commit troops"—or whatever his phrase was— "unless we have the support of the American public." I thought that was very interesting. Because if there are enough demonstrations of concern anticipating the possible invasion of Nicaragua and protesting the already existing intervention, it sounds, from what he said, that they may actually be a deterrent. I'd like to think that poetry, political or otherwise, contributes to that deterrent. Poetry is and should be part of resistance movements, including the anti-nuclear movement.

Invocations of Humanity: Denise Levertov's Poetry of Emotion and Belief

Joan F. Hallisey / 1986

From *Sojourners: An Independent Christian Monthly* (February 1986), 32–36. Reprinted by permission of Joan F. Hallisey and *Sojourners,* 2401 15th St., NW, Washington, DC 20009; (202) 328-8842; fax (202) 328-8757.

Considered to be one of the greatest living American poets, Denise Levertov is also a long-time activist for peace and justice. Indeed, she sees the often conflicting spheres of poetry and politics as organically and necessarily connected.

It is a central grace in both her poetry and her politics that Denise Levertov maintains a passionate, delicately nuanced love for the daily details of human life alongside an active and uncompromising battle against the forces that seek to limit or destroy life. She has not given in either to the poet's temptation to leave out the horrible when describing the beautiful or the activist's temptation to omit the beautiful when describing the horrible. Because of this she is a voice that can be deeply trusted—a rare and precious thing.

Author of more than 19 volumes of poetry and two books of literary criticism, Levertov travels extensively to give readings and lectures and to teach poetry writing. Retired from a full professorship at Tufts University, she has also taught at Vassar College, Stanford University, Drew University, and several other academic institutions.

Much of Levertov's poetry is influenced by her travels to Mexico and postwar Vietnam and by her birthplace and childhood home, England. She currently lives in Somerville, Massachusetts.

It was while Levertov was poet-in-residence at Tufts that she and Joan Hallisey first met in 1976. Hallisey was working on her doctoral dissertation, which focused in part on Levertov's war poetry. When Hallisey and her professor disagreed about her interpretation of Levertov's work, Hallisey decided to ask for an interview with the poet herself. Her interpretation met with Levertov's approval. They have been in touch ever since, and Hallisey has published several articles on Levertov's poetry since 1976.

Joan Hallisey is an English professor at Regis College in Milton, Massachusetts, and a member of a Pledge of Resistance affinity group. She is involved with the Catholic Connection, a social action center in Boston.

Hallisey: How do you think your mixed religious heritage and early background contributed to your sense of vocation as poet?

Levertov: I feel that inherited tendencies and the cultural ambiance of my own family were very strong factors in my development. My father's background of Jewish and (after his conversion) Christian scholarship and mysticism, his fervor and eloquence as a preacher, entered my imagination, even though I didn't, as a child, recognize that fact. And though in adolescence I rejected my parents' world as restrictive and embarrassing, I could not help seeing, despite my teenage doubts, that the church services were beautiful with their candlelight and music, incense and ceremony and stained glass, and the incomparable rhythms of the King James Bible and the *Book of Common Prayer.* Similarly, my mother's Welsh intensity and lyric feeling for nature were deeply influential—and I had more recognition of this.

I didn't go to school, nor had my sister (nine years older) done so except briefly. As I have written in the introduction to my section of the new *Bloodaxe Anthology of Women Poets* [published in England by Bloodaxe Press, 1985]:

> The reading I did myself, and the reading-aloud which was a staple of our family life, combined to give me a passion for England—for the nuances of country things, hedges and old churches and the names of wildflowers—even though part of me knew I was an outsider. Among Jews a Goy, among Gentiles (secular or Christian) a Jew or at least a half Jew, (which was good or bad according to their degree of anti-Semitism) among Anglo-Saxons a Celt, in Wales a Londoner who not only did not speak Welsh but was not imbued with Welsh attitudes; among school children a strange exception whom they did not know whether to envy or mistrust—all of these anomalies predicated my later experience: I so often feel English, or perhaps European, in the United States, while in England I sometimes feel American. . . .
>
> But these feelings of not belonging were positive, for me, not negative. . . . I was given such a sense of confidence by my family, in my family, that though I was often shy (and have remained so in certain respects) I nevertheless experienced the sense of difference as an honor, as a part of knowing from an early age—perhaps by 7, certainly before I was 10—that I was an artist–person and had a destiny.

That knowledge was my secret—but the fact that everyone in the family did some kind of writing meant that it wasn't a *guilty* secret, just a private matter which I wasn't ready to reveal.

To note what I've written in that introduction again: I "grew up in an environment which nurtured the imaginative, language-oriented potential I believe was an inherited gift; and gave me—or almost seduced me into—an appreciation of solitude which, since writing poetry is so essentially a solitary occupation, has always stood me in good stead."

Hallisey: Over the last several years, you have spoken out both as a citizen and as a poet about various issues.

Would you comment on the ways in which you see yourself addressing the martyrdom of Archbishop Oscar Romero and the four American women, the Reagan administration's obsession with supplying military aid to Central America, and oppression of peoples, whether it be battered women and children or those suffering from poverty and hunger in our own country and elsewhere.

Levertov: In regard to the deaths of Archbishop Romero and the four American women, the drama of their deaths seemed to cry out for something to be written, for they were the most visible part of the great iceberg of deaths in Central America.

As a citizen I am opposed to Reagan, and as a citizen I have signed the Pledge of Resistance. What has that got to do with me as a poet? Well, I am a citizen who is a poet and a poet who is a citizen. My political views and opinions sometimes come directly into my poetry; at other times, they don't. There are poems about the nuclear threat and about Lebanon and about El Salvador in *Candles in Babylon* and *Oblique Prayers,* but the Pledge of Resistance is a matter of my citizen life, not my poet life, at this point.

In response to the last part of your question, one thing I have found myself doing is using the fact that, as a published poet, I have an audience; I address that audience, in person and in print, but not necessarily in poems, on issues that engage my political concern. Indeed, I often risk shamelessly haranguing my readers and listeners. And why not, for the above causes? I mean, who would refuse?

I do not see myself as "alleviating" any of the pain of battered women and children or of the hungry or poor. But if my reputation as a poet can help organizations like OXFAM to raise money which *can* help, that is surely the least one can do. I would never "use" poetry itself—what I *use* is whatever prestige I have. But because the issues—justice and peace and "the fate of the earth"—are always on my mind, they do also enter my poems, and then I have the chance, *through* poetry, to stir others' minds or to articulate what readers feel but have not found words for.

It is my hope that both approaches—the prose of speeches and conversations and the poetry that articulates engaged emotion and belief—have a political function, just as letters to Washington or demonstrations or acts of civil disobedience do.

Hallisey: In "A Poet's View" you speak about the important role in the struggle for peace and justice currently being played by certain branches of the church, both Catholic and Protestant, and about how this has helped to dispel the sense of embarrassment and uncongeniality that previously had been an impediment standing between you and the experience of a fellowship of belief. Would you comment on where and how you see this being accomplished?

Levertov: Well, the answer to that certainly has to be, "All over!" Speaking of "churches" in the wider sense, many denominations have become more active in the peace and justice movement in recent years, or they have stepped up their activity, it seems to me. Those that were active in peace movement support during the Vietnam War have gone into the anti-nuclear movement, sanctuary, etc. The greater role played by women and laity in the churches recently has probably helped a lot, too. And then there's the U.S. Bishops' Peace Pastoral. The ideas of liberation theology have infiltrated, too, even where they are not totally accepted. Issues have been raised, so the whole climate, in a broad range of denominations, has changed.

So then the question has to be asked, how does this relate to my work as a poet? I think that finding the churches, as I have experienced them in recent years, no longer to be places of embarrassment and uncongeniality, finding that many people already in the peace and justice movement also were involved with some kind of religious observance or experience and that this involvement was much more widespread among such people than I suspected—all of this frees me up to make allusions and use a vocabulary which earlier would have felt awkward to me. But even if that awkwardness had not existed, and I had used or wanted to use such a vocabulary years ago, I would have felt it to be more alienating to my readers than I do now. It is still a problem, though, because if I speak—as I do in some recent poems—in religious terminology and of theological concepts, that's going to put off some of my readers. Maybe my Christianity is unorthodox, but it's still a Christian unorthodoxy, liable to offend both skeptics and members of other faiths.

So it remains to be seen what the reaction to my new poems will be. They're certainly not going to be everybody's cup of tea! But this is the kind of risk any artist has to be ready to take: if some new element enters one's life, it will enter one's work, which is at the center of one's life, and change it in some way. Those who liked what one did before will not always be prepared to follow through these changes. That's an old story! But I'm anticipating, for up to now I haven't lost my public.

Obviously, as an artist, I just have to do what I have to do; and I never have readers in mind beforehand. I am not naive about it, and I realize that this may create problems for me vis-a-vis my public, because they may start putting me in a "box," and they will not hear what I am saying if they think it comes out of a certain box.

Hallisey: In "A Poet's View," you speak about your own spiritual journey toward belief in "the God of the Incarnation" during the last several years. Could you tell us how this journey influences your understanding of your vocation as poet?

Levertov: I cannot really answer this without jeopardizing my creative work, I'm afraid. It would have to be asked ten years from now, retrospectively! It is fatal to one's artistic life to talk about something that is in process.

Hallisey: In *El Salvador: Requiem and Invocation,* you reflected on the martyrdom of Archbishop Oscar Romero and of the three American nuns and a lay sister. Would you share with us the evolution of this powerfully poignant oratorio and the significance of the meaning of "invocation," as well as "requiem," in your libretto?

Levertov: Not long after the murders of Archbishop Romero and the four American women in El Salvador, I was asked by composer Newell Hendricks to provide a text for him to work with in composing an oratorio. I suggested El Salvador as a theme and these martyrdoms as a focus, and he was receptive to the idea.

Drawing on my knowledge of Mexico to help me imagine the landscape and culture, I did some research into Central American pre-Colombian and later history as a preparation for my work. And I obtained from the Maryknoll Sisters some copies of letters written home by the four assassinated women and excerpts from Archbishop Romero's homilies.

What I then attempted to write was not conceived as a poem but as a working text for a composer. That is to say, I wanted to avoid certain nuances of rhythm and pitch in my words (which in a poem I would be very much concerned with attaining), in order to produce instead something deliberately incomplete, something broadly sketched which would call for precisely that development the still unwritten music would give it.

I supplied Newell Hendricks with the text in three installments, and he worked on the music in that same sequence. The joint project took us around a year to complete. Until its performance in May 1983, I did not hear the music, except for a brief orchestral rehearsal tape, as I was in California during the rehearsal period.

I had, however, included in my text a few "stage directions," as it were, for in order to meet the challenge of my task at all, I had to *imagine* the music in some degree. Newell followed through on all my concepts most intuitively and produced what I and the large audience felt was a very strong and remarkable piece of music.

The overall intention that determined the structure of the libretto was three-fold: First, because this was a performance piece written for an audience, not for solitary readers—an audience probably different from those who buy my books—I wanted to bring home to that audience the horror of what was going on in El Salvador.

Second, I wanted to inquire into how it got that way and thereby to make, essentially, a political point about imperialism and the economics of imperialism, and how violence and tension in a nation have roots in an oppression which has to do with economics and land use (for profit, not for feeding people).

And third, I wanted to return to the present and to try to give a sense of the significance of all these deaths, an understanding of them as *martyrdoms,* with the understanding that martyrdom does not just mean victimization but stands for something, signifies something, has a message—that is what distinguishes a martyr from a victim. (A martyr is also a victim, but not all victims are martyrs.) And the message of these martyrs seems to be embodied in those utterances I quoted from them, especially in what I quoted from Romero, which is then summed up and paraphrased in a passage at the end which is sung by the Half Chorus:

> Those who were martyred
> bequeathed, a gift to the living,
> their vision:
> they saw, they told in their lives that violence
> is not justice, that merciless justice
> is not justice, that mercy
> does not bind up
> festering wounds,
> but scrapes out the poison.

> That no one has to comply
> with immoral laws,
> that power abused is powerless to crush
> the spirit.

You asked me to speak about my use of the word "invocation," as well as "requiem," in the libretto. An invocation is the act of invoking assistance, especially, but not exclusively, from a higher power. (Peers can also invoke one another for help.) An invocation is also a form of making a demand in justification of one's cause, and it has the sense of "calling for earnestly." When Romero said to the national guard and the soldiers and the police:

> Brothers, you belong
> to our own people! You kill
> your brother peasants!
> Stop the killing—for no one
> has to comply with immoral orders,
> immoral laws,

he was invoking their humanity.
   Then we have the words of the Questioner:

> What do they ask,
> the martyrs,
> of those who hear them,
> who know
> the story, the cry,
> who know what brought
> our land to this grief?
> What do their deaths demand?

This assumption that their deaths *do* demand something is "invocation" in the sense of "calling for earnestly." And this is further developed in the words of Romero and the four women:

> We ask that our story be known
> not as the story of Salvador only;
> everywhere, greed
> exploits the people,
> everywhere, greed
> gives birth to violence,

> everywhere, violence
> at last is answered with violence: the desperate turn,
> convulsed with pain,
> to desperate means,

which is also "making a demand in justifying one's cause."

Another passage says, "Those who were martyred/bequeathed, a gift to the living/their vision . . ." which harks back to, "What do their deaths demand?" By bequeathing this vision, they are making a demand, so that also is "invocation."

The next Half Chorus speaks about the longing for peace and says that what is happening, even now, in the territories under the control of the revolutionaries, what they are trying to organize is, "for Peace. For this/our martyrs died,"—for this new society, for this different vision of society. "Their deaths enjoin upon us"—there again it's in terms of the linked meanings of "invocation": to call for earnestly, to enjoin upon, or to demand.

Then in the last chorus there is a further recapitulation of the story, not only of the deaths of Romero and the sisters, but also of the deaths of all the "anonymous" others. And the chorus tells us that,

> . . . horror
> won't cease on the earth
> till the hungry are fed,
> that the fruits of the earth
> don't grow that a few may profit,
> that injustice here
> is one with injustice anywhere,

and that we *are* our brother's keeper and that we are "able to change," for "This is the knowledge/that grows in power/out of the seeds of their martyrdom."

The passage about present violence and about the structure of life in hidden villages fulfills the meaning of "invocation" as "to demand in support or justification of one's cause." And the last part talks about how the deaths themselves are a kind of summoning or incantation, a conjuring up of something—the making of an "icon," one might say—and this is what makes us see these dead as useful martyrs and not pitiful victims, because they present an image which is, in itself, an appeal. The first meaning of "to invoke" is to call upon a higher power for assistance, but this takes up the second meaning and is calling upon *us,* is calling upon human power to recognize this appeal.

But then, finally, you have the prayer of Romero and the four sisters:

> Let us unite
> in faith and hope
> as we pray
> for the dead
> and for ourselves.

This refrain, repeating the words he spoke just before he was killed, is an "invocation" in the sense of prayer, and it is a "requiem," too.

Hallisey: Despite the darkness that is etched in some of your poetry, one senses that a movement toward hope is present in poems like "Mass For the Day of St. Thomas Didymus" and in "Beginners," where you say, "We have only begun to know/the power that is in us if we would join/our solitudes in the communion of struggle." If you are, indeed, hopeful, why?

Levertov: Well, my religious faith is at best fragile, but if, in fact, that which I hope is true *is* true, then I think God's mercy may prevent the annihilation of our planetary life, despite human stupidity and violence. I also have strongly that sense of so much being "in bud"—so many things being in the beginning of growth, the first shoots of some different consciousness, of moral evolution, despite the fact that we go on more and more effectively doing the awful things that human beings do.

In other words, on the one hand, you have a new, or at least newly widespread, questioning of whether war, even conventional war, can ever be a tolerable means of settling differences, at all. But on the other hand, technology has continued to make war ever more devastating and far more civilians get killed than in wars in the past. And we've invented the obscenity of nuclear war. It's a neck-and-neck race, it seems, between what is "in bud" and what arrogant technology keeps devising.

As the 87-year-old atomic scientist and Nobel Prize winner, Professor Rabi, said at a recent teach-in on the occasion of the 40th anniversary of the first bomb test, we keep trying to apply technological solutions to moral problems—and moral problems are susceptible only to moral solutions.

But I have some temperamental optimism. And though, as I said before, I can't lay claim to an unshaking faith, there is the deep hope implied in the words, "With God all things are possible."

An Interview with Denise Levertov
Terrell Crouch / 1986

From *Sagetrieb* 8:3 (Winter 1989), 99–113. Reprinted by permission of Terrell Crouch.

In late 1986, I was working on a thesis on the early poetic development of Denise Levertov. The following interview was recorded on 11 November 1986, the day after she gave a poetry reading at Bates College in Lewiston, Maine.

TC: I'm interested in your metamorphosis from "an English Neo-Romantic" into a more American, W. C. Williams-style poet. First of all, I would like to know if you think these are artificial categories? Is there such a thing as English and American style, or is that narrowing down too much?

DL: Well, I think it was English insofar as that particular Neo-Romantic style was, as documented by Kenneth Rexroth in his anthology (*New British Poets*, 1949), a phenomenon that took place in England. I don't think the same thing was taking place in this country. And so you could say it was English in its very nature and could never have happened here. It's one of those absolutely unanswerable questions, like what would've happened if I'd been born with blue eyes? It's an historical fact that various events caused, partly in reaction to the war, which after all was a very different war in England, for the English, than it was for the Americans. Probably. But who could say?

TC: Would you say that Williams was your strongest influence?

DL: Yes. Williams, along with the sheer impact of America. Williams provided a way for me to deal with that impact. If I had had only the tools, so to speak, of my own neo-romanticism, it's hard for me to imagine how I would have absorbed and reflected the changes in my own life. Again, that's one of those unanswerable things. But Williams *was* there. His poetry was there. I did read it.

TC: Williams spoke about using the American vernacular as a vehicle for poetry. I think many people were amazed that you managed to capture that so quickly, in a few years, learning the American idiom and putting it on paper.

152

DL: Well, although I had published my first book before I had met Mitch [Goodman—Levertov's former husband], or had come to America, I was still very young in myself, and very impressionable. Some of the other switch-overs were older. Auden, for example, was already fully formed when he came to America, as well as a good deal older, and also, I think, a much more fixed quantity in his ideas and diction and so forth. A Public School boy, after all, in the English sense. The other thing is, don't you think that some of my use of Americanisms in the early poems really is extremely obtrusive? They stick out like the proverbial sore thumb. It doesn't sound all that natural. When I reread them I can see myself enthusiastically and strenuously making myself over. For instance, I had a job in a big office as an assistant proof-reader, and we used to sit in this glass booth, and outside was this huge room, like the whole floor of a department store, filled with typists. When they'd finished typing they'd bring their typescripts to the two of us, Matilda and me, to be proofed. The typists didn't all know that I was actually English, and when I would speak to them, in order not to be thought to be putting on the dog, to be snooty, I would deliberately change my accent. Not really turning my t's into d's, but I did Americanize my speech quite deliberately, because if they didn't know I was really English they might think I was being snobbish. So there was a lot of that going on.

TC: When I heard you read last night I was surprised to hear such an English accent. It does change the sound of your poetry.

DL: Twenty, twenty-five years ago my accent sounded less English than it does today. The reason for that is partly because of those years, my very early years—I mean in the '50s in America. I was enthused about coming to America, and I was very enthused about American poetry, and so my accent, for several reasons, became more American. But then I think it leveled off, and there is a mixture. Since about 1970 I've been back to England quite a lot, and within about five hours of being there I'm quite unintentionally say-ing tomahto, not tomato, and so forth. I think that has made my speech get much more English again in the last ten or fifteen years.

TC: In an interview with me, Robert Creeley characterized your very early poetry as being generalizing, and your later poetry, with Williams' influence, as much more specific.

DL: Oh, absolutely. That's one of the big things I learned from Williams. Have you seen the early book of mine, the English one?

TC: *The Double Image*? Yes. There are a few of those poems here, in *Collected Earlier Poems 1940–1960*.

DL: Yes. Well, if I mention a tree, there'll be a generic tree. Later on, the tree would become an oak tree or a birch tree or whatever it specifically was. I don't think that English poetry is more apt to generalize than American poetry. I think I was groping for a poem, and as I got better—this was one of the things that helped me to get better: I became more specific. That specificity is so important to poetry. There are times when you can be general, but if you just generalize as a habit, or because you've never confronted the particular, I don't think that leads to honesty. I don't think that leads to good poetry.

TC: Do you think that's to some extent a function of youth? That when you're younger you haven't had as much particular experience, or at least as much experience expressing it.

DL: Yes, and more than that even, one is apt to get enthused by the general emotive character of certain words.

TC: I'm also interested in the question of the line break.

DL: I think that article I wrote on the function of the line explains it, and I think the next one to it, called "Technique and Tune-up" (*Light Up the Cave* 61–78), deals with the line somewhat, too. I think those explain fairly well what I think the line can do. I've never thought of it as being by breath, because . . . whose breath? If you've got very large lungs, is that automatically going to give you longer lines? Or if you've got emphysema, are you going to write lines with only one syllable?

To me, the main function of the line, which nobody knows, except some of the more intelligent speech department people seem to recognize it, is its effect on melody. It is the *source* of melody in poems. In the kind of exploratory forms that I write, the main source of pitch pattern is line breaks. Some of it comes directly out of expressive ordinary speech, and in that sense there is a pitch pattern in prose, too. In talking, one doesn't speak on and on in a monotone like a robot. But the way in which this is organized in poetry is different from speech and from prose. It's dependent on an intelligent, *intuitively* intelligent, use of the line-break. And this can heighten and accentuate intonation, bringing it close to music. There is that momentary, that less than momentary, that fraction of a momentary hesitation—yes, one incorporates it in the score. The line-break is a tiny little hiatus in one's train of perception.

TC: Would you say that hiatus leads the reader to pause for a second and think, contemplate?

DL: No, it has a more subliminal effect. Think of it, as a rule of thumb, as half a comma. This is just a way of expressing it because it's such a tiny amount; it's not very exact, but thinking of it as half a comma, that's not long enough to think. It *is* long enough to register *something*. A pause obviously is something which affects rhythm, because rhythm is as dependent on the spaces between beats as it is on the beats. That's how they constitute rhythm, don't they? The interplay of both beats and silences. However, rhythms can be tapped out on a single note, but melody calls for a difference in pitch. Melody affects what one receives as intelligence, as information, because it is *expressive, beyond* the way rhythm alone is expressive. And so if you read these lines—these first three lines ("The Hands," *Collected Earlier Poems* 38) which form a sentence—in a monotone, paying attention to the rhythmic structure but not to the pitch pattern, you don't get the same perceptive information as you do when you let the pitch pattern, that you've brought about by those pauses, take place. Example: [recites in a monotone] "Don't forget the crablike / hands slithering / among the keys." That's got the rhythm right. But now if I want to have both rhythm and intonation: [recites in her normal reading voice] "Don't forget the crablike / hands slithering / among the keys." O.K., now you're getting something different, and again, if you ignore the lineation, and you simply read it as a sentence, putting "hands" along with "crablike," you get something different again. [Reads again.] See how the intonation pattern, the pitch pattern, the *melody*, changes? So, the use of the line-break for me is a matter of utilizing the way in which the *observed* line-break moderates . . . organizes . . . regulates the melody. It not only has aesthetic effect (which may be interesting, and valuable—which is part of the art). Since words have specific meanings, as pure sound in music doesn't, line-breaks regulate the *affect*.

TC: Creeley said that he also based much of his early style on Williams, and then he was amazed when he heard Williams read and found that he didn't pause at the line-breaks.

DL: I have something to say about that. In the first place, I don't know when Creeley first heard Williams read, but the recordings, I think, all post-date his first stroke. And that must be taken into account because he no longer had [complete control]. I don't think that Creeley heard Williams read much before I first met Williams, because he hadn't met Williams more than a year or some months before I first met him, I'm pretty certain. And at that time Williams didn't have complete control of his voice. He paused involuntarily, and had difficulty getting to some words. The other thing is, and you can only take my word for it, because there aren't any living witnesses, but when I would read, at his place, poems of his own to him, Williams *fully* approved of the way in which I read them, and I always read them paying *strict* attention to line-breaks. And so I would really take issue with Bob about that.

TC: Do you think that Williams was as interested in the sonic and melodic qualities of his poems as you are in yours?

DL: I think he was passionately interested in it, but I also think he was— (it was one penalty of his leading two full lives, his life as a doctor, and his life as a writer of poetry. And also, it was a temperamental thing)—he was extremely careless. The books that came out during his lifetime are full of errors which he never took care of. For years the *Selected Essays* had tacked the end of one essay—they'd lopped it off one essay—onto another. I kept pointing this out to New Directions, and finally they corrected it. I think the first time they reprinted it they just reprinted the error. They had tacked something about Whitman onto an essay about García Lorca or vice versa. These things just went right by him. I think he also made typo errors in a lot of his manuscripts. And when he corrected proof he did a lousy job. He just wrote hastily. He gave a lot of care and thought, but he also didn't pay meticulous attention to details. I think this was the result of a kind of generous, expansive temperament, *and* the fact that he was both a full-time writer and a full-time doctor, which is actually an impossibility, but which he did however manage to bring about. There was a price to pay.

TC: Did he try to convince you to write exclusively in the triadic line?

DL: Oh, no! Absolutely not. I don't think I had written anything in the triadic line before he died.

TC: Mitch told me a little about how you would go to Williams' place, where you would read some of your poetry and some of his own poetry to him. Would he offer advice? Would he say, "I think you should change this line"? Would he be that specific.

DL: What a fool I was not to write things down. Well, of course I had a lot of letters from him, some of which have been published in a long-since defunct magazine. But they've not all been published. Some of them were so complimentary to me that I thought it would be inappropriate to release them to the world. But I've got them all safe, and eventually I will. I might be able to do so soon. But no, I don't remember him saying "This line," or "This word," or something. The few times when he didn't like something it would be because he thought the *general* diction of it, or something *general* about it was. . . . One poem of mine that he didn't like very much was "Le Bateleur" (*Collected Earlier Poems* 37). Le Bateleur is a Tarot Card figure. I don't really know anything about Tarot Cards, but I had been reading about the Tarot at that point, and I had also been watching a bank clerk counting bills out with that incredible skill, like someone shuffling cards, and the poem really is about the way this money keeps coming back to the bank. I mean, it's just circulating there. But he didn't like that one. He never really went into detail about why he didn't like it, but I think it must have been because he felt it was a strange metaphor, something like that. I don't particularly like it myself. I liked it well enough to include in the City Lights book (*Here and Now*) though.

And there was another poem that he criticized, but then he wrote me a wonderful letter about it afterwards saying that he had thought about it and he was completely wrong, that he'd misunderstood it. I don't remember now what poem that was.

TC: One poem that Creeley mentioned that Williams apparently really liked was "Mrs. Cobweb" (*Collected Earlier Poems* 42). Do you remember him saying anything to you about that?

DL: I *think* one of his letters talked about it.

TC: Did you save any manuscripts from those days?

DL: Actually, there are a lot, in different places, as I've discovered, much to my astonishment. But I think that most of what there are is letters. I think it's absolutely awful for people to sell their collections of letters from other people—where we've deposited our souls in them. Many people have done it, especially at a point when Texas was paying a lot for such things, but I think it's dreadful, really; it destroys all intimacy when you're writing to your friends. However, someone did a bibliography as part of a thesis, and sent me a copy, which listed all these different places that have things by me in them. So I wrote to them.

TC: Is that the Phoenix Bookstore bibliography?

DL: No, no. This was a thesis. The Phoenix Bookstore, Bob Wilson, bibliography is of course very much out of date. In any case, this woman, or whoever it was, had listed many collections that had manuscripts. I was astonished, and I wrote to many of these university libraries asking if I could have xeroxes of them. Some of them said, "Yes, you can have copies of them—it'll cost you so much per copy and we've got, say, two-hundred items." And so I didn't pursue the matter any further. Some sent a list of what there was, itemized, as: a letter to so-and-so, or a manuscript, or whatever.

TC: But these wouldn't be early copies, manuscripts of early drafts of particular poems?

DL: In some cases there were "manuscripts." And how they got there I don't know. Occasionally, someone would ask me for manuscripts and I would give them away, years ago, but I don't do that now. I don't have manuscripts of early poems. If I do, they would be in some quite inaccessible box, and I probably don't even have them. I do have fair copies made at the time, in hand writing, but they aren't exactly manuscripts. And even those, it would be pretty hard to get my hands on.

TC: I asked Mitch and he thought that you had not been particularly influenced by the Zen movement, or philosophy, that many people were picking up on in the '50s. But much of your poetry, even the title *Here and Now*, seems to have the same attitude toward "the dust in the street"—living in the present moment and realizing the "authentic" in every instant, every thing.

DL: I think that's very true, but I think it was coincidental. Zen doesn't have a monopoly on those kinds of perceptions. *Much later*, there was an exhibition of Zen painting at the Boston Museum of Fine Arts. That would have been around 1970 or '71, and I was very moved by certain things in that exhibition, but that's beyond the time period you're talking about. When I read a little bit of Suzuki I found the Zen Koans that he quoted very sadistic and I didn't like them at all. The parallel form, to me, is the *Hasidic Tales*. I felt an atavistic rapport with the *Hasidic Tales* as recounted by Martin Buber. But I had heard some Hasidic tales from my father as a child, too.

The Blyth books on Haiku, however, were very significant to me. But not with a sense of discovery so much as with a sense of confirmation of things that I felt anyway.

TC: Would you categorize yourself in any way as a mystic, or a mystical poet? Do you think that your religious impulse is mystical?

DL: I would never call myself a mystic, anymore than I would call myself a revolutionary. I think that for anyone to call themselves either of those things would be extremely presumptuous. And certainly, in my case, unfounded. "Mystical" is something else. Yes, I'm extremely interested in what is commonly called or thought of as "mystical experience," specifically Christian mystical experience. I've become very interested in and I've written a whole bunch of poems about Julian of Norwich.

I've just been reading a long interview with Dom Helder Camara, the old Brazilian bishop, or archbishop, who is one of the people who have clashed with the Vatican sometimes. One doesn't hear too much about him now, because he's also sort of retired, but a wonderful person, and I think that some of the things he says are mystical in nature, whether or not one . . . perhaps one could call him a mystic. A mystic has to have actually had visionary experiences. Maybe that poem of mine about the two angels . . . do you know the one? ("A Vision," *Poems 1960–1967*, 223). I think that was a tiny little mystical experience, because it wasn't a dream, and it wasn't something I was thinking about; it was more like that image flow I was talking about last night [at her reading at Bates College—see *Breathing the Water*]. I well remember I was lying in bed and there was a sink in the room, a wash basin, and Mitch was brushing his teeth in the corner by the wash basin, and I closed my eyes for a moment and I *saw* these two figures, and I *knew*, as one knows in dreams although I wasn't dreaming, what they signified. I re-opened my eyes and Mitch was still brushing his teeth. The next day I wrote the poem, all in one go, actually. There are those flashes on things that one has in that receptive state, where one is between sleeping and waking, but they're not dreaming. It's when the mind . . . people who do bio-feedback call it some pseudo-scientific name which I can't remember.

TC: Alpha waves?

DL: Yes, right. Well, to call a person who sometimes has those kind of flashes a mystic is hyperbolic. Truly hyperbolic. Many mystics are people whose visionary experience comes out of a lot of concentration on sacred matters, I think, but that's a different order of experience to the mere flashes, although the flashes are great things for poets to experience. Or for anyone, actually. It's just a matter of being in touch with your intuitions and your inner life and sometimes getting a little access to . . . I mean, I saw fairies when I was little. Does that make me a mystic? No.

TC: It's one of those words that everyone uses slightly differently.

DL: It's *very* loosely used in our time. As is the word "spiritual."

TC: You mentioned that you had written "A Vision" in one sitting. Mitch said that, especially in the '50s, you would often wait until you knew a poem was absolutely ready, and then you would tend to write it all at once, with very little revision.

DL: That is *somewhat* true. I definitely believe in waiting until a ripe moment. And how to tell when that moment has come is not something that one person can transmit to another, really, at least I think. I tell my students this is so, and I do so in the hope that just knowing that there is such a possibility of waiting and such a possibility of feeling that the right moment has arrived will make them alert to it, but to describe it. Besides, it might be a different sensation for someone else. But I do also revise. *Some* poems have emerged complete. If you have *Oblique Prayers* there I could show you one.

TC: Of course you've written quite a bit about that process—your essay on "The Tulips," for instance (*Poet in the World* 20).

DL: Yes. Now this poem, "The Mourner" (*Oblique Prayers* 17). Two weeks before I had been working on a translation of a poem by a French poet, whose name I forget, which describes North African burial practices where apparently the body is placed in a more or less fetal position—upright, not lying down. And so I worked on that and put it aside and wasn't thinking about it at all, and one morning I awoke, not so much *from* a dream as *with* this image, and even these words sort of popping out of my mouth, and I just grabbed a pencil and paper and wrote them down. I think that the experience out of which it comes is a long and deep one, but the articulation of it in this poem was facilitated by my having accidentally worked on that poem, and it came out absolutely complete except that I originally had another word for "immense"—of only one syllable. I can't remember the word now, but see the diction here? "Infinitesimal" is certainly of Latin origin, and so is "immense," and maybe the other word I had was a more Anglo-Saxon-rooted word, so that they did not fit together. And then I put in an extra comma someplace. Now I *cannot* see where it might've been.

TC: Do you have poems flash back in your mind after you've completed them, or even published them, and suddenly think, "I should've used a different word"? Or do you let them go?

DL: I let them go. But when I reread, for instance, "The Hands," which you showed me, I wouldn't feel very happy reading it aloud now. I *don't* feel that all those line-breaks are quite right, somehow. It seems too choppy. But I wouldn't change it, or tinker with it now, because I'm much too far away from the origins of it, so I would only make it worse, actually. But if I had the same feeling about hands on the keyboard, that same realization about them *today*, I think I would have written a poem very different in its rhythmic realization.

TC: In your essays you've written about what has come to be quite in vogue, now called process writing, which is taught in composition courses all over the country these days. Process writing emphasizes the *process* of working out a piece of writing through several drafts rather than just the final product, as it's typed and handed in. I believe you've also written that you have to begin to write a poem in order to know what the poem is going to say to you. This seems to differ from knowing that the poem is ready and then suddenly having it realized on the page.

DL: Oh yes. The knowing that it's ready doesn't mean that you know what the poem is going to be.

TC: You're not going over the words in your head?

DL: You know that you're ready to begin. You have a dim conception. And then you come to a point where you have . . . a phrase, a line, a cadence, a point of entry. That is my experience. It's from that point of entry that you can go, but the place where you *think* you might be going doesn't always turn out to be where you are going.

TC: So again it's the "every step an arrival" kind of process, where you have to go from one word to the next rather than trying to generalize ahead of time?

DL: Yes. You've got a general sense of direction, like setting out on a road, but you don't know what crossroads you're going to come to. And so, as in other aspects of life, you have many moments of choice coming up before you. And all you know is that you're heading westward, or whatever compass point you're headed for.

TC: What writers today would you advise me to read if I want to understand more about your poetry?

DL: Well, I've been writing such a long time, since early childhood, but I don't feel those whom I read, that I admire and get a lot out of, that I read for my own pleasure—I just don't think they're going to be illuminating to anyone about my own work. In other words, if they're influencing me, it isn't in any perceptible way. I *think*. Now that's not really for me to say. That's for somebody perhaps in the future to look back on and see how much osmosis of influence there is anyway between people all writing in the same period. I love the poetry of Galway Kinnell, of Lucille Clifton. I like a lot of William

Stafford, but not all. I think he publishes too much, but some of it I like very much. I'm very, very fond of Yannis Ritsos, who writes in Greek, but he comes through very well in translation, even by different people. He seems to be very translatable, because it's always Ritsos no matter who translates him. And Wendell Berry. Those are some of the people I like and feel a rapport with. Much more than I do with Duncan and Creeley today. I made that statement years ago, and people still say, "And she thinks the chief poets of her generation are Robert Duncan and Robert Creeley." Not that I think less of them, but they interest me less because I feel less affinity with their concerns and manners of writing, each with their own idiosyncrasies—have *long* felt less, as the years have gone by. I feel much more affinity with Galway and Wendell, for example.

TC: Do you know Gwendolyn Brooks?
DL: No, I don't. I heard her read just recently in Cleveland, but I've only met her years ago, briefly.

TC: What political action groups would you support today?
DL: Because of the sense that I came to at some point during the '60s, of a pacifist position being impossibly priggish in face of what the Vietnamese people were doing, I moved reluctantly, and never really wholeheartedly, from a pacifist position to a non-pacifist viewpoint, and have subsequently moved back to a pacifist position. There were all sorts of problems about this, because again, like so many others in the Peace Movement, *what* is one going to, *how* is one going to confront the struggle of, say, Salvadoran guerrillas? How is one going to look upon the Sandinista revolution, which overthrew Somoza and produced the now embattled but very decent society in Nicaragua today? Is one going to go tsk! tsk! because of the use of force? I still see that. At the same time, I see that violence produces more violence, and is deforming to the people who have to use it, who feel that they have to use it for the most understandable reasons, and are heroic in their use of it. But it *still* is bound to have a terrible, deforming effect on them and on the subsequent society if they manage to succeed, because it validates militarism. And I don't know what the solution is. I don't pretend to know, and I think that the only way for a person who believes in the potential power of nonviolent action is to cling to that belief, not to be judgmental about people who in desperation are being led to take up arms, and to try to learn to be nonviolent in one's own methods—and to just hang in there in this ambiguous position. It's a kind of fence sitting. It doesn't sit easily with me. But one

cannot see a solution and yet one believes that in the long run a certain proffered solution, namely armed struggle, is inefficient, because it brings about a repetition of the very conditions it struggled against. One has to remain in the state of suspension, actually. I know I'm not alone in feeling this conflict. One has to keep on asking the questions; one has to keep on pointing to instances of creative non-violence where they have existed, and giving loving support in so far as one can to the poor and desperate.

So, as for groups that I support today . . . of course all the anti-nuclear groups, whether it's Greenpeace or Mobilization for Survival or . . .

TC: Greenpeace is doing some incredible things. They recently sank two ships by pulling some kind of plugs beneath the water line. Did you hear about that?

DL: Yes, in Iceland. And in Central America there are many groups. Madre. Witness for Peace is a marvelous group. Someone not religiously connected has remarked, I saw it quoted somewhere, "The only left-wing you've got left is the religious left." It's not absolutely true, but it's pretty true. Another is the Sanctuary movement. OXFAM is a really, really fine organization that doesn't just hand things out, but is very informative.

An Interview with Denise Levertov

Jean W. Ross / 1988

From *Contemporary Authors: New Revision Series*, Vol. 29, eds. Hal May and James G. Lesniak (Detroit: Gale Research, 1990), 250–53. Reprinted by permission of Gale Research, Inc.

CA: In "Some Notes on Organic Form," collected in *The Poet in the World*, you wrote about how, in the making of a poem, "content and form are in a state of dynamic interaction," form being discovered in the work rather than determined beforehand. Does at least some idea of its form usually become apparent early in the writing of a poem?

Levertov: Yes. It varies from one poem to another, particularly in relation to the length of the poem. But of course, yes—it does. One is not writing in a literal trance.

CA: Usually, though, there's that interaction between content and form going on until the poem is really finished and tidy?

Levertov: That's right. It isn't that you start off not knowing and then you abruptly know and then you go along knowing until you get it finished. It is an ongoing, extended process, with not knowing blending imperceptibly into knowing.

CA: You had an unusual education, not in schools, and you seem always to have come upon just the right influences at the right times. Do you have any thoughts about whether this good fortune might have been more than luck?

Levertov: The fact that I didn't go to school was a kind of luck. I happened to have had the kind of parents who didn't send me to school. As for things that happened later on, I think one thing leads to another. The kind of thing you're referring to as good fortune or luck—I don't mean every kind of good luck, like winning bets at the racetrack, but the kind of life-history good luck—is a matter of a sort of accretion, the influence of one event upon another so that a context occurs which is a lucky context. Once you're in it, then things happen which don't really happen out of the blue; they happen because you're in a particular place at a particular time.

CA: It's lovely that you sent some of your poems to T. S. Eliot when you were twelve, too young to be shy about doing such a thing. What sort of advice did he offer in his reply to you?

Levertov: How I wish I hadn't lost that letter! He said to learn to read poetry in some language other than one's own; that was one good piece of advice. Basically, I think, it was just sort of *keep on keepin' on.*

CA: Coming to the United States in 1948, at a time of other big changes in your life, you were faced with the differences in spoken language that you've said the poetry of William Carlos Williams especially helped you to adapt to. Was there a period then of mainly learning and adjusting before you were writing as much as before?

Levertov: I don't know whether the actual quantity of writing was particularly different. I think during the first two or three years of my son's life I was writing less, as most women find who are writers and who have a child—they don't get very much writing done in that time.

CA: How would you assess the influence of that change in the speech you were hearing, coupled with reading American poets, on your own poetic use of language?

Levertov: It's plain to see in my poems of that period, I think! They begin to sound less "literary," the diction broadens, the rhythms come closer to speech, and there are fewer echoes of other poets—except, for a while, of Williams himself.

CA: You're very concerned that readers approach poetry with their hearing attuned to its musical qualities. Does music—the kind that comes from instruments and voices—play some real part in your writing or in setting a mood for it?

Levertov: I listen to a lot of music, but I don't know that I can say it plays any direct part in my writing. Occasionally while writing I put on a record of something that has the "feel" of what I'm trying to do. My poem about the death of Chausson (in *Breathing the Water*) did emerge from listening to some of his music while picturing his death in a bicycling accident.

CA: You've written about dreams and their relationship to your poetry. Have the dreams that seem to figure in your work changed in any way—in intensity or clarity or pattern, for example—over the years?

Levertov: There was a period of my life when my poems were much more directly related to dreaming than in recent years, because I was remembering and writing down my dreams a lot, which I haven't done in recent years. They haven't been playing such a large part in my work the last few years, though that's not to say they might not again.

CA: One of your poems I especially like is "By Rail Through the Earthly Paradise, Perhaps Bedfordshire," from *Footprints.* Do you feel a special excitement in traveling?

Levertov: I do like traveling, but the poem's not about travel as such but about England—ordinary common or garden dear England—in particular. I don't think that poem was written the first time I went back to England after a long absence; I believe it was a later trip. But I grew up there (not in Bedfordshire, however!) and I have very particular feelings about it.

CA: In "Goodbye to Tolerance," written in 1973 while you were very actively protesting the U. S. involvement in Vietnam, you criticized poets who were not doing likewise. You continue to use your poetry as a voice against social and political injustice. Have your feelings softened at all towards those poets who do not?

Levertov: I never demanded of other poets that they write anti-war poems, but that they activate themselves in whatever way they were able. If they were *able* to write poems about it, fine. But if they stood apart from everything— never signed any protest, never demonstrated, never took a stand—that is what I criticized, not that they didn't write anti-war poems. I think there was a certain mealy-mouthed kind of poem which poets who weren't doing any of those things were sometimes publishing at that time, just as if nothing were happening. That certainly irritated me. But I would never demand of anyone that he write a politically-engaged poem, because you cannot write well to order, though you may sincerely wish to. You may not be inspired. I've never demanded on-tap inspiration of anyone.

CA: I think you included in your criticism in that essay not just poets but people at large who were taking what they considered a sort of objective, reasoned stance about the war.

Levertov: That's right. What sort of objectivity can you have about the deliberate maiming (by napalm, by fragmentation bombs, and various "anti-personnel weapons") of civilians as an attempted strategy of demoralization? It was not a game of chess.

CA: Are you in touch currently with poets from countries where writers are censored?

Levertov: Not particularly, no.

CA: You mentioned earlier Eliot's advice about becoming familiar with poetry in another language. How do you feel your own translations of other poets's work have affected your original writing, if indeed they have?

Levertov: Translations are an excellent thing to be working on when you're not in a very productive phase yourself. As for other ways, I can't really think of any particularly. I don't feel my work in translations has been of direct influence on my own creative work. They are an extension of it, rather—and I think this is probably true for most poets who translate (except when a translation is undertaken as a sort of commission or obligation, and then it is a literary task to be done as well as possible, but cannot have the same charge).

CA: You have bemoaned, in the good company of many other people, the erosion of language by misuse, the growing general ignorance of language, and the lack of knowledge of history on the part of many younger people today. Do you sometimes feel because of these conditions that you are writing for a diminishing readership?

Levertov: Yes!

CA: You must confront this especially in your teaching. Any idea about remedies?

Levertov: The remedies have to start at a very early age, and they have to do, really, with the condition of the whole society. Everything else is Band-Aids.

CA: Through the years your work has elicited a good bit of written response from academic critics. Have you found much of it to be perceptive and useful to readers and students?

Levertov: The poet can never really answer that question, because the poet isn't the reader, but the writer. However, not to quibble, I must say I have found some of it has been perceptive. When the writer says that something is perceptive, he or she means that the critic understood what the writer was trying to do. One is not, obviously, the best person to evaluate one's own work. Whether something in praising or dispraising the writer's work is perceptive or not is not for the writer to say; he cannot be objective in that way. But certainly I have come across things which got it all wrong, and I've come across others which were gratifying in that the response one might hope for seemed to have occurred.

CA: You care very much not only about the form of individual poems, but about unity and order in your collections. Is it usually readily apparent to you when you have enough poems, or the right combination of poems, to make a good book?

Levertov: Absolutely not. Usually I've got enough numerically, and I therefore think, Oh, maybe I've got a book here. So I start looking at what I've got. At first it seems to me as if it's hopelessly disparate. It isn't until I've laid everything out on a large surface like a floor and shifted things around into groups that, if I am in fact ready for a book, the pattern begins to emerge.

CA: Have experience and time made the process of writing poems in any way easier for you, or harder, or otherwise different?

Levertov: There are certain skills that anybody acquires as they go on doing something. But to say that writing a poem is easier for me at this stage of my life than it was thirty years ago would certainly not be true. In fact, it's probably more difficult because one is that much more cautious and demanding of one's self.

CA: You teach at Stanford part of the year and spend part of the year at your home in Massachusetts. How is your writing affected by living in two places and by moving between them?

Levertov: It doesn't seem to be adversely affected. I write in both places.

CA: Does the teaching affect your writing in any way?

Levertov: It would if I were teaching all year. Since I'm only teaching one quarter a year, it doesn't seem to get in the way of writing that much. In fact, this year while I was at Stanford I was more productive than I have been during the summer here at home when I'm living a busy but unscheduled life. So I can't really say with certainty. I know, because I did it for many years, that I don't want to teach full-time anymore. I wouldn't get enough writing done if I did. But sometimes I'm quite productive even at a period when I am teaching. However, if I could afford to, I'd give up all the racing around the country giving readings that I do in order to make up the rest of my income. I love going to Stanford, but ideally I guess I'd give that up too if I won the Irish sweepstakes or something.

CA: Many people say that teaching takes the same kind of energy as writing, and that makes it hard for them to do both things at the same time.

Levertov: I think it takes an entirely different kind of energy. It's just that one's time gets chopped up into so many obligations. My crushing burden of mail, always backlogged, is a much worse problem than my teaching has ever been. When one sees that one probably has ten to twenty years left, at the most, it gets pretty scary.

CA: Does the community of writers in each place you live differ considerably?

Levertov: I have a circle of friends in both places, but they are by no means all writers. Here particularly I avoid the literary scene. I know too many people, and it's too much social bother. And out there I have lots of academic friends who are writers of one kind or another, but I don't see many poets. Some of my friends are poets, but I don't live in a literary community in either place.

CA: In a larger sense of community, what kinds of audiences do you see at readings now, what sort of response to poetry in such a public setting?

Levertov: I read all over this country. I read a lot in the Midwest, for example, Texas, all over. There are regional differences in audiences, almost state by state. In university or college settings, the institution usually determines the nature of the audience and the degree of enthusiasm.

CA: In "An Approach to Public Poetry Listening," you wrote about the business we spoke of earlier of hearing the music of the poem, and about bringing the whole self, not just the reasoning mind, to poetry. In that regard, how did you feel about the recent public television series on poets, "Voices and Visions"?

Levertov: I only saw a few of the segments. They varied; some were better than others. They were all pretty skimpy, actually. I don't think they particularly helped people approach poetry in the way you've mentioned. It would be more useful if we had more radio poetry.

CA: Do you have any particular thoughts about the poetry that's being written currently? Any directions you'd like to see change or continue?

Levertov: I dislike L-A-N-G-U-A-G-E poetry, which ignores the consensus of understanding of what words denote; I find that arrogant, a kind of elitism that denies the human communion. Of the poets I've gotten the most from this year, 1988, quite a few of them are translated. One is Polish, one is Estonian, and there are several other European ones. Those happen to be the poets I've found the most stimulating, along with a handful of English-language poets.

CA: What are your greatest social and political concerns now?

Levertov: That's a big question. Central America . . . trying to stop the trade embargo on Nicaragua, not to speak of stopping more funding of the contras, which Reagan is still trying to obtain . . . South Africa. . . . I am praying for a Democratic victory—not that I think it will solve all problems, but four more years of the Republicans would certainly be a catastrophe. Hoping that Jesse Jackson's influence will be felt after a Democratic victory, as it has been during the campaign. The usual things about the arms race, about the environment. Today I was talking to the fishmonger: I bought some fish from him that's farm-raised, and he was pointing out to me which fish comes from the deepest sea, and far out at sea. He's in the business, and yet he's concerned. He is avoiding fish from coastal waters, even though he knows the fishermen that the store buys from and they don't buy anything that was caught in the harbor. All the environmental problems . . . and then AIDS . . . cocaine-addicted newborn babies . . . the destruction of the rain forests. . . . Maybe as people begin to feel the effects in their own lives there is beginning to be a ground swell of protest? Unless there is, we haven't a hope—if we don't do ourselves in in one way, we'll do it another. But I still hope for change, and believe work and prayer can produce results. I have a button that says Picket and Pray. There's still a chance to turn things around. *Glasnost* and *perestroika* are what we need in the USA, just as much as in the Soviet Union—especially *perestroika!*

Feminism, Poetry, and the Church
Nancy K. Gish / 1990

Unpublished telephone interview conducted in September 1990 from the home of Nancy K. Gish in Maine. Transcribed from recording device attached to telephone. Printed by permission of Nancy K. Gish.

Gish: Your poetry has been seen as distinctly feminist. I have found it movingly so in poems like "Pig Dreams," "She and the Muse," "The Goddess," "Cancion," "The Soothsayer," "The Dragonfly Mother," all of which I have taught in Women's Studies classes as well as poetry classes. Yet you have said that was not your specific aim. What, in your poetry, do you feel has had such an impact on feminists?

Levertov: Now I would like to come back with a question, "What is it that people find *feminist* about those poems." Can you tell me?

Gish: I can tell you from *my* perspective, seeing myself as a feminist and many years director of a Women's Studies Program. "Pig Dreams" seems to me to portray the discovery of Sylvia's life as a woman, and it ends with an address to Isis. That three-line poem is moving and disturbing to me; the idea of identifying the self as a woman with the divine is very powerful, and the Christian tradition has not done that, for me at any rate. And so what you have is precisely that extraordinary discovery of one's self as both living and female in the world, its implications, the maturation, leading to a direct address to Isis. I guess that's what I would say it is.

Levertov: Well, you see, did you ever see the original publication of those poems, with the pictures?

Gish: No.

Levertov: I wish you would take a look at it. It was issued by Countryman Press in Vermont. It is available. It's around; it's not out of print. I think it cost $12.50 or something like that. The genesis of those poems is described on the jacket copy. And the pictures were the inspiration for the poem, along with Sylvia herself. She was a real pig whose owner was an artist, a very primitive kind of artist; actually her work has become—it's still primitive and always will be—but it's become more developed since that time. But at any rate, she had done a lot of large pastels of her pig, and I originally thought that I would like to capture them—"Sylvia does this; one day Sylvia did that" and so forth—and that we would do a children's book together. Sylvia's owner was a high school sweetheart of my son's, and she used to spend a lot of time with us. She sort of ran away from her parents one summer to us and she became a friend of mine and continued to be so long after they had broken up. So I started asking her more questions about Sylvia, and the more she told me, the more these poems started to develop, which really were then not for children. I mean there are a couple of them that children enjoy very much, like the one where Sylvia plays in the snow, but some of them tend to be heavy—the one about her mating, I would think—for kids. But you see critics, and sometimes just your intelligent common reader, sometimes attribute to the poet a kind of intentionality that is quite incorrect, a degree of intentionality and also intentionality of a particular kind in relation to a particular work that is incorrect. And so Sylvia was always a pig to me. She was a house-trained pig, who house-trained her piglets. She was a Hampshire pig, black and white, and she was absolutely a character. And now that a person can read a universal message that has to do more with human females than with pig females into those poems is okay, but I as the author am taken aback at that intention being attributed to me.

   Gish: Well, I don't even know so much if intention has anything to do with it, because I don't know if one has to attribute intention or conscious intention.

   Levertov: Well it does, because you're asking me questions about my attitude to feminism. So in that context it does.

   Gish: Well, what about something like "Cancion," where you have a series: "as a rock I am this, as a bird I am that, but as a woman, oh as a woman"—what is the last line?

   Levertov: I can't remember but I know the poem you mean. But I *am* a woman. I was speaking for myself, and of course if you speak honestly for yourself, then you find that you have, as it turns out, spoken for others too. So when a woman is writing something out of their own outer or inner experience, it will bear the mark of, clearly, of their gender, just as when a man does, it will bear that mark; that is simply a fact of life like, you know, an extension of one's anatomy. So often critics do attribute intentionality in the sense that a critic is liable to say that the writer was trying to speak for the nature of woman in such a poem. And as far as I'm concerned, that is not what I was doing.

Gish: Let me put it another way . . .

Levertov: Excuse me. In a sense, you see, one could take poem by poem and, you know, individual instances, and I suspect that they would almost always, as far as I'm concerned, come out with the same kind of answer or response that I've been giving about those two. I mean, do you want to try it with one of the other poems that you mentioned? I can't remember what else you did mention as instances.

Gish: Okay. Let me just make a comment first. It seems to me that when you say that when a woman speaks, inevitably it bears the mark of gender. . . .

Levertov: If she's speaking out of her own inner or outer experience. If she is writing in a fictive mode, then this is not so, or if she's writing poems in which the personal pronoun does not appear or should not appear, has no place. I mean I have a poem written recently about a heron that I watch, and a friend said to me that it was interesting that my poem about the heron was about a heron and that x, y, or z's poem about the heron is about that poet looking at the heron. So I think that poems in which the author does not appear in the way in which in my heron poem the author does not appear—if they become anonymous, or you don't know who wrote them—you're not going to be able to tell whether it's a man or woman, I think. So I did not mean that there is an imprint of gender which appears in everything that a person writes, but that in certain kinds of poems where they are drawing specifically on their own life experience in an entirely personal way, the subjective kind of poem, then—and even then not always. But, I mean, *that* poem speaks of womanhood, womanness. That's one of the words in it, "when I am a woman." Well, by an act of projection of the active imagination, presumably a man could have written that poem, or I could have written a poem that was my imagination of something going on in the life of a man.

Gish: I guess I would say from my point of view, from a feminist point of view, that that imaginative act has been historically very hard. And that one of the forms of power that your poetry has had for me—and this is really only partly related to what I'm doing now in this article, but it's obviously connected—is that it has given a voice to certain kinds of female experience that have not been voiced, and I went to an Irish poetry festival and heard Eavan Boland talk about this issue, and she talked about the fact that we talk about Irish poetry, but we cannot talk about Irish poetry but only about Irish men's poetry because the rest has been silence. And until those silences are filled, there is not *Irish* poetry. And she said, and I think she's said this in print as well, that she had to say that it was only in American women poets that she has been able to find a voice that she could use, and I guess that's what I mean by "feminist," not necessarily doctrinaire statements.

Levertov: If that is what you mean by "feminist," then what we're calling "feminist" is the testimony of what it feels like, the testimony of what a woman has felt or what a woman has seen or how she has seen it and so forth, not a point of view either deliberately or consciously or ideologically formed and adopted, but simply testimony. So that, let us say, when you are reading a novel by a man, which is a wonderful novel, and in which the women strike you, as a woman, as really real women and so you feel that man imagines those women very authentically, okay. But it's still, when it's a woman that has written about a woman, she hasn't had to take the same leap of imagination actually because she's testifying out of her own experience, and she has to take that leap of imagination if she's writing about male characters, and this comes into it somehow. But at any rate, what we're talking about as feminist—at least in regard to your first question, the poems that you're referring to as having a feminist character—you're claiming that feminist character for them and say that you've taught them in Women's Studies courses because they offer testimony from the voice of a woman. Is that correct?

Gish: I'd say that's absolutely correct, but I would say that it is not separate from certain kinds of feminist ideology, based in the notion, for example, that the personal is political, which is now a cliché, and that to speak as a woman is something women must do; they must find a voice. And I think that many feminist theoreticians make that claim, that women must find a voice which is their own voice. So I suppose what happens when I speak about those poems—take something like "Cancion" which I come back to because it's short and I can make the point clearly—whether you intended this consciously or chose it or whatever, one of the fundamental traditional male ways of accounting for woman is to account for her in terms of nature— "woman is a flower; woman is water; woman is a rock," whatever. She is the natural world. And it has always seemed to me—and in fact my students will initiate this without me—that this is a poem that begins with three negations, that when I am placed in this mode, which is not my own choice, then I am this or that or the other, but when I am a woman . . .

Levertov: That is not what I meant. It's in *The Freeing of the Dust*, and you see the first thing is "when I am the sky." The next thing is "when I am the sea," "when I am the earth." And you or your students have read those as what others attributed to me as a woman. I, however, am testifying to being sometimes the sky, sometimes the sea, and sometimes the earth. And sometimes a woman. I can't tell you everything that I meant by it at the time because it's quite a while, and I'm not going to attempt a real explication de text, but I was definitely not saying that these were things attributed to me by others, by men or any other others, but these were part of my own experience.

Gish: Does it matter if you didn't consciously intend that if historically that is what poets have done to females?

Levertov: I think it matters quite a lot because it's a matter of reading a poem with precision and not hanging on to it, sort of manipulating it to mean what you want it to mean. And the syntax should give it the impression that I intended. It doesn't say "when I am called the sky." It says "when I am." And I think that that should be taken seriously. That's why I really object to that interpretation, which I think is what people with an agenda tend to do to anything; they apply their own agenda to it, to the disregard of its own structure.

Gish: I understand that you're saying that feminism isn't your conscious intention. Would you say that your poems do not function as feminist poems?

Levertov: Some of them perhaps, on a case by case basis, function as feminist poems in the sense of, maybe, giving courage to other women. Perhaps with the obviously silent past still a heavy weight on the shoulders of so many women, the speaking in whatever way of any woman is in itself an encouragement to them. That kind of thing—yes, they would function. I mean, I didn't have any problem speaking. I started to write poems as a very young child. It never occurred to me not to or that there was anything standing in my way.

Gish: It's interesting because I did the same thing as an academic. I didn't notice that there weren't any women academics at the University of Michigan and went right on doing a Ph.D.

Levertov: You didn't realize you'd been the token woman.

Gish: But on the other hand, I've only in the last couple of years written poems, and I do feel that my poems were stolen from me as a child.

Levertov: And I dare say they were. If you feel that they were, you've probably got good reasons for it. But I would like to point out that there were many, many countless numbers of men who have had their poems stolen from them.

Gish: Yes, I know that.

Levertov: They've had them stolen in the same way that their tears have been stolen from them and many other ways. There is a certain kind of feminist self-pity that I strenuously object to. Not to deny the history of women. But women who see exclusively the oppression of women tend to forget other kinds of oppression. "But my oppression is better than your oppression."

Gish: It is so difficult to use the word "feminist" because it has taken on certain kinds of meanings. I think that the creativity of women, the history of women as artists, as writers, as women who acted, is as powerful and important as the fact of their oppression. We don't differ on that.

I would like to get back to the issue of Christianity. It seems to me that there have been three major ways women have functioned in a patriarchal church. They have left it altogether and repudiated religion. They have taken up other forms of spirituality—specifically, feminist spirituality and goddess religions—but many women have stayed within the church. And there is a complication there because of the nature of the church, if not the nature of religion. I'd like to put together two questions: Do you feel your poems are moving away from the concerns which gave them a "feminist" label, whatever you may think of that label? And do you remain, as a Christian, unorthodox? Is St. Thomas Didymus still someone with whom you identify as an unbeliever seeking belief or do you feel more able to accept a traditional form of Christian belief?

Levertov: Let's back up a bit then to the first thing: Has my focus of interests changed, sharply changed? I would say, "definitely not." The process of moving from agnosticism to belief has been for me profoundly influenced by such people as Archbishop Romero, Dorothy Day. Thomas Merton and other people—although those are Catholic, not all of the people who have been of interest to me have been Catholic, but a lot of them have—and they are all people whose commitment to peace and justice is absolutely outstanding. And so my commitment to peace and justice is in no way changed. My politics haven't changed.

That's my answer to your first question, which wasn't, as you originally framed it, specifically about feminism.

Gish: What I said was, "Do you think your poetry is moving away from the concerns on which its feminist label was based or are you approaching similar issues in a new way?"

Levertov: Let me rephrase my response. It is not moving away from the political concerns that have characterized it for most of my life. Those elements in my poetry which have caused it to be characterized as feminist are ones about which I am still committed.

Gish: Let me just throw out a set of poems that was one of the first and most powerful to me, that I saw as feminist. It was the combination of "The Earthwoman and the Waterwoman" with "The Dragonfly Mother" because it was such a rethinking of how women respond to one another as mother and daughter. And possibly because my own mother was so important to me.

Levertov: Okay. Well, let me say first of all I have to respond with an account of the *facts* behind those poems. "The Earthwoman and the Waterwoman" was descriptive of two women whom I knew in Mexico, thirty-five, thirty-six years ago. One of them became an ongoing friend, and that was the waterwoman one. The waterwoman came into an incident in my life one afternoon when I was really going to go and be at this rally. Well, I mean I wasn't the only speaker. There were half a dozen speakers, and it was one of those things where you shout a few words into a microphone to a totally peripatetic crowd, and one more speaker, one speaker more or less, doesn't really make any great difference. So this friend came over, and we talked and so forth, and she left, and I made the decision not to go to the rally. And I usually always keep commitments. And I thought, "absolutely, I'm exhausted. I must have a nap." And I did so, and while I was taking my nap, I had a dream, which produced the poem, and it also really was sort of a message: "You don't always have to go out there and mill around. You also have permission to stay home and do what you are more profoundly about." So that is the background of those two poems. Now let's get back to your question.

Gish: I love that message. I wish I could learn it myself.

Levertov: One gets that message and that permission not once and for all, but you get it and then you need it again, later, and I wrote a poem just recently that also came out about something parallel, something similar.

Gish: Let's go back to the question about Christianity. Do you think of yourself as still unorthodox or more traditional in your form of belief?

Levertov: I think that I'm probably more orthodox than when I wrote whatever article that was, but as far as St. Thomas Didymus is concerned, and as far as the man—the person who says "Lord I believe, help Thou my unbelief"—I think that attaining or arriving at (attaining sounds too willful) arriving at, becoming, arriving at certitude as compared to belief, I think that is something with which I may have to contend all my life. I mean I may never arrive at that kind of certitude. I've known a few people who had it. I read somewhere a statement. I can't remember who said it, but it puts it very well, that difference: "Belief is believing there is God; faith is believing that God believes there is you." Something like that. I haven't got it quite right. "Belief is loving God; faith is believing that God loves you." Something like that anyway. So I think that the figure of St. Thomas Didymus, like the old man that said those words "I believe, help Thou my unbelief," is a figure who goes on being important for me. For every believer who is honest with themselves—it's not a station you pass through and then you never lapse.

Gish: What does this have to do with speaking as a woman with a woman's voice, which you seem to say you often do whether or not it is a conscious feminist voice? I seem to hear in you an identification of "feminism" with a certain extreme ideological position that many feminists take, but it doesn't necessarily have that meaning for me. But what is the relationship between speaking as woman and believing in a religion which has, at least historically, whether valid or not, grounded itself in a primacy of maleness?

Levertov: Since I started writing when I was five, this constant consciousness of "I am a woman, I am a woman speaking as me" has never been part of my consciousness: it just isn't part of it. I am a human being. And I am *me*. Of course if you stop to think about it I am a woman. I am also a woman in that I've had a child. I've borne a child. But it isn't something that—as a poet I'm a poet. I'm not a woman poet; I'm not a man poet. I'm a *poet*, and that has always been my consciousness. I don't know how else to say. So leaving poetry out of it for a moment, as a person, who is a woman, how does the male terminology or male-dominated concept, how do those things square with me? Well I've come to realize the fact of the great pain felt by so many women about all that, and of course I think that in the liturgy where it says "brothers," nowadays in most churches that's been amended and says "brothers and sisters." On the other hand, I'm much more bothered by the changing of beautiful, rhythmic, poetic language to make it gender free. In many instances where it wasn't just a matter of adding "sisters" along with "brothers" but more complicated sort of sentence structure, I'm much more bothered by the aesthetic desecration of beautiful language, that might be set in a time, that takes place in those revisions, than I am by the use of male terms. And I have always felt perfectly comfortable with the use of the masculine pronoun. I accept that they are meant and always were meant, in many instances, to be comprehensive. I have avoided in recent years the term "Man" with a capital "M" and substituted "human" or spoken of "our species" rather than "Man" or "Men." And I think that's good. But on the other hand, I have never had a personal difficulty with accepting that when people spoke of the history of "Mankind" they meant all human beings. So when I've changed my terminology, it has been out of deference to the feelings of others rather than out of personal feeling.

Let me return to something else. In Biblical language—well what was Biblical language? But the historical Jesus was male. OK. What was the alternative? If you're looking at the Incarnation this person *has* to be either male or female. Because it couldn't really be an it. This is part of the duality of time and space, and the kind of existence of any kind that the human mind is capable of grasping. The human mind can certainly imagine amalgams of two contrasting categories but is not really capable of completely transcending duality. If we consider matter itself, there's either matter or non-matter. Maybe contemporary physicists would have some other term. Things either are or are not: there you have a duality. That's part of the condition of being living creatures on this planet.

So if Incarnation was going to be in human form rather than as a flower or a dolphin, as I talk about in one poem, I mean, it wouldn't have been very pointful to be a hermaphrodite, symbolically, I don't think, and the entry, the Incarnation, of God into time and space and history had to be in a specific place. There are no generalities in such a situation. Oh God, this is getting heavy, isn't it? It isn't any problem for me to believe that if Jesus is the Incarnation of God, that he was incarnate as a male figure rather than a female figure. Because for one thing, in the Palestine of his time, the opportunities for fulfilling his mission were greater. He was coming into what was already a male-dominated culture.

Gish: What about the fact that this has now led the church as an institution, specifically the Catholic Church, to interpret that as meaning that males and females have essentially different roles and purposes in the world?

Levertov: Although I'm Catholic I disagree with this. I have sort of moved into the Catholic Church with all my objections to many things in the Catholic Church because some of the people whom I most admire and whom I consider most active and effective in the area of peace and justice are within that church. Some of them are women, and they also are intensely critical of those things which you and I, I am sure, share in critique of the Catholic Church.

I think the Catholic Church should permit married priests. Mandatory celibacy only came into the Church not at the very beginning, you know.

Gish: It was the eleventh century I understand. And I was told by a professor in a theology school that one of the fundamental reasons was property rights because they didn't want the priests leaving property and money to women and children.

Levertov: Yes. All the things like that. But the Catholic liturgy and mystical tradition are what I feel most nourished by among the different kinds of churches that there are, and I feel that if one is going to take from the Church as I have for years, then it is dishonest to always criticize it and remain outside. One should criticize from within, if one is a believer, and I am. I was a communicant in Catholic Churches, sometimes with the knowledge and sometimes without the knowledge of the priest that I was not, in fact, Catholic, and it was against the rules.

Gish: Do you believe that women should be priests?

Levertov: Well, I have sort of mixed feelings about it. I have known women priests in the Episcopal Church, and I have never felt quite confident in them. In principle, yes they should be. A lovely nun that I know was talking about how, in counseling someone, essentially she is doing—in the way of the profession—what the priest does, but she has not the right to give absolution. And she absolutely feels that she should have, and I feel that she should have too.

See, I think these changes are going to come in the Catholic Church. There's a tremendous movement in the Catholic Church, in America, for change. It's different in different countries. The Catholic Church in Italy is very backward. The Vatican is awful, is awful. The Church is full of priests and nuns and lay people who deplore the Vatican and are struggling for change. But not by leaving.

And I felt that it was a strange moment for me—quite recently really—to have made the decision to join the church. Historically it's a peculiar moment, really, but I see things in a somewhat longer view. I think that in some ways the battle is joined and I think that there may be big changes in twenty years.

Gish: I'd like to ask about the seeming reduction in the physical presence of women as subject and content, especially in *A Door in the Hive*. For example, there are poems about Julian of Norwich in *Breathing the Water*. In *A Door in the Hive*, as far as I can see, it's down to perhaps three poems specifically focused on women. And there is enormous commitment to praise of great men.

Levertov: It's purely coincidental. Until you pointed it out to me, I hadn't realized that, but it's not a program. I cannot account for it. A book goes off to the publisher, and it takes, usually, nine months, like a baby, before it actually appears as a book. So the next book consists of poems that start getting written at some point after that one went off to your publisher and have accumulated until one feels that there are enough for a book. And then that one goes off. And, in some ways until one feels, in my case anyway, that there are enough poems accumulated that one had better do something, that it seems to amount to a book, that it can be a composition.

Aside from *To Stay Alive*—which was an enterprise, a long poem—none of my books has been, while the poems were being written, thought of in that way: "I am writing a book." And people kept on saying to me, "Are you working on your new book?" And I say, "Well, not exactly. I suppose eventually they'll be in a book, but I'm not writing a book." Some people look on that differently. One can see from the nature of some books that that is so, but I don't work that way, with that one exception of *To Stay Alive*.

And therefore the fact that this book, *A Door in the Hive*, has very few women in it is just happenstance. I can't really account for it. I still have just as many close friendships with women as I've always had, but they haven't given rise to any poems, it just hasn't happened.

And what will happen in the future I cannot predict. I absolutely cannot predict. I don't have anything in mind at the moment that would be a sort of satisfaction to you or reassurance in that respect. But then I don't have anything very much in mind. I don't know where I'm going in poetry. Anything could happen—(laughing) and I just wish it would.

A Conversation with Denise Levertov

Jewel Spears Brooker / 1995

From *Christianity and Literature* 45:2 (Winter 1996), 217–24. Reprinted by permission of *Christianity and Literature* and Jewel Spears Brooker.

The Conference on Christianity and Literature sponsored a reading by Denise Levertov at the 1994 Annual Convention of the Modern Language Association in San Diego. In addition, CCL presented the poet with a Lifetime Achievement Award, and president Jewel Spears Brooker interviewed her for *Christianity and Literature*. The interview, which had to be conducted by mail, was completed in November 1995.

JSB: The poet has been viewed in different ways in different ages—as entertainer, teacher, prophet, priest, legislator. Some of your writing suggests that the poet may be a historian, a witness, a participant. Does the poet have special responsibilities? Are they constant, or do they vary with circumstances?

DL: The only responsibility peculiar to the poet is to poetry, language, art, the aesthetic conscience. Historical moments elicit response, more in some individuals than in others; if that individual is a poet, that response may take the form of poems, but that is an opportunity, not an obligation. As for obligations, as I've said before, poets share the same obligations as others. No more, no less. A poet can be historian, witness, participant—but that is always an individual response. Walt Whitman wrote about the Civil War, Emily Dickinson did not.

JSB: In essays on poetry and politics, you sometimes allude to the responsibility of the poet in public discourse. Some of your poems seem to be rhetorical in the classical sense of the word—that is, concerned with persuasion, with moving the reader to action. What are some of the challenges with moving today's readers? How, if at all, is your poetic shaped by an awareness of the need to engage the reader?

DL: I don't consider my work "rhetorical," designed to persuade to action.

If any of it "awakens sleepers," that may lead some readers, sooner or later, to actions they might not otherwise have taken. But my poems do not tell people what to do. I never think about an "audience" when I'm writing. As I've written, and as I've tried to teach students, one locates that in oneself which needs a certain poem, and writes for that inner listener. Then it goes out into the world—and I rejoice if it corresponds to what others also need. But I don't write for them. Of course, poems that articulate political rage and grief are bound to seem rhetorical, it is true, because in them opinions and passions become indistinguishable; and it would be disingenuous to deny consciousness of their possible effect. But their *motive* is not rhetorical.

JSB: What about the reader's imagination? Do poems about pain or about God require special imagination in readers? What resources can the poet draw upon when faced with illiterate or unimaginative readers?

DL: Of course the reader must have a receptive imagination, no matter what the theme, and be reasonably literate, too—though a less than fully literate person can sometimes respond to the sensory aspects of a poem better than an over-analytic intellectual who may be poorly developed in sensuous response.

JSB: In "My Prelude" you invite your reader to associate your muse with Wordsworth's. "One summer evening, led by her. . . ." In *his Prelude* Wordsworth invites the reader to associate his muse with Milton's. Milton is present in some of your poems too ("They Looking Back," for example), and images suggesting your own evolving version of paradise lost and indeed paradise regained are scattered throughout your work. In the opening lines of *Paradise Lost*, Milton's evocation of the muse modulates into a prayer to the Holy Spirit: "And chiefly thou, O Spirit, that dost prefer / Before all temples th' upright heart and pure, / Instruct me, for thou know'st." Could you comment on the evolution of your muse—from the early muse that "remain[s] in your human house, / and walk[s] / in its garden" ("To the Muse") to the spirit that moves through so many of your later poems—"Blessed is that which . . . bears the spirit within it. / The name of the spirit is written / in woodgrain, windripple" ("Mass for the Day of St. Thomas Didymus")? Has your muse changed in character over the years? Have you come, as many Christian poets have, to recognize in poetic inspiration a place for the Holy Spirit?

DL: I don't really subscribe to the "muse" idea. I've used the word more or less playfully in the past. But I've never really entertained the sense that I had a more or less embodied figure dictating to me or whispering in my ear. In "To the Muse" it was a figure of speech. In "The Goddess" that was the Goddess of Truth, not the muse as some readers seem to have thought. And in "She and the Muse" I was having fun with the idea of lovers as muses. I would consider it impertinent, if not blasphemous, to claim the Holy Spirit as a muse!

JSB: Many of your writings—that poignant sketch of initiation, "When Anna Screamed," the elegies for Olga and your mother and Murel Rukeyser, the marriage and divorce poems and "A Woman's Document," the poems about women as hypocrites and men as deaf mutes—thee and more deal with your consciousness of yourself and others as female. Could you comment on your evolving sense of yourself as female and perhaps say how these special gendered experiences have shaped your epistemology, your spirituality?

DL: I can't really address this question. I have always simply taken for granted the fact that I am female, and I have never understood the problems of consciousness of gender which seem to have become prevalent. To me the question (which of course others have asked me sometimes) is as baffling as it would be to be asked how my life has been affected by having brown eyes.

JSB: Much has been made of the neo-Romantic origins of your work. But what about the old Romantics? You once mentioned that in your youth you enjoyed reading Wordsworth, Keats, and Tennyson. You refer to Keats in your essays, especially to Negative Capability and to this world as the Vale of Soulmaking. You often refer to Wordsworth too. His natural supernaturalism, his insistence on presence, his experience of joy in the things of this world, his emphasis on the role of the imagination in cognition—all of these seem important in your work. How do you understand your kinship as an artist with the greater Romantics, and most especially could you comment on your reading of and attitude toward Wordsworth?

DL: My early (and abiding) love of Keats and Wordsworth is inseparable from my early (and equally abiding) love for the English countryside. In the case of Keats, the other strong factors were the sensuous music of his poetry (which is what I also enjoyed in Tennyson) and—when I got into my teens—the personality so vivid in his letters. And in his *attitude* to poetry. In the case of Wordsworth, certain lines have great music too, but as you well know, Wordsworth walks and Keats dances. I loved the details of nature in Words-worth, and the evocation of rich solitude, and much else. I took in and ab-sorbed much of his more philosophical content unconsciously. Keep in mind that I was (and remained) a solitary reader, unexposed (thank God) to academic requirements and critiques and analyses.

JSB: In a 1972 interview with Ian Reid, you defined the imagination as "the power of perceiving analogies and of extending this power from the observed to the surmised. . . . The poet sees, and reveals in language, what is present but hidden—what Goethe . . . called the *open secret.*" Is imagination, then, part of knowing, of cognition? If so, in what way is it creative? Is there a sense, as Wordsworth claimed there was, in which the imagination in the process of perceiving actually *creates* life out of the dust?

DL: I would stand by what I said in 1972. But, yes, I also see the imagination as creative—it combines the analogies and "open secrets" it perceives and fashions from them new works. This, I believe, is the act of synthesis that Coleridge called "esemplastic power." And, of course, the materials of the poet (or any artist) are not solely that which is perceived but include the medium itself—in the poet's case, words, syntax, sounds, rhythms. This is what the famous dictum "Poetry is not made of ideas but of words" means. And William Carlos Williams' "No ideas but in things" likewise includes among "things" the physical entity, language.

JSB: You also say in this fascinating discussion that imagination is inextricable from doing, from process, that just as the painter only sees when he is painting, the poet only sees when he is writing—"the vision is given in the work process." In the final books of the *Prelude*, Wordsworth discusses imagination as more of a state than an act—"reason in her most exalted mood," a "spiritual love," an "intellectual love" resulting in a fusion of intellect and feeling or, as Eliot would put it, from a unified sensibility. How, if at all, does this emphasis on love—in Keats's and Hazlitt's terms, on sympathy—fit into your present thinking about the imagination?

DL: I think the state, rather than the act, that Wordsworth refers to (and I would relate this to your other allusions also—"unified sensibility," "love," "sympathy," etc.) is what Rilke spoke about in describing his perception of a dog not as an "in-spection" which involves seeing through the dog, using it as a "window upon the humanity lying behind it," but as *Einsehung*, an "in-seeing" which allows one "precisely into the dog's very center, the point where it begins to be dog" (see my *New and Selected Essays* 235–36).

JSB: One more question about the imagination please. A dozen years after the Reid interview, you write about the imagination from the point of view of a Christian poet. And, again, your comments seem extraordinarily rich. If in 1972 you were saying, "I imagine that I may know," here you seem to extend it to "I imagine that I may believe." Instead of saying, as Stevens does, that "God and the imagination are one," you make a crucial distinction—arguing that it is through the exercise of the imagination that "one moves toward faith, and possibly by its failure that one rejects it as delusion. . . . Imagination . . . is the perceptive organ by which it is possible, though not inevitable, to experience God" ("A Poet's View"). Now this seems clear enough in the case of Julian of Norwich, as your wonderful sequence, your own *Showing*, reveals. But for poets who are not mystics, and for the rest of us, could you comment, please, on what seems to be a vital point: the connection between imagination and faith?

DL: I am certainly not a mystic! So I have no way of knowing how mystics' faith related to their imagination, other than what anyone can deduce from their testimony. For a poet (and poets don't tend to be mystics: the poetic and mystic modes of experience are quite different, I think, though some mystics may also be poets), imagination (which, obviously, comes with the territory) is a prerequisite for faith, though all poets must have imagination and only some have faith. Poets are typically too mentally active and questioning to have the kind of faith that is an extension of trust, the kind of faith a simple and perhaps uneducated, or at least unsophisticated, person may have, the faith of "un coeur simple." And yet poets are "right-brain" people. So if they do attain faith, it must involve the imagination. It is perhaps their substitute for the childlike direct assumptions of the naturally pure in heart.

JSB: In "A Poet's View" you describe something that was becoming evident in your poems, especially in *Candles in Babylon, Oblique Prayers,* and *Breathing the Water*—a movement from an altar to the unknown gods to an awareness of God (capital G) to an understanding of "God as revealed in the Incarnation." The Incarnation is central in a number of your poems, for example, "Mass for the Day of St. Thomas Didymus" and "On the Mystery of the Incarnation." Would you comment on your deepening understanding of the Incarnation as it figured in your gradual conversion to Christianity and as it figures in your present faith?

DL: I cannot add anything to what is in the poems.

JSB: In "Origins of a Poem" you suggest that art is an incarnational experience, an act of "realizing inner experience in material substance" (*The Poet* *in the World*). And in "A Poet's View" you reaffirm that your aesthetics are incarnational. In a 1989 essay you mention that you have come to appreciate *Four Quartets*. I am wondering if this might have something to do with Eliot's incarnational poetic, his emphasis on the word made flesh, and his incarnational theology, his emphasis on the Logos, particularly in Part V of each section. Could you share some of your reflections on *Four Quartets*?

DL: I turned against *Four Quartets* in the mid-60s when Eliot's lines came to seem limp and lacking in vitality compared to those by Williams, Pound, D. H. Lawrence at his best, and Jeffers. When I reread the *Quartets* in the late 80s, they seemed less flabby, and I again felt the beauty of many parts of them (though there are sections that I still find flat and over-abstract). It is true that I found their content more interesting by the time of rereading than I had in the 60s, but my primary problem had been with the quality of the writing.

JSB: In view of your consistent interest in issues related to war—from "Listening to Distant Guns," your first published poem, to the more recent "In California During the Gulf War"—I am wondering if you would be willing to comment on today's war in Europe. Is Bosnia a European problem, none of our business? What, if any, is our responsibility as Christians when we see entire populations sorted like bags of flour—the old and very young exported, the girls sent to rape camps, the boys murdered on the spot?

DL: I certainly don't have any answers to all this!—except to say that violence breeds violence and that world disarmament is the only sane and righteous yet seemingly unattainable strategy. If the U.S., France, and other manufacturers would stop making and *selling* weapons of every kind, it would be a first step. Yet even if that were to occur, what vast, virtually inconceivable problems would remain: every kind of injustice and inequity, the sources of hatred and resentment and despair and thus of violence. Personal conversion to non-violent action of all human beings is what's needed, and it is—obviously—not a realistic hope, at the present state of human evolution. If we don't destroy the planet first, we can perhaps hope for further evolution . . . spiritual evolution.

JSB: In reading over your work again, I am impressed with the many intersections between your long-held political positions and the theology of your later work. It seems, for example, that one of the consistent principles in your writings and indeed in your life as an activist is that in the final analysis deeds are more important than words, works more powerful than faith. "Even the ascent and descent of the angels depend on my deeds," as the epigraph from *The Jacob's Ladder* puts it. In a 1990 essay you again shy away from the Protestant idea of a faith that works in favor of the Catholic idea of "works that enfaith." You are referring, of course, to the work of writing, but could you comment on this general idea—this emphasis on works—as a more comprehensive principle in your personal, political, and spiritual life?

DL: Faith *without* works (unless, say, in a physically incapacitated person) is surely hypocritical. That is surely clear to any Christian. Whereas works without faith are no less valuable than works *with* faith (maybe even more valuable since the saintly atheist, for example, would be acting under a handicap). As for the person whose physical situation precludes works in the sense of action, his or her attitude to caregivers, say, or to fellow-prisoners if confined, also constitutes a form of "works." At the extreme, human value resides in being, not doing—but when action is possible, it is often the only truthful *expression* of being. Or, if you can, do; but if you can't, all is not lost. One thinks of the Hasidic story about "Why were you not Moishe?"

JSB: In conclusion, I want to focus on what has been a favorite metaphor of yours, life as a pilgrimage. In 1967, in a talk presented to a coalition of poets and theologians, you mentioned that *Pilgrim's Progress* was one of the childhood books that most affected your imagination, and there or elsewhere you revealed that Bunyan's hymn on valor was one of your childhood favorites. You have written of your struggle to bring together "for myself my sense of the pilgrim way with my new, American, objectivist-influenced, pragmatic and sensuous longing for . . . living in the present" (*The Poet in the World*). And in a recent essay you say that "though I own a house and have steady work, I am by nature, heritage, and as an artist, forever a stranger and pilgrim" ("A Poet's View"). You have come a long way, have crossed many geographical and spiritual worlds, in your more than three-score years and ten. Could you comment retrospectively on your own pilgrimage and, perhaps, if you wish, comment on the road ahead?

DL: Though I now have a nice edition of the unabridged *Pilgrim's Progress*, I've never waded through it all. What I read as a child was a children's abridgment. The "To Be a Pilgrim" hymn was in the *English Hymnal* (with a different tune than the one mainly used in America. I think maybe it was arranged by Vaughan Williams). The concept, the sense of a land with geographical features and various personages with descriptive names, and [the idea] of *quest* were what impressed me so indelibly. Some of these same factors were among those which, at a slightly later age, I loved in Malory's *Le Mort d'Arthur*—the romance of wandering and of quest. . . . Thus, eventually, of life itself—the inner life, the artist's life—as journey, as personal *Bildungsroman*. . . . I can't comment on my life as a whole, as your question invites me to, nor on what may lie ahead for me.

JSB: Thank you, Denise.

Index